P9-DEY-722

Kellogg on Integrated Marketing

Kellogg on Integrated Marketing

The Kellogg Marketing Faculty
and
the Faculty of Integrated
Marketing Communications
at the Medill School of Journalism

Northwestern University

DAWN IACOBUCCI AND BOBBY CALDER
EDITORS

John Wiley & Sons, Inc.

Published by John Wiley & Sons, Inc., Hoboken, New Jersey.
Published simultaneously in Canada.

ISBN 0-471-20476-5

Printed in the United States of America.

10 9 8 7 6 5 4 3 2

CONTENTS

FOREWORD

EVOLVING MARKETING AND MARKETING COMMUNICATION INTO THE TWENTY-FIRST CENTURY

DON E. SCHULTZ

Northwestern University has a long and historic tradition in the development of marketing, marketing communication, and advertising thought and practice. In 1903, Walter Dill Scott, then the director of the psychological laboratory at Northwestern University and later president of Northwestern University, wrote one of the first books on advertising titled *The Theory of Advertising*. Shortly thereafter, in 1922, Fred E. Clark, on the faculty of what was then the School of Commerce (which later became the Kellogg Graduate School of Management) wrote *Principles of Marketing*—one of the early and leading texts on marketing theory and practice.

That tradition has continued over the years. The Kellogg Graduate School of Management has continually ranked as one of the top business schools and the top marketing program in the world. The Integrated Marketing Communications (IMC) program at the Medill School of Journalism has been defining and redefining what marketing communication is and should be in an interactive and networked economy. In short, Northwestern University has been the cradle of both marketing and marketing communication education, training, and thought and it continues to be one of the leading residences for scholars and academicians. Thus, the development of this new text on Integrated Marketing is the latest in a long record of marketing and marketing communication innovations.

What is "Integrated Marketing" and why and has Kellogg and IMC developed these new concepts? This Foreword explains the basis for this new approach.

A Natural Evolution

This latest innovation in marketing and marketing communication thought and practice is a natural evolution for the faculties of the two schools. Kellogg and IMC have recognized the new marketplace and marketspace changes that have occurred over the past decade. This new Integrated Marketing text, an interdisciplinary approach, has been developed to provide new insights, theory, and applications to this emerging field. This joining of the two faculties in one text seems only natural. It is more a return to historical roots than a new alliance.

The Medill School of Journalism, where the IMC program is located, was part of the Northwestern School of Commerce, predecessor to the Kellogg Graduate School of Management, until 1938. In that year, the Medill School was separated and given school status. Advertising continued to be taught in both schools until 1961 when all advertising resources were consolidated at Medill. But, while separate, the two schools continued to work together, a tradition that continues to this day.

While there has been continuing cooperation between Kellogg and IMC, the two have found separate paths in the world of marketing and marketing communication. Kellogg has historically focused on the broader issues of marketing and marketing management primarily from the corporate and consumer points of view. IMC, which originally was an "advertising only" program, focused on the client, agency, and media areas of communication. In the late 1970s, the Medill undergraduate advertising curriculum was phased out and faculty began to focus on graduate and continuing education, primarily in advertising and sales promotion.

In the middle 1980s, the Advertising Department added direct marketing, sales promotion, and corporate public relations to its curriculum. It consequently moved its focus more to the corporate or client view of marketing communication than from that of the advertising agency.

In 1991, the Advertising Department, recognizing the emerging areas of electronic and data-driven communication, merged the four tracks into what is now the Department of Integrated Marketing Communications, the first such program offered at any level at any school. With that change, IMC began to focus on customer-centric data and database-driven communication programs. That change moved the entire field of communication out of tactical activities into the managerial and strategic use of marketing communication to drive corporate and shareholder value. Thus, it is only natural that Kellogg and IMC should come together once again to provide leadership, guidance, and direction for the entire field of marketing and marketing communication. That is particularly appropriate as we enter a new and more challenging field of networked, interactive, and global marketing and communication in the twenty-first century.

WHY INTEGRATION IS NEEDED

Many scholars and practitioners ask: Why Integrated Marketing?, Why Integrated Marketing Communication?, or even, What is Integrated Marketing—haven't marketing and marketing communication always been integrated? Hasn't the marketing concept always been to focus on the customer and then provide products and services to meet customer needs? If we truly are a "marketing organization" aren't we naturally integrated? So, what's so new and different about "Integrated Marketing" or "Integrated Marketing Communication?"

In this book, faculty members and practitioners will address and answer those issues and concerns. Yes, the concept of marketing is naturally integrated. However, it is commonly integrated only from the view of the marketer, not from the view of the customer. Thus, the practice of marketing around the world is often quite different from that found in textbooks and organizational flowcharts. For the most part, modern marketing is built on a marketing theory that is Industrial Age. That is, it focuses primarily on production, distribution (or place), pricing, and promotion—the traditional 4Ps of marketing. That approach was relevant and appropriate for the 1950s to the 1960s era when it was developed. It was hugely successful when product shortages abounded, the population was increasing rapidly, and nations were coming together to build more common cultures and the focus was on supply more than demand.

The marketplace has changed. Today, we live in an interactive, globally connected, customer-driven, service economy where time and speed are of the essence. The traditional approaches to marketing and marketing communication, based on the efficiencies of mass production and mass consumption are giving way to mass customization. In today's markets:

- A lap-top computer can be built to the customer's order, shipped, and received in less than a week.

- Communication no longer takes place primarily by letters and correspondence but by e-mail and Web sites.
- There is no "established price" and all products and services are essentially negotiable.
- The focus is on the supply chain where commonly much more value is created than on the factory floor.

Most all these changes have been brought about by technology—usually, information technology. That is what this book is about: the growth and use of information technology in the development of marketing and marketing communication.

To understand this change and to understand why Integrated Marketing is so important to all marketing organizations around the world, you must understand the basic shift in marketplace power that has created the need for this change.

A Shift in Market and Marketplace Power

Marketing was not invented for the benefit of customers and consumers; the buyers. Instead, it was invented for the benefit of sellers. As mass production developed, sellers often found their ability to produce products outstripped their ability to find buyers. True, the growth of logistical networks, transportation systems and mass distribution helped, but even those could not move products through the market faster than the seller could produce them. In other words, the producers and sellers needed new and improved ways to get customers and prospects to purchase and consume. They needed demand creation, not just production and supply skills.

Initially, the focus was on selling. But, selling was often slow and difficult. As mass markets emerged, sellers adopted the concept of marketing, that is, the mass movement of products and services through demand creation (one of the goals of marketing). As media systems developed, particularly after World War II, selling organizations found they could reach millions of customers and prospects with various forms of advertising and promotion easily and efficiently. Thus, were born the practices and traditions of what we today call "modern mass marketing" and "modern mass communication."

In this type of mass production, mass distribution, mass communication system, the seller held all the cards and all the marketplace power. He or she decided:

- What products to make.
- What distribution system to use.
- What prices to charge.
- What and how much information or communication to distribute about the product or service.
- Who to inform.
- When to inform them, and on and on.

All the power lay with the producer or marketer. The customer was often considered simply a "consumer" or someone who could be persuaded to buy and use again and again by the manufacturer or producer, based on the skills and capabilities of the seller or, better yet, the marketer.

The producer or product-driven marketing system of the 1950s to 1970s looked something like Figure F.1. In the product-driven marketplace, the seller or producer or marketer controlled all the elements, that is, raw materials, plants and factories, workforces, and the like, so he or she wielded tremendous power in the marketplace. The greatest tool the marketer had,

Figure F.1
Product Driven Marketplace

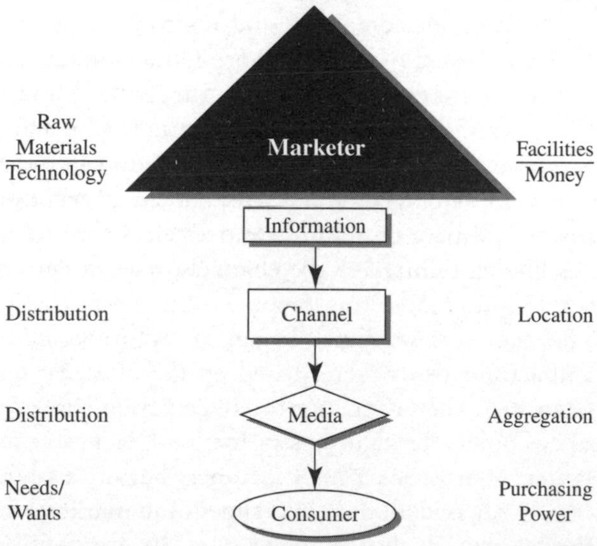

though, was technology, generally information technology. Technology allowed the marketer to:

- Understand consumer demand.
- Identify price points.
- Manage logistics.
- Control inventories.

Furthermore, all this information technology was held by the producer or marketer, with little in the hands of the other players. With all the tools and techniques, the producer could dominate the channels, such as the wholesalers and retailers, dominate the media or communication systems, and ultimately dominate the consumer or customer or end-user.

In a marketplace such as this, the integration of marketing and marketing communications was relatively important, but only to the marketer. All the marketer had to do was find ways to produce products, get them into the distribution system, advertise and promote, and watch the customers buy. Channels or distribution systems bought what was offered. Communication programs, developed by the marketer and delivered through the media, built consumer demand. In short, consumers responded; they went to the stores and bought. It was a perfect system for the marketing organization, but not so good for channels and end-users (e.g., channel members had few choices and little power).

Then things began to change. In the late 1970s and early 1980s, technology in the form of computers and in-store point-of-purchase or point-of-sale systems began to develop in the United States. That began to shift the power in the marketing systems to the retailers and distributors. The reason? The computer technology allowed the channels to gather more and more information about actual consumer behaviors in the marketplace, information the manufacturers did not have and could not easily get (e.g., a manufacturer would have to coordinate over all retail outlets). Thus, as information technology shifted to the channels, the marketplace began to look like that in Figure F.2.

As Figure F.2 shows, the channels began to capture much of the power from the manufacturer or marketer based on the information about customers and consumers they were able to collect. By being able to identify the individual customers through various forms of data capture (e.g., scanner data), retailers and other channel members began to understand how customers actually responded to various types of marketing and marketing communication efforts. With this knowledge, channel members began to

Figure F.2
Distribution-Driven Marketplace

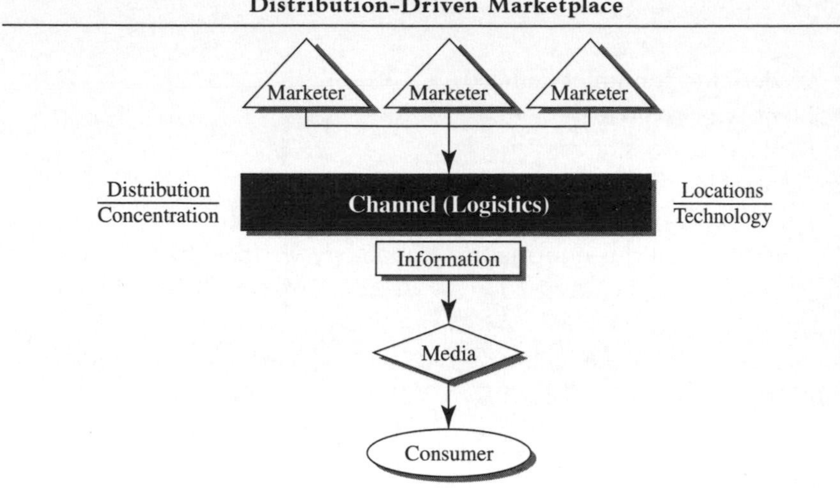

dictate the types of marketing and marketing communication programs that their suppliers would, could or should develop. Thus, today, in most mass marketing systems, the retailer or channel is much more powerful in determining what customers and consumers are offered than is the manufacturer—a power shift that continues to evolve.

In a distribution-driven marketplace, integrated marketing and integrated marketing communication programs have to be developed between the manufacturer and the channel. It is not really necessary to integrate the programs with the consumers because the power balance is still primarily in the hands of the marketing organizations whether they are the manufacturer or the distributor.

In the early 1990s, the system changed radically. With the advent of the Internet, the World Wide Web, and other forms of electronic communication and data interchange, power shifted once again, this time from the channel or distributor to the consumer. As consumers and customers got more and more information technology (i.e., the Web, the Internet. E-mail, faxes and the like), they effectively took power from the marketer and the distributor and created what we know today as the interactive and networked marketplace (Figure F.3).

As the customer or end-user gained information technology, the technology enabled him or her to develop more effective and more efficient market information gathering techniques. The customer was, for the first

Figure F.3
Customer-Driven Marketplace

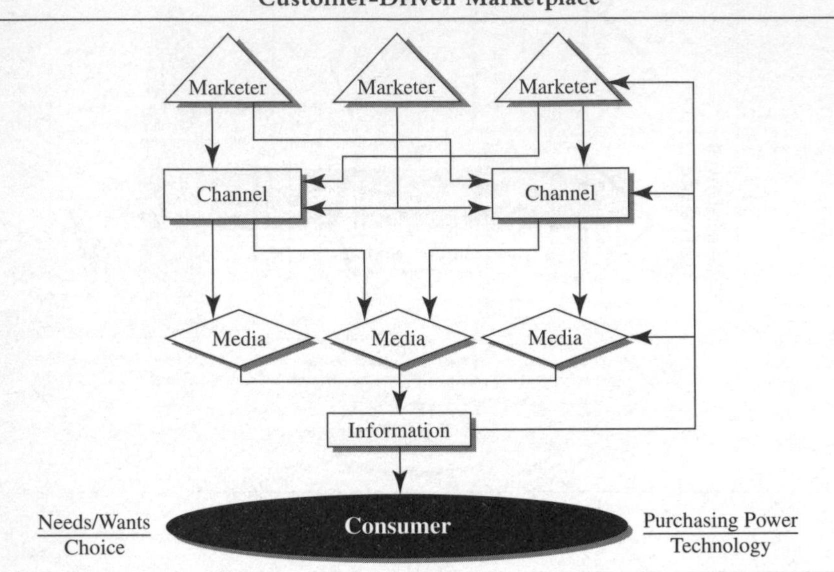

time, able to survey the entire marketplace, not just the areas in which they were physically located. These new technologies enabled the consumer to shop the world, to compare prices, to negotiate for the products and services they needed and wanted. In essence, the more information technology the consumer or customer gained, the more power he or she had in the marketplace. Perfect market knowledge in the hands of customers makes for a very difficult situation for traditional marketers and distributors.

The result of all this change is a continuing shift of information technology and therefore, marketplace power, from the manufacturer to the distributor to the customer—the "Marketing Diagonal" as shown in Figure F.4.

As information technology slides down the Marketing Diagonal, from the manufacturer to the customer, the power in the marketplace shifts as well. Equally important, however, is that marketing and marketing communication shift from being primarily outbound systems driven by producers and distributors to an interactive marketplace in which customers accept, access, and acquire product and service information as their requirements demand.

Figure F.4
Marketing Diagonal Chart

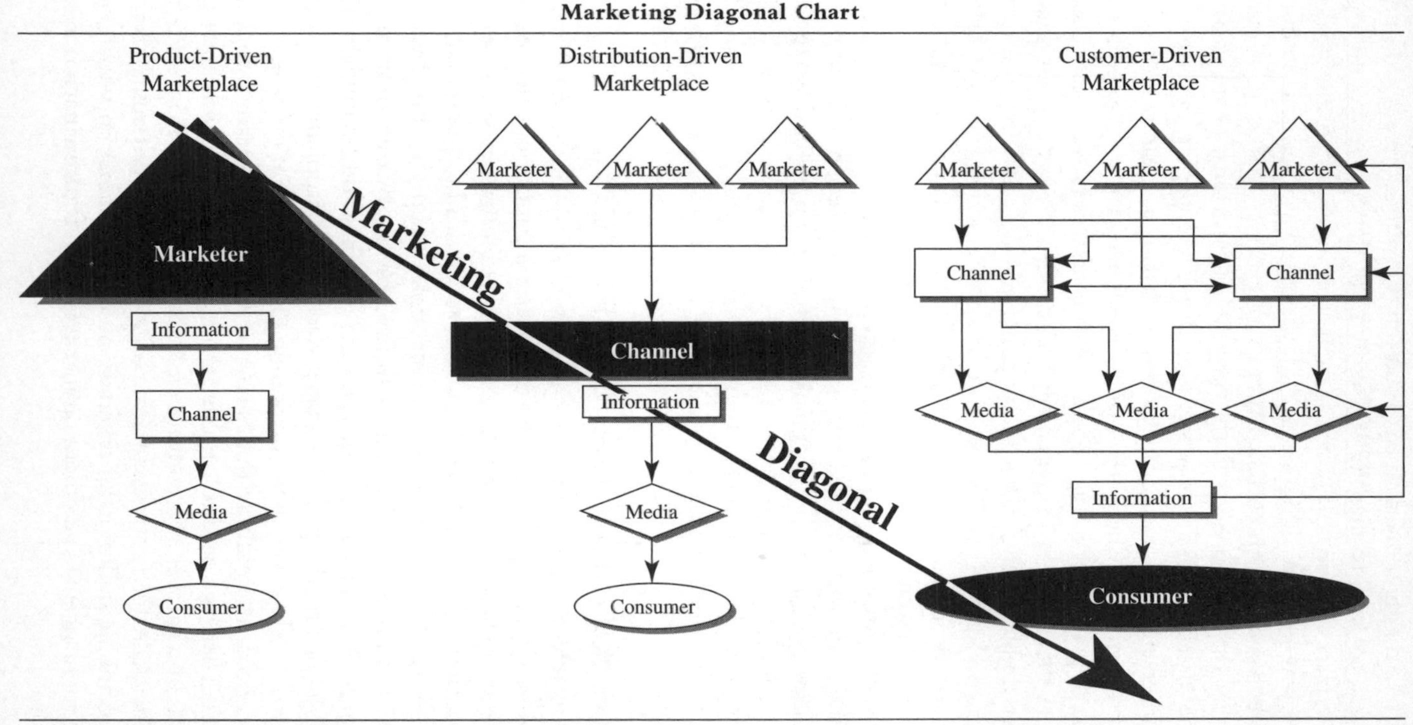

While the three marketplaces and the transitions are easy to understand, they are not easy to manage. The growth of the networked and interactive marketplace and the shift of power to the consumer or customer makes it easy to see why Integrated Marketing and Integrated Marketing Communication have become such important issues to all types of marketing organizations whether they still operate in the product-driven arena, or they have shifted to the distribution–driven system, or they are engaging in true networked and interactive marketing approaches we define as customer-driven.

In the product- and distribution-driven marketplaces, integration of the marketing and marketing communication elements were not required. As long as the marketer or the channel controlled the system, integration was rather simple—it was what the organization did, not how it affected customers and prospects. As the shift to an interactive and networked marketplace occurred, integration became mandatory. To market in the customer-driven marketplace of the twenty-first century, the firm must start with customers and prospects, their needs and wants, their potential, and their opportunities and integrate all the marketing and communication activities. Simply having products or distribution systems makes little difference if they cannot be connected to the customer in some way. Thus, integration of the marketing system, by starting with customers and working back to the organization, is challenging organizations around the world.

THE KEY IS CONVERGENCE

Fortunately, the information technology that has created this marketplace power shift can be leveraged by marketing organizations to meet the new needs and requirements of the twenty-first century marketplace. The ability to capture, store, manage, and analyze data and to respond to customers and consumers has increased exponentially for marketing organizations. Thus, the marketer is no longer limited by mass views of customers and prospects but can actually focus on the behaviors of individuals. This new "one-to-one marketplace" has been widely publicized and often criticized. Indeed, the challenge of the marketing organization of the twenty-first century is how to combine mass and one-to-one marketing into a coherent whole. There is a need to combine traditional mass and individualized marketing in what we call "convergence," as illustrated in Figure F.5.

The challenge for the marketing organization in the twenty-first century is to combine traditional marketing, much of which is still very relevant in both sophisticated and emerging markets, with the new approaches offered

Figure F.5
Convergence Chart

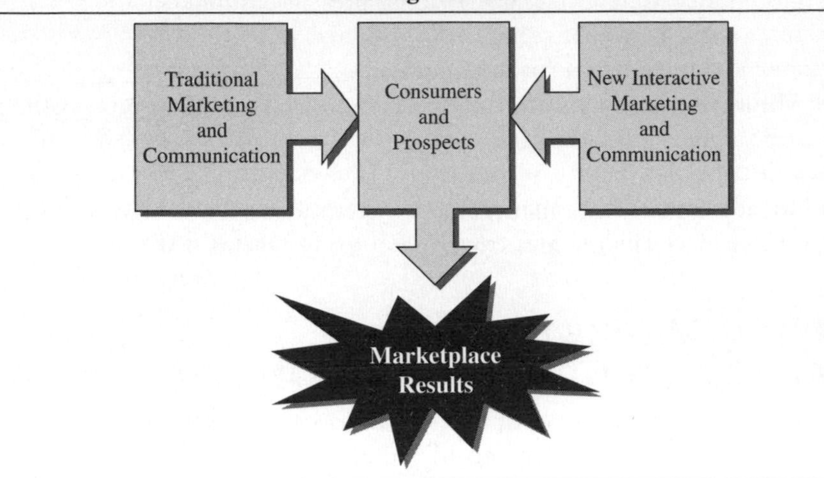

by electronic systems. In many cases, the same customer or consumer who sees a television commercial also surfs the net. It is the same person who buys online who also goes into traditional bricks-and-mortar stores to purchase products. In short, it is a combined, converging, interactive, interconnected, and networked system of customers, marketers, distributors, and technology that challenges today's marketing organization.

To deal with this new, complicated marketplace, the traditional step-by-step marketing plans and programs dictated by the 4Ps simply will not work. We need new processes, systems, and approaches. In this book, the Kellogg and IMC faculty outline an integrated marketing concept that can be implemented as a marketing management system; in other words, a process for a process-driven marketplace.

As you will see, the Integrated Marketing Management System developed by the Kellogg and IMC faculty puts the marketing concept into practice. The approach starts with customers and consumers. Through the use of information technology, we can conduct various marketing activities starting with finding relationship subsegments, measuring customer profitability, and then moving on to dynamic pricing and the development of integrated channels and distribution systems.

The Integrated Marketing process guides the manager in focusing on the key ingredients:

- Acquiring new customers,
- Communicating with and managing present customers,
- Integrating customer service into the mix,
- Rewarding customer loyalty, and then
- Mining the customer information base to find customer cross-selling and migration possibilities.

In short, it is a marketing management system focused on the true meaning of marketing: finding and satisfying customer wants and needs.

MIXING MARKETING AND MARKETING COMMUNICATION

Traditionally, marketing communication has been viewed as a subset of marketing, that is, it has been considered as ways in which the marketing organization could develop and distribute external communication programs about its products and services to potential customers or prospects. For the most part, in a product- or even a distribution-driven marketplace, marketing communication was often viewed as a tactical luxury, something the organization could turn on or turn off as it felt necessary. The real value of the offering was believed to be inherent in the product or service with its unique attributes, things that separated the product or service from competitors. Often, these attributes were called "sustainable competitive advantages."

While a sustainable competitive advantage is an excellent objective, it is increasingly difficult to gain or maintain. Technology has allowed competitors to quickly replicate or even improve or enhance any manufacturing development. In service organizations, competitive advantage is even more tenuous. For example, a new product developed by a bank or financial institution now has a life-span of about 20 minutes, or the length of time it takes the competitor to match it and offer it to its customers. Thus, the entire spectrum of competition has changed and will continue to change.

Over the past several years, marketing managers have begun to realize they can no longer compete on traditional product or service differentiation. They must compete on something they can create, manage and enhance over time—increasingly, that is the brand. Accordingly, we have seen a substantial increase in interest, involvement, and development of brands and branding capabilities as one of the key ingredients for a successful marketing organization. Both Kellogg and IMC have spent many years studying, developing, and implementing concepts and approaches that help organizations build strong, effective, and most of all sustainable brands in the marketplace. Therefore, the approach in this book is not based on an Industrial-Age approach to marketing where the emphasis is on product attributes and benefits. Instead, it is focused on an Information-Age approach which posits that brands are the one and perhaps only sustainable competitive advantage the marketer has or will have in the marketplace.

The approach in this book is based on an Integrated Brand Management process. Yet, this brand management is not that which has been practiced traditionally in fast-moving consumer products firms. Instead, our brand management approach views the brand as the primary competitive differentiator for products, services and organizations that build on-going relationships with customers and consumers. In truth, it is the brand with which the customer or consumer has a relationship, not the product or the service or the price or the discount coupon. It is the emotional tie the customer has with what he or she perceives to be the value, benefit, and, yes, even psychological comfort that a strong brand brings to the marketplace.

Historically, brands have been thought to have been the result of the mass marketplace communication investments and approaches. That is, the brands were created through massive amounts of media advertising through clever and creative messages, icons and packages. Today, we are beginning to understand that brands are instead based on customer experiences. It is the value the brand provides the customer over time, not the short-term creative or "edgy" television commercial that builds customer loyalty. Thus, managing brands is really about managing customers and that is what Integrated Marketing and Integrated Marketing Communication are all about.

Yet, detractors have said that Integrated Marketing will not work. Either the product, service, or brand is a mass market entity, developed and supported with media expenditures and publicity, or it is an individualized, mass-customized product or service that relies not on the brand but on the actual value delivered to the customer, created and developed by personalized, one-to-one communication approaches. Integrated Marketing recognizes that both are needed.

In an integrated system, marketplace familiarity and acceptance are required, and that often calls for mass market and mass marketing programs. At the same time, customers need to have the contact and personalization of one-to-one programs. We visualize the system as something like that shown in Figure F.6.

Figure F.6
Umbrella Graphic

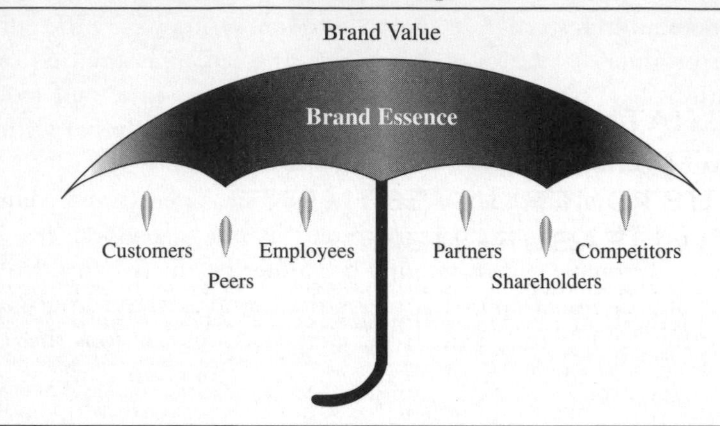

To succeed in the interactive and networked marketplace of the twenty-first century, the marketing organization needs to create what is often called a *brand umbrella*. This brand umbrella is:

- The broad, market-encompassing essence or value the brand presents to both customers and other stakeholders.
- The familiarity of value and worth that comes from the brand name and brand recognition.
- What imbues Mercedes, Virgin, Tiffany's, Evian, Dell, and Starbucks with the market cachet that says they are market leaders.
- What provides specific benefits and values to all stakeholders.

Underneath that broad brand umbrella, there are specific benefits that customers and prospects want and need. Those are and can be delivered by various one-to-one forms of marketing and communication. This tailoring is what creates relevance for individuals and groups of individuals to find specific benefits under the broad brand umbrella. That relevance and its benefits are what we meant in Figure F.5 when we talked about convergence.

Convergence is important not just in the physical distribution of marketing and communication programs, but also in terms of the ability of the brand to provide differing values to a broad spectrum of customers and users by varying the marketing and communication approaches as needed or required. Thus, Integrated Marketing and Integrated Marketing

Communication provides value to all levels and all sections of the market and customers—this is what really drives the need for integrated programs and processes.

Integration and Return on Investment (ROI) or Return on Customer Investment (ROCI) Measurement

One of the major challenges for all marketing management is to provide verifiable methods of measuring the return on marketing and marketing communication investments. The lack of so-called "marketing metrics" has long plagued the field. Measurement, accountability, or simply determining what the organization got for its marketing investment are the key elements of an Integrated Marketing process.

What makes measurement possible in an Integrated Marketing process is the underlying knowledge that the organization has about its customers and prospects. As Professor Mulhern illustrates in his chapter on measuring customer profitability, by knowing the value of a customer, marketing firms can set up investment strategies and return calculations on an ongoing basis. While there is still much work to be done in this area of marketing metrics, particularly in activities such as communicating with customers, measuring returns on customer service and loyalty programs, Integrated Marketing is a major step forward in terms of making marketing an accountable, strategic activity in the management of the firm.

Where Do We Go from Here

This book should not be considered the "end-all" in marketing. Indeed, it is more a work-in-progress which illustrates the improvements that the faculties of Kellogg and IMC have made to this point. No doubt there will be more and greater progress in the future as we address such issues as globalization, measurement of brand equity, and the like. But, in the spirit of progress, Northwestern University, with this book, maintains its commitment to the development of new thoughts, new concepts, new approaches, and new practices in the fields of marketing and marketing communication. With an over 100-year tradition to keep up, we cannot stop now.

CHAPTER 1

OVERVIEW OF KELLOGG ON INTEGRATED MARKETING

DAWN IACOBUCCI and BOBBY J. CALDER

Current marketing practice is simultaneously exemplified by the seeming paradoxical extremes of mass branding and one-to-one relationship marketing. This book merges these two streams into a single, integrated concept. The chapters in this book describe the mass and relationship approaches and a vision of how these marketing philosophies can be combined. The contributing authors address methods for handling specific marketing activities to take advantage of these synergies.

The foreword, "Evolving Marketing and Marketing Communication into the Twenty-First Century," is written by Don E. Schultz, the pioneering thinker of integrated marketing communications and founder of the group by the same name at Northwestern University. Schultz describes how integrated marketing communications can and should be justified in terms of return on investment, thereby demonstrating the importance of this integrated vision for marketing in the future. Schultz shows how the two independent streams, mass and relationship marketing, parallel the history of the Marketing Department in the Kellogg School of Management and the Integrated Marketing Communications center in the Medill School of Journalism, both at Northwestern University. Communications to customers began as mass, undifferentiated efforts, including tactics of advertising, sales promotion, and even public relations. More recently, tailored approaches, such as direct marketing, allow an organization to become "customer-centric," primarily by being database-driven. Schultz demonstrates the importance of coordinating the communications to customers not only across media, but also, for example, across global reach and channel outlets, including the Internet. This coordination is not intended simply to streamline business practice and logistics. Rather, Schultz lays the groundwork for a theme that appears in most of this book's chapters: Marketers seek coordination and consistency in messages to build brands.

Kellogg on Integrated Marketing differentiates and simultaneously integrates classic, mass branding efforts with relationship, one-to-one marketing. The positions are defined and illustrated. In Chapter 2, Bobby J. Calder and Edward C. Malthouse describe a model for the *integrated marketing* concept and show how it can be implemented as a marketing management system and a guide to directing specific marketing activities.

Kellogg on Integrated Marketing continues with the authors addressing the daily activities of the marketing manager. Most of these activities share the principle goal of enhancing brand equity. Tom Collinger, in Chapter 3, "The Tao of Customer Loyalty: Getting to 'My Brand, My Way,' " considers what has probably become the premier marketing truism—the importance of customer loyalty. While marketers would presumably agree with the goal's importance, Collinger describes the challenges in achieving that goal. He recognizes that loyalty is not attained simply by offering a superior product or price, delivery system or customer service privileges, and so on. Rather, Collinger sets forth guidelines in the search for loyal customers and, with each step, describes some signals that you can use to assess your own company or your own brand to diagnose whether your company or brand is on its way to achieving customer loyalty.

In Chapter 4, "Using Interaction Maps to Create Brand Experiences and Relationships," Andrew J. Razeghi and Bobby J. Calder explore the varieties of relationships that customers have with brands and the implications of the anthropomorphic process of attributing personalities to brands. They present a logic and methodological process for mapping a customer's interactions in a consumption setting (e.g., with a service provider). This detailed charting can be used to describe the current state, as well as to postulate an ideal, goal state, in which the customer interactions with the provider may go beyond the conventional, far to the innovative, to approach higher levels of customer satisfaction. The authors demonstrate the utility of this mapping approach to the case of the Celebration Health Care organization.

Lisa Fortini-Campbell discusses how you might best communicate with your customers in Chapter 5, "Integrated Marketing and the Consumer Experience." She reminds us that a marketing manager should not make assumptions about consumers' perceptions of a brand—rather, marketing managers should go out there and listen to their customers. Customers often value brands for many reasons that could be largely unanticipated by the prevailing wisdom of the brand manager. Fortini-Campbell describes how customers form impressions and make assumptions about even apparently minor features of brands (e.g., price, channel availability, packaging colors). She shows how readily customers' impressions of brand features are tied to their perceptions of the brand's overall equity. She offers two analytical tools. First, she describes how to create a brand inventory of every piece of information about a brand—every one of a customer's contacts with the brand. Second, she uses these inventories to diagnose qualities about the brand and to form a mapping of the brands, and competitors' brands, into perceptual maps characterized by customer emotions, including delight, annoyance, disgust, and frills.

Only those managers not paying attention to current marketing phenomena would not have heard the otherwise unusual phrase *Viral Marketing*. In Chapter 6, "Strategies for Viral Marketing," Maria Flores Letelier, Charles Spinosa, and Bobby J. Calder substantiate what has heretofore been largely buzz. The authors present ideas that explain how customers help, or hurt, the marketing process. They describe opinion leaders, those sources of desired buzz. The chapter shows how important it is to learn about the various communities, or segments of interacting customers who are driven by different motivations, and ways to engage these different groups, given that they value different benefits. The chapter is rich in examples—from BWM to Martha Stewart.

Lisa A. Petrison and Paul Wang remind us in Chapter 7 that the key to customer loyalty, brand equity, and, ultimately, profitability is the job of "Acquiring the Right Customers." Marketers know that it costs a lot to acquire customers, and the authors elaborate on such marketing efforts. Petrison and Wang describe the scenarios for which acquisition is a sensible strategy. They discuss traditional means of acquiring customers, including mass media and direct marketing, and they offer their present vision of more optimal, longer term-oriented, direct customer contacts. These direct contacts are facilitated with data and information that can be used to profile the customer, and then to assess a customer's desirability and status. Petrison and Wang offer us a means of answering the question, "Is this customer a 'good' one, worthy of acquisition?"

In tune with the marketing goals of Chapter 7, Edward C. Malthouse, in Chapter 8, "Database Sub-Segmentation," walks us through the task of how we might find relationship segments. Traditional market segments are often too large to be useful, and one-to-one marketing efforts are still technologically and logistically unrealistic. Meeting somewhere in the middle, more refined than big, rather heterogeneous segments, but more actionable than segments of size one, Malthouse shows us how to use a variety of data sources and analytical techniques to achieve this more optimal middle solution. He talks about enlisting buying segment information, such as geographic-based data, and integrating it with data-mining exercises on a company's extant database, such as their lifetime customer value assessments. With these data sources and options among technical tools, the marketing manager can understand much more clearly which customers are profitable and those that are not worth the company's targeted marketing efforts.

Continuing with this logic, in Chapter 9, "Customer Profitability and Diagnosing a Customer Portfolio," Francis J. Mulhern shows us how to precisely measure customer profitability. He reminds us that profitability requires the measurement of customer revenue streams, but also costs. He describes and assesses the usefulness of a variety of indices that describe the range in profitabilities of customer segments. He works through these indices using an example of ready-to-eat cereals.

In Chapter 10, "Decision-Guidance Systems," Nigel Hopkins, Adam Duhachek, and Dawn Iacobucci describe qualities of the ideal information system for the marketing manager. Current practice falls short, in part because opportunities for customer insights are not used strategically. Better planning allows for more efficient research efforts, and more precise analyses allow for more actionable and useful results. Marketing managers do not want extensive, well-coordinated databases as an end in themselves. Rather, these are but high-technology tools to facilitate serving customers, building brands, and truly understanding the marketplace.

Chapter 11, "Scoring Models," demonstrates how the marketing manager can plan effectively and spend marketing dollars efficiently by optimizing customer contacts. Edward C. Malthouse demonstrates how to use several data-mining techniques to try to predict customers' future purchase behaviors. He works with concepts such as lifetime customer value, customer retention, and even an understanding of customer defection to inform the marketing manager which marketing tactics have been, and would be, most useful. Malthouse presents two illustrations—the applications of his ideas to catalogue purchases and to magazine subscriptions—to demonstrate how complementary data sources can be used to build a database and a scoring model. He also demonstrates how the marketing manager can evaluate the usefulness of those scoring models.

In Chapter 12, "Integrating Marketing and the Web," Eric G. Berggren, Bobby J. Calder, and Richard I. Kolsky talk about the topic that everybody feels knowledgeable about, yet all too often is proven otherwise. The Internet provides a tremendously powerful opportunity to reach customers, and there is no reason this channel cannot be used in a highly successful manner.

The authors first analyze and revisit some of the classes of errors made in primitive attempts by companies to harness the potential energy of the Web. Next, they share their vision of how to succeed. (Hint: Do not forgo your marketing; e.g., segmentation, positioning of the brand.) They offer two in-depth case illustrations of integration in action: Priceline and eBay.

Kellogg on Integrated Marketing closes with two perspectives. Bobby J. Calder considers "An Illustration of Integrated Marketing" in Chapter 13. In Chapter 14, "Reflections on Becoming a Great Marketing Organization," Stephen Burnett tells stories of lessons learned and lessons shared from a variety of customers of the Kellogg School of Management's executive programs in marketing. Kellogg has earned its reputation as the premier marketing business school in part because of numerous successes, such as implementations in companies by managers who came to the Kellogg training programs with questions and who left as marketing strategists. We hope that this volume continues to contribute to the stimulation of raising marketing questions and effecting useful marketing solutions.

CHAPTER 2

WHAT IS INTEGRATED MARKETING?

BOBBY J. CALDER and EDWARD C. MALTHOUSE

Marketing has always meant, and will continue to mean, responding to consumers (or, in the case of intermediaries, customers) to increase sales. The alternative has been, and will continue to be, to seek other sources of competitive advantage, such as technological innovation, access to resources, and competitive barriers. The concept of marketing is unchanging.

This does not mean, however, that our guiding philosophy of marketing—how we think about implementing the marketing concept—should remain unchanged. For some time now, there has in fact been a growing recognition of the need for change.

The loudest calls for change, for moving away from the traditional view of marketing, have come from what we think of as "fill-in-the-blank before the word *marketing*" business books and articles. What we need is *relationship* marketing, or *loyalty/retention* marketing, or *one-to-one* marketing, or *database* marketing, or *experience* marketing, or some other "______ marketing." Most of these present interesting ideas but they have not been sufficient to point the way away from the traditional view of marketing. Perhaps the only exception has been the notion of *integrated marketing,* which is the term we adopt here for describing an emerging and potentially comprehensive new philosophy of marketing.

We first describe the themes that have emerged under the banner of integrated marketing. Then we contrast these themes with a portrait of the traditional view of marketing. We conclude by summarizing some of the reasons for rethinking the traditional view and providing a sketch of how a new, integrated view of marketing might look. Other chapters in this book elaborate on the details of many of the issues raised by this philosophy.

THREE EMERGING THEMES OF INTEGRATED MARKETING

The term *integrated marketing* has been broad enough to encompass three different, but related, themes. The strongest theme has been the contention that marketing should be more targeted. Rather than focusing on large numbers of people with common offerings, marketing should target fewer people with more customized offerings. The epitome of this is direct marketing, or direct mail, where solicitations are carefully crafted to people with highly specific interests or lifestyles. The advantage is that the marketing effort is not wasted on those who are less likely to respond. Moreover, the tailoring of the offer to a relatively small group maximizes the fit of the offer to the consumer's needs. The ability to customize the offer includes not only the use of targeted media (direct mail, telemarketing, etc.) but also the design and delivery of the product itself.

Much has been made of the advantages of tailoring and the increasing ability of companies to accomplish it. These advantages are very real. Much waste in the marketing effort is eliminated. Moreover, increasing the fit of the offer to the consumer goes to the heart of the marketing concept. It must be said, however, that tailoring has been reduced by some to a magic bullet approach to marketing. Its advantages have been stretched to the point of advocating "segments-of-one" as an objective in and of itself. It is as if the goal of marketing were defined to be the delivery of a unique product to every individual consumer. This denies the fact that part of the appeal of any brand is that its value is shared and acknowledged by other people. A true segment-of-one approach stands to lose much of this appeal. It may be one thing to have a pair of jeans that are perfect for me; it is another thing entirely if these jeans do not stand for something among my peers. It is not just what I know about the jeans, it is what other people know about them and what this conveys to me.

The advantages of tailored targeting are undeniable. Marketing needs to move in this direction. However, this does not imply a complete customization of offers. Nor does it imply that a segment-of-one is the ideal marketing target. We need to approach targeting in terms of optimizing response and minimizing wasted effort. It is in this sense that enhanced targeting represents a desirable advance in our philosophy of marketing. *Marketing needs to be integrated over more finely targeted segments of consumers.*

Another valuable theme emerging from calls for integrated marketing has to do with consumers themselves. There is a need to view the consumer whole. A consumer is not just a person who buys our product—a brand of jeans or a particular make of car—at a point in time. Consumers are more complex than this. The same consumer may buy other clothing items to go with the jeans or another vehicle for his or her household, and this may occur over some time. It follows that taking a more multidimensional view of the consumer may lead to larger opportunities than the one-time sale or even repeat purchase of a single product.

One dimension that requires more attention is time. A consumer may purchase a compact car today. But that same consumer can be expected to have a higher income as he or she gets older. Later, he or she may buy a larger, more luxurious family car. If we can anticipate this and take a more wholistic view of the consumer, we can market to the consumer in such a way that we aim from the beginning to sell the consumer both cars, quite possibly explicitly linking the purchases in the consumer's mind. We could even do something that might not be financially justified in selling the consumer the compact car; for example, including a luxury feature or having more amenities in the showroom. This takes into account the *long-term value* of the consumer. (As with segments-of-one, it should be noted that this issue is sometimes exaggerated too. It is sometimes discussed as lifetime value, as if the goal were to extend the marketing time horizon as far as possible.)

Another key dimension is choices of related products. If we know the consumer's preferences for jeans, this should allow us to sell sweaters, belts, shoes, and other related items more effectively. This extends beyond obviously complementary products. Knowing that a person wears a brand of jeans may just as well extend to selling shorts for the summer. The opportunity is for more systematic *cross-selling and up-selling*. (Again, this should not be an end in itself. Embracing cross-selling as an objective in and of itself may well annoy consumers. The objective is to use cross-selling in a way that makes sense to consumers.)

This logic applies to any dimension of consumer behavior. A consumer's protection needs become an opportunity for taking a brand across many different platforms, from insurance to alarm systems. The opportunity is for *cross-platform branding*. Marketing needs to be integrated over time and other dimensions of consumer behavior.

A third theme of integrated marketing concerns how we communicate with consumers. We need to move beyond a focus on measured media. In many ways, television advertising has become the norm for communication. It allows marketers to reach large audiences efficiently with highly visual, entertaining messages. Even when television is not economically justified, other communication decisions are often framed in terms of what can be done in the absence of television (how other media can be used to make up for a lack of television).

Even in industries that still rely more on personal selling than measured media, there is a tendency to approach consumers or customers as if the sales situation were a media exposure, another way of getting across the message. A pharmaceutical detail-person is likely to approach a doctor with a very scripted, media-like presentation.

There is a need to view communication more broadly, to see it as more than media-delivered messages. Consumers have many *contact points* or *touch-points* with brands. Many of these are not media exposures. A consumer certainly uses the product. Inherent in this usage are contacts that can be important from a communications point of view. A consumer's opening of a box that the product comes in can be a major opportunity for communication. A call to an 800 number can be a communications opportunity. Consumers talking to other consumers represent an opportunity for *viral* marketing.

We need to move away from an overemphasis on media exposures as the objective of communications. Any contact with a brand is a communications opportunity. *Marketing needs to be integrated over both measured media and other communication opportunities.*

THE TRADITIONAL FUNCTIONAL VIEW OF MARKETING

We have reviewed the three major themes emerging from calls for integrated marketing:

1. Integrating the marketing effort over more finely tuned segments.
2. Integrating over time and other dimensions of consumer behavior.
3. Integrating over both measured media and other communication opportunities.

Another way of looking at the need for change is to revisit the traditional view of marketing. For many decades, this view has stood as the guiding philosophy of marketing. For many people, it is so natural that by now it can seem the only possible view. By taking a fresh look at this view, and by trying to bring its major features into bold relief, we can perhaps see the rationale for change more clearly.

An overview of the traditional view of marketing is shown in Figure 2.1. First, marketing is approached as a business function. It is one of several functional areas such as finance and production. Part of the rhetoric of

Figure 2.1
The Traditional Functional View of Marketing

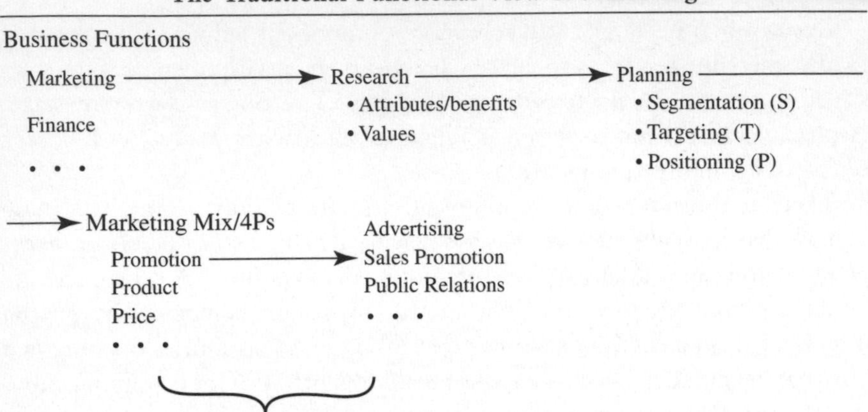

marketing may be that "marketing is everyone's job" and there may be high-level marketing executives in place, but most marketing activity is still viewed functionally. Marketing primarily exists to execute activities that are among the many functions that must be performed by the enterprise. These activities may be guided by a strategic marketing plan, but strategy is closely linked to the marketing tactics of the firm.

Marketing research is used to supply information about the needs and wants of consumers as they relate to the product offerings of the firm. The focus is ordinarily on identifying the key attributes or features of products that are most important for consumer wants and needs, possibly including identification of the benefits provided that actually satisfy the consumer's needs. In some cases, it may be possible to *ladder-up* to higher-order benefits or values that, if associated with the product, typically through advertising, can produce even greater levels of satisfaction.

Ideally, marketing research feeds into a marketing plan that gives direction to marketing activities. The critical elements of the plan are specifying how the market for the product is segmented and selecting the segment(s) to be targeted. Targets are profiled with both demographic and psychographic descriptions. The ultimate objective is to state a *positioning* for the product that reflects the insights of the marketing research into the key attributes and benefits for each segment. (Sometimes the positioning is stated in the form of a promise to the consumer or as a brand personality or another specific device.) Usually, it is possible to target only one or a very limited number of segments. The positioning statement for a segment drives marketing activities by stressing that these activities all relate to the key attributes and benefits. All together, this is sometimes referred to as the *STP process* (segmentation, targeting, and positioning process).

Marketing is primarily about the functional translation of the planned STP into activities. These activities are often collectively termed the *marketing mix,* which is made up of the "4Ps." The product needs to be promoted, and this is one P. The positioning also needs to be related to the product itself in terms of accentuating key attributes and benefits, the placement or distribution of the product, its pricing, and so forth. This logic can be extended to other activities, even more than the classic four Ps. Each of these in turn can be further broken down functionally according to increasingly specific activities (see Figure 2.1). Promotion can thus be divided into advertising, sales promotion (coupons, in-store displays), public relations, Web site, trade relations, and the like.

The major underlying concern that guides marketing thinking with this philosophy is the *orchestration* of all of the marketing mix, 4P-type activities according to the positioning of the product. There is a need to coordinate across all activities so that the STP process drives each activity. The classic role of the *brand manager* in consumer package goods firms is to affect this kind of coordination. Orchestration is difficult and often requires a brand management form of organization because many activities also involve the functional expertise of other areas. Therefore, it is necessary, for instance, to involve technical or production people in orchestrating product decisions. Without brand management, orchestration requires cross-functional teams, and organizational issues become even more complex.

When it works, the traditional philosophy results in consumers who are aware and knowledgeable about the fit of the benefits of the product to their needs and who can clearly perceive this fit in the design, delivery, and pricing of the product. This clarity and consistency in turn fosters a commitment to the product that translates into repeat purchases.

In our view, there is no question of whether this traditional functional view of marketing is right or wrong. It is a demonstrably useful way of thinking about marketing. It is certainly superior to the contrasting "sales" view of pushing products at consumers. The only question is whether it has weaknesses that need to be addressed.

Weaknesses of the Traditional View

Traditional marketing thinking, even when executed well, sometimes encounters difficulties. Despite the emphasis on marketing research and insight into key attributes and benefits, this view still leads to an emphasis on the product as it exists, or as it is technically conceived. Marketing is viewed as driven by the consumer in that functional decisions are made with the consumer's needs in mind. However, product positionings are often too product-centric and ultimately too similar to the positionings of competitive products. This leads to a feeling on the part of consumers that many products could satisfy their needs and that many marketing efforts amount to overblown hype.

The problem of product-centric positioning is compounded by pressure to define segments too broadly. To maximize the available market, large segments are considered desirable. This often means that the positioning for a segment must work for a very large number of people. Finding a positioning that works for all of the people in a large segment means that the positioning has to be very general or abstract. Clarity is lost in the process, and the positionings for competitive products are more likely to be similar. Moreover, it is difficult to compensate for this tendency by targeting many (possibly smaller) segments. Marketing activities must be performed differently for each segment and managed so as not to confuse consumers. Even if different positionings are found for different targeted segments, it becomes difficult to implement these with separate marketing programs. There are classic successes (Tide and Cheer), but these are hard to duplicate.

Beyond all this, the traditional philosophy of marketing works best when a high level of orchestration is achieved. It is more limited when areas (typically areas outside promotion) resist coordination with marketing. Unfortunately, this is all too often the case.

Orchestration also becomes problematic when companies neglect the functions of research and planning. Some companies try to do planning without research or, possibly even worse, go from research directly to the marketing mix. The consequences of trying to orchestrate the marketing mix after skipping the research and/or planning steps can be ugly indeed.

These problems with the traditional view of marketing are not addressed in most companies. Segments are commonly too broad, positionings too general. Orchestration is limited mostly to promotion. Consequently, opportunities for tailoring brands to segments are missed. Consumers get a sense that the product is for them, but they do not experience a close tie to the product; they identify more with the specific product and less with a larger brand concept. They see the product as a one-time or repeated decision that is a small part of their overall behavior. Media advertising may well be the most salient thing to them.

When we reflect on the traditional functional view, we see how its weaknesses coincide with the integrated marketing themes that we began with. Integrated marketing is a way of capturing the missed opportunities inherent in the weaknesses of the traditional view of marketing.

A VISION OF INTEGRATED MARKETING

It remains to offer a more systematic view of what integrated marketing is. Or, more accurately, we offer a vision of how thinking about marketing could evolve to take into account the weaknesses and opportunities of the traditional view. We see this as more evolutionary than revolutionary, and perhaps best confined to discussions of specific topics such as the ones contained in this book. However, it might still be helpful to give an overview of what integrated marketing might look like. For purposes of the present discussion, we will continue to deal with marketing to consumers or intermediary customers, but it should be acknowledged that the same logic applies to marketing to other stakeholders such as investors or employees.

As depicted in Figure 2.2, we see integrated marketing as a process originating with corporate strategy. It should rise from a corporate strategy that recognizes that operational excellence by itself is no longer a viable strategy. Operational excellence is a given, a requirement for doing business in most industries or product categories. The real strategic challenge is to be different[1] or even to revolutionize the industry or category.[2] Thus, for a quick-service restaurant chain, it is not a strategy to offer cleaner, more convenient stores. A strategy would be to offer stores with healthier menu items that transform the nature of fast food.

With a strategy in place, enter marketing. Marketing is the means to the ends of corporate strategy. Marketing deals with how the firm makes the strategy happen. The critical step is this: Marketing must conceive of an idea that could make the strategy work in the mind of the consumer (customer). What could a healthy fast-food restaurant be to a consumer? To put it differently, how might it make sense to a consumer? Perhaps our healthy fast-food

Figure 2.2
A Vision of Integrated Marketing

Corporate Strategy
Brand Concept
Experience
Contacts
Integrated
Customized Experiences
Sub-segment 1
Relationship
Different Contacts
Sub-segment 2
Relationship
Different Contacts

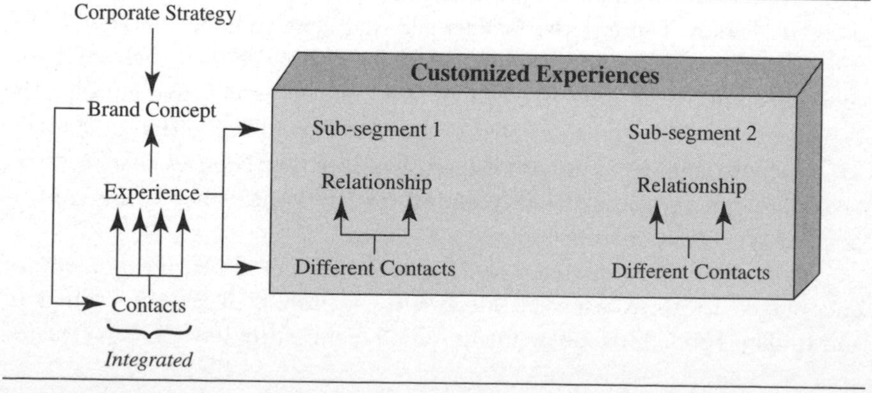

strategy could be the idea of *simple fresh foods prepared while you watch in a way that allows you to control the ingredients so that you know that what you are getting is good for you.* The idea is a concept that accomplishes the strategy by making it meaningful and relevant for the consumer.

The brand concept drives consumer thinking.[3] The concept is not merely a positioning that highlights aspects of the product. In a sense, it *is* the product. It is the idea that defines how the consumer should experience the product. But for this to happen, we must manage contacts with the consumer so that these contacts in fact produce an experience that matches the concept. The experience comes from these contacts: watching the food being made, seeing what the person making it looks like, hearing a friend explaining why the tomatoes are tasty, and, yes, perhaps seeing an ad. The contacts need to be managed in an integrated way over time and other dimensions of consumer behavior to yield the experience dictated by the brand concept. Marketing, as shown in Figure 2.2, becomes a continuous feedback loop. Marketing management becomes a core business process; it is not just a set of functional activities.

One further elaboration of this vision of integrated marketing is necessary. The philosophy described emphasizes the experience that consumers derive from contacts. A natural extension of this logic is to think in terms of sub-segments. Overall, the marketing effort may be directed at a fairly broad segment of people; for example, people concerned about eating in a healthier way. Because this segment is diverse, it is ordinarily possible to identify sub-segments. For any one of these sub-segments, we can then find contacts that are used only for that sub-segment and, therefore, define a relationship with the sub-segment based on a customized experience.

The guiding logic here is that experiences can be customized. Segments can be divided into sub-segments for this purpose. Some people who are concerned about eating in a healthier way think in terms of avoiding things that are harmful; others think of adding things to their diets that make them healthier. There is the *avoider* sub-segment and the *functional food* sub-segment. Different contacts could be designed for each of these sub-segments to customize the overall experience in a way that enriches the experience of the brand concept. As shown in Figure 2.2, different contacts for different sub-segments produce customized experiences that in effect take the form of personalized relationships (the experience being contingent on who the consumer is).

To illustrate, the *functional food* sub-segment could be given a menu or encouraged to go to a special side bar in the store that contains things to add to their food. This sub-segment would feel that they were being treated in a special way, thereby customizing the experience and fostering a sense of relationship. The principle is that sub-segmentation can be extended over time to create more and more relationships based on differential contacts that yield customized experiences. This can be done in a way that enriches the base experience and further reinforces the brand concept.

CONCLUSION

Integrated marketing means change. And there are two ways of thinking about change. You can think about where you are coming from. Or, you can think about where you are going.

We certainly would agree that it is possible to think in terms of the evolution of the traditional view of marketing. This does make thinking about the organizational and financial implications of change easier. There is merit to the argument that, at least to some extent, the issues raised here can be addressed within the traditional functional view of marketing.

At some point, however, it is necessary to face change head-on. The vision of integrated marketing sketched here may seem like uncharted territory, especially considering its largely unexplored, organizational, and financial implications. Nonetheless, it does offer a picture of real change.

No matter how change is approached, we hope that there can be agreement that change is necessary. Going-forward marketing:

- Must be more strategic in creating strong brand concepts that make corporate strategy happen.
- Must focus on a full range of contacts with consumers as they unfold over time and lead to a total consumer experience that is aligned with a strong brand concept.
- Must customize consumer experiences in a way that still allows for marketing to large numbers of consumers.

Notes

1. Michael Porter, "What Is Strategy?" *Harvard Business Review* (November/December 1996), pp. 61–78.
2. Gary Hamel, "Strategy as Revolution," *Harvard Business Review* (July/August 1996), pp. 69–82.
3. Bobby Calder, "Brand Design," in *Kellogg on Marketing,* ed. Dawn Iacobucci (New York: Wiley, 2001).

CHAPTER 3

THE TAO OF CUSTOMER LOYALTY: GETTING TO "MY BRAND, MY WAY"™

TOM COLLINGER

Name a company, a product, a brand, or a service to which you are loyal—really loyal. You could not be convinced to sample a competitor.

Who is this company; what is this brand?

Examine your behavior regarding this company. Have you always been loyal to it, as far back as you can remember? Or, is yours a new fascination, driven by a singular or memorable event? Are you fiercely committed to the brand, or could you be convinced to buy from the competition when you need to? Do you feel compelled to dissuade friends from buying from the competitors? Do you feel as if you are actually performing a sort of public service, helping friends by telling them of your feelings for *Your Brand Name Here?*

Now, why do you think you feel this way? Do you know? Does the answer live in a completely logical, cognitive place, one that requires little thought—something like these reasons:

- They make better shoes.
- It just tastes better.
- It's the safest car on the road.
- They have better deals.
- It's a brand from my childhood.
- They *know* me.

Or, does the reason for your brand loyalty live somewhere just outside your ability to explain it? Has a product, brand, or service crossed that barrier from being "their product" to being "your brand?" Is it so far inside you now that it is practically in your DNA?

Over the past three years, I have worked with more than 400 marketing professionals—some in the most senior management posts, with the majority in middle management—in workshop settings. Through these individuals, I have been able to gather input and data from two distinct areas on the subject of customer loyalty:

1. Their own self-reported brand passions as consumers.
2. Their knowledge of their customers' behavior.

Through them, I have also been exposed to thousands of consumers, *their customers,* with relationships to the brands for which the marketers work.

In a recent workshop, a woman found herself defending her relationship to Crest toothpaste because, as she put it, "My family has always used it." I asked her to explain. I might just as well have invited her to explain why she is tall, or Catholic, or left-handed. When asked what would happen if she had to make the choice between using Colgate, Crest's archrival, or nothing at all, she was unable to decide. Choice had abandoned her. Habit is what she proudly boasted in defense of her toothpaste-buying strategies. Habit can be based on pleasant memories of brands from our childhood.

Occasionally, a consumer is affected by one of those unpredictable, unexpected surprises that can catch you off guard and cause you to connect with the brand in a wholly new way. For example, an insurance company came to the rescue when you were in real need. Or, the typically unsympathetic airline went the extra mile that time you lost your luggage. Or, the credit card company called to tell you that there was an uncommon quantity and type of charges on your card and asked if you were aware of it, or if someone might have stolen your card. For these kinds of brand connections (and there are others), the motivators typically exist somewhere outside our consciousness. Are the reasons for our feelings of loyalty driven by the reason articulated by the man who was a very dedicated Coca-Cola drinker? He would not drink anything else. I asked him why. He paused, reflected, and admitted: He had no idea. He began to explain, paused, and said it again: He just did not know why.

Yes, marketers, loyalty still lives. There is no doubt that it is the real consequence of highly effective work by companies that know loyalty to be the gift the consumer gives them when that connection has been made. We all have it for something, or some company(s), and, in some cases, for many things.

How Do We Earn Loyalty?

Much research has been done on the phenomenon of customer loyalty. Frederick Reichheld's book, *The Loyalty Effect,* does a great job of lending some science to this otherwise elusive art.[1] One of his great breakthroughs was the quantification of the differential between the costs to acquire a new customer and those of maintaining a current one. Reichheld frames the economic benefits associated with successfully earning loyalty, and, in so doing, he has dared marketers to find a way to earn it, because the power of having it is so profound and an obvious business strategy.

The challenge is to understand loyalty well enough that we marketers can affect it, create it, and, at the very least, sustain it when and where we have earned it.

Market Forces Pushing Loyalty: First, *Loyalty Programs*

Marketers are working to improve loyalty at a growing pace. There has been an explosion of database marketing, points- and miles-based frequent user programs, typically referred to as *loyalty programs.* In addition, more and more companies are adopting or converting to more customer-centric strategies.

As a result, companies are training the consumer to expect to get something more than just the product or service in exchange for repeat purchases. Points and miles are now a new currency. They are transferred, donated, traded, and even passed down to heirs.

Companies have been born or morphed to build and support these programs. The catchall phrase, *customer relationship management* (CRM) has now taken over as the strategy, tactics, and technologies designed to win customer loyalty.

New and significantly improved technologies have been born to support these programs, resulting in customer identification cards, smart cards, credit card tie-ins, point of sale readers, personalized URLs, and so on. Add to this the myriad tools for marketers, from enterprise resource planning tools (ERP) to middleware tools, designed to make all these technologies work together, as well as the issue-specific tools, such as:

- Marketing automation.
- Call center automation.
- E-mail response management.
- Salesforce automation.
- Web site personalization tools.

Customers are changing their expectations, marketers are evolving their customer strategies designed to win loyalty, and these changes are, in some cases, rewriting all the rules.

Second, Being Where the Customer Is: Shifting from Managing Channels to Managing Customers

The history of channel management has been one in which companies seek to control one or multiple channels of distribution in ways designed to avoid conflict within and across the channels. This strategy has recently given way to one of channel integration, in which companies seek to manage customer relationships across multiple channels to ensure the customer can get *My Brand, My Way.* The challenge for marketers is to enable the customer to see, shop, and buy products the way they want, when and where they want. Otherwise, the customer can vote for an all too eager competitor who can deliver. As a result of this consumer demand, we have seen a change emerging: Manufacturers are now facing the consumer.

IBM sells direct through IBMDirect.com. IBM did not compete only in the computer category; through the 1970s, it was the 800-pound gorilla in the industry. The firm thoroughly dominated the computing industry with a majority-market share. Its dominance also, by management's admission, handicapped its ability to take a leadership role in the personal computer market. With Dell's and Gateway's direct-to-consumer models proving to deliver real value-added customer benefit, IBM needed to respond. It has elected to compete this way, building strategies to effectively manage its disparate channels of distribution, now to include a 24/7 store called *IBM Direct.* Dell has practically forced all the major manufacturers to step up in the same fashion.

GM and Autobytel sell direct. There is an old saying, "As goes General Motors, so goes America." Now GM is reaching out to consumers to invite them to shop and even buy autos the way they want to.

Sonystyle.com sells direct. Sony was among the best-regarded manufacturers whose well-crafted and extremely well-managed channel strategies demonstrate how to sell products at places like Kmart, as well as the highest of high-end audio and video retailers. Now Sony sells its electronic products direct to the consumer.

Tupperware sells at Target. In July 2001, Tupperware announced it was taking another major step toward being where the customer wants it to be, signing a joint venture with Target Stores that marks the first time Tupperware is available in a retail environment.

General Mills sells direct. I have always mixed different types of cereal in my bowl to vary the consistency and levels of sweetness. It turns out I am not alone, and this insight has been identified by General Mills (see mycereal.com) and leveraged by enabling consumers to do just this. I can tell the firm that I want to buy cereal composed of 40 percent Cheerios, 30 percent Wheaties, and 30 percent Lucky Charms; and they will ship this mix to me at home—another example of *My Brand, My Way*.

Manufacturers now know that, to earn a customer's loyalty, they must be where the customer is and provide service the way the customer wants it. These moves to direct selling are symbolic of a very significant shift.

How Important Is Loyalty? Why Bother?

Loyalty is interesting to consider, first as a consumer and, perhaps more importantly, as a marketer. But, is it important? Absolutely. Consider the following aspects of the importance of loyalty.

1. Getting customer loyalty is *it*. In 2000, the noted global executive search firm Heidrick & Struggles published the results of a survey that invited CEOs to identify the issues they considered to be of greatest importance for them.[2] Seeking and improving customer loyalty was the most frequent response given by more than 40 percent of U.S. CEOs.
2. Loyalty overlooks a screw-up. In the wake of the Firestone and Ford Explorer recalls in 2001, research was fielded to understand the impact of recalls on purchaser loyalty. The numbers in Table 3.1 suggest that the power of customer loyalty is so strong that a single recall, if handled well, has no impact on repurchase loyalty.
3. There is an effect of viral (word-of-mouth) marketing (e.g., "I'm mad as hell"): The Web has enabled groups of aggravated consumers to find a forum to vent their frustrations, both at substandard industry performance (e.g., planemad.com) and at specific companies.
4. A version of Pareto's Law still rules. That 20 percent of the market is responsible for 80 percent of the volume is a guideline. Some market

Table 3.1
Relationship between Numbers of Automotive Recalls and Customer Satisfaction

Number of Previous Vehicle Recalls	*Loyalty (%)*
0	57
1	57
2	56
3–4	52
5 or more	48

Source: Polk Manufacturer Loyalty Excelerator™ (more information is available online at: www.polk.com, under their loyalty "products.")

leaders know that the numbers may be even more substantial from the most loyal of the customer base.

5. Wall Street now values customer loyalty. The financial difficulties of Priceline.com have been attributed to its underlying business model, which does not encourage, or experience, repeat purchase activity among its core customers.[3]
6. Customers expect more personalized attention. Every major hotel chain now has a "preferred customer" check-in. Albertson's supermarket chain provides on-the-spot discounts clearly advertised for frequent shoppers only. In a recent survey of buyers' experiences completed by Brann Worldwide, 41 percent of customers surveyed indicated "they would stop doing business with a company that offers a special deal or rate for new customers, but does nothing for loyal customers."[4]

However, the slide in loyalty continues. The consumer is frequently still saying, "You haven't convinced me." A study by R. L. Polk found that among Generation Xers, the 25 million consumers between the ages of 20 and 35, manufacturer loyalty was more than seven percentage points lower than the industry average.[5] In addition, the study found

- Credit card companies and long distance providers now routinely accept customers' requests to renegotiate rates, reducing the customer relationship to the attribute of price alone.

- The growth of comparative shopping robots (software that can autonomously accomplish a task) on the Web has enabled comparison shopping to be done in the most overt of ways. Comparison shopping engines (CSEs) influenced $1.4 billion, or 3.7 percent, of the total $38 billion in Business-to-Consumer (B2C) e-commerce sales in 2000.

Thus, while we may agree that loyalty is important, we realize it is also challenging to achieve.

LOYALTY IS IMPORTANT, BUT HOW DO WE GET IT?

In particular, how do we achieve loyalty in a way that serves customers by understanding and leveraging their unique qualities? We know that the benefits of mass production and mass communication tend to deemphasize customer differences, but loyalty generation today requires marketers to know and recognize the differences among special market segments.

We also need to seek loyalty in a way that improves business. The cynic translates loyalty-based initiatives as "soft" nice-to-do initiatives that are replaceable during difficult market conditions. The evolved business sees loyalty development as a companywide initiative, a business strategy: Satisfy the high-value customers to make more money. In other words, as Willie Sutton said about why he robbed banks: "It's where the money is."

Loyalty must also be achieved via strategies that are managed in a way that builds on a brand's character and values. Warnaco, the manufacturer of Calvin Klein jeans and men's underwear, declared bankruptcy under Chapter 11 in June 2001, citing the deterioration of the brand's values as a driving force. When these high-value brands began to be highly discounted in mass merchandiser outlets, the perceived value of the brands eroded.

Loyalty must also be achieved with a methodology that introduces more facts and more data into the process that is all-too-often relegated to a "program" rather than a strategy, or as a "creative idea" rather than a measurable way of building business.

There Is No Simple Answer to Earning Loyalty

We know this, intuitively, but there is proof that the silver bullet does not exist. Companies that have not learned this lesson continue to funnel resources into so-called *loyalty programs* alone, as an independent initiative, disconnected from their core business. Earning loyalty is a companywide focus, not a program. Consider these examples:

- In the face of the pilot "slow-down" that United Airlines' customers experienced in the summer of 2000, even the loyal customer getting the most "goodies" in the Mileage Plus program said, "the goodies aren't enough" and moved to other airlines.
- Even among companies with active loyalty programs, 44 percent of customers surveyed in the Brann Worldwide Buyers Experience audit indicated that they would stop doing business with a company when they "join a membership program and collect points, but when I try to redeem them, I find that they're either unavailable because they're in limited supply, or I can't use them for what I want, when I want."[6]
- In the same survey, 42 percent of customers surveyed indicated they would stop doing business with a company "that makes me navigate through many push button options when I call them, even when all I really want to do is talk to a live person."

It Is Not Enough Just to Have the Best Product or Service Available

Walt Disney World consistently delivers one of the most highly satisfying customer experiences. Every cast member (employee) is trained and empowered to do whatever it takes to exceed the expectations of customers. The firm's continuous growth since inception more than 25 years ago is proof that this strategy works, but is it enough?

If it were, Disney would not have also identified the guest who most frequently stays on site at the park and then sought to improve this group's experience a bit more. But it has. Disney learned that the one hurdle these guests face, like everyone else, is standing in long lines for the best rides. Disney now offers special guests the opportunity to get into the theme parks two hours early.

It Is Not Enough Just to Have the Best Prices

Wal-Mart is about savings. The firm pioneered cost-cutting with its supplier partners to pass along savings to customers. It aggressively promotes price rollbacks in its advertising, but is it enough? If it were, Wal-Mart would not have also partnered with a bank to offer a points-based affinity credit card to increase the benefits and rewards of shopping at Wal-Mart.

It Is Not Enough Just to Have the Best Privileges for Best Customers

The Hyatt hotel chain has one of the best-developed frequent-guest programs, called *Gold Passport*. Those who are card-carrying members enjoy the privilege of avoiding the long lines at check-in. The program provides points for visits and for money spent in the hotel, all redeemable for exotic vacations at their resorts, but is it enough?

If it were, Hyatt would not need to deliver the occasional unexpected surprise in the form of a bouquet of flowers or bowl of fruit or note from the hotel manager with a complimentary cocktail offer in the hotel bar. These unexpected surprises do not arrive on a regular schedule, so they are not part of every visit. Hyatt must know that these actions have the result of increasing customer satisfaction and loyalty, beyond the points.

It Is Not Enough Just to Have and Provide the Best Information

In the late 1980s, American Express pioneered the year-end account summary, which provided card members with a comprehensive recap of their entire year's spending, classified by type of purchase. This innovation preceded the advent of Quicken and Microsoft Money, making it even more valuable as an information-based tool. Amex did not charge extra for this information, merely adding it to the benefits of membership, and adding to the brand's value.

Amex has continued to leverage the power of information as an attribute building value to the brand, through things like targeted permission-based e-mail services and its account center, which enables the aggregation of all online reports for everything related to financial management. This company has a history of using information wisely, but is it enough? If it were, Amex would not have also introduced Membership Miles, or the Optima Card co-branded with Delta Skymiles, enabling miles to be earned for purchases made.

It Is Not Enough Just to Have the Best Unexpected Surprises and Delights

Nordstrom has become legendary in business schools as the model for building an empowered sales force that connects with customers daily. Salespeople are schooled in exceeding customer expectations and are rewarded for doing so. Stories about them have become urban legends, exemplified by the one about the customer who successfully returned a set of tires to Nordstrom even though the store does not sell tires. Nordstrom truly uses unexpected surprises and delights as a weapon, but is it enough?

If it were, it is unlikely the firm would also have its highly publicized and successful semiannual sales. However, it does, because it knows that one arrow in the quiver is not enough to compete.

It Is Not Enough Just to Have the Best Delivery System

Amazon (Will there come a time when this brand name will not evoke debate among marketing professionals?) is rewriting the book on many things, and its story continues to be a fascinating one. Among the things Amazon has created is an almost perfect buying (as opposed to shopping) experience. With a customer's permission, the site e-mails suggestions for new books or CDs based on similar interests of like customers and allows a "one-click" shopping decision. Literally, with one click of the mouse, we can say, "Yes, I want it, send it, bill me"; and in three days, it is on the front doorstep. This is a near-perfect, frictionless delivery system. It is indescribably and, for now, incomparably easy, but is it enough?

If it were, Amazon would not also advertise 40 percent off on book titles, but it does because Jeff Bezos knows, as all market leaders know, that there is no single solution, no one attribute that results in a perfectly loyal customer.

In Sum, the Tao of Customer Loyalty Is That There Isn't a Silver Bullet

The six examples point to one of the obvious conclusions that professional marketers have always known: There is no simple, or singular, solution to earning customer loyalty. Nevertheless, there are methodologies that put far greater controls into the hands of companies, giving them the advantages they seek in the hunt for customer loyalty.

In our new millennium, there has been a rapid migration toward the adoption of CRM as this single silver bullet. The right technologies, driven by the right strategies in the hands of an enlightened workforce, seem to be the new motto of customer loyalty. There has been an explosion of tools enabling marketers to obtain, and then use, customer information to greatly improve the shopping and buying experience, but this, too, is not enough. A recent study suggests that less than half of the technology installations designed to improve the CRM process are considered successful.

What can work, however, is a process driven by a clear point of view about earning customer loyalty, which in turn drives increased profits. In addition to increasing the ability to achieve the profitability goal, the journey will unearth many more rewards.

THE PROCESS IN SEVEN STAGES

Depicted in Table 3.2 are the seven stages to successfully earn customer loyalty. Each stage is fully examined in turn. The diagnostic signals showing that a company understands the principles and has activated them in their strategic visions and daily business practices are also described.

Stage 1: Set the Vision

If the strategic intent of the company does not include a goal of increasing or improving customer loyalty, all bets are off. Regis McKenna recently opined that the responsibility for marketing now falls on the shoulders of the CEO, because a company's (and by inference, the CEO's) vision must be directly translated to and through marketing decisions. McKenna said:

> Marketing is becoming an integrated part of the whole organization, rather than a specific function. Who's responsible for setting the direction of a business? Who sets the marketing direction for Cisco? For Apple? For Microsoft? More and more, it's the CEO who is becoming the Chief Marketer.[7]

The Signals. The *signals* must be overt and clear. Look for signs in the annual reports of companies that have proven to be successful in earning

Table 3.2
The Stages of Building Loyalty

The Issues		*The Stages*
1. Where are we going?	→	Set the vision
2. Who's important?	→	Identify best customers
3. What are they worth?	→	Value them
4. What will I accomplish?	→	Set goals
5. What do I do for them?	→	Set attributes
6. How do I get the work out?	→	Communicate
7. Did it work?	→	Evaluate

customer loyalty. Read the interviews with senior management to see what they are talking about. Look for words such as *loyalty, customer satisfaction, repeat purchase,* and *retention* as signs of companies that are driven to exceed customer expectations with strategies designed to improve loyalty.

Conversely, be suspicious of the way loyalty is addressed if it resides exclusively in the form of a "Customer Loyalty Program." There are danger signs in this or in cases in which competitors add these programs but neglect to add real and sustainable value.

Stage 2: Identify Your Best Customers

In a workshop I led in 2000, an individual from one of the top five accounting and consulting firms told a story about an embarrassing meeting the company had hosted only months before, when a newly hired CFO at one of its client companies asked to review all the assignments done for his company in the prior 12 months, including the related billing fees. The accounting firm brought its records, as did the CFO. It turns out that the accounting firm understated the projects and the fees by 50 percent because it did not have a method of aggregating all client projects globally. Rather, the firm accounted for projects by clients on a country-by-country basis, consistent with the way they are organized by profit centers. In the absence of this information, the firm was unable to identify its best customers globally. The firm did not even know its clients.

In the past year, I have met with dozens of companies to learn that this anecdote is not uncommon. Most of those with whom I've met fall into one of these two categories:

1. Companies that have not identified their best customers.
2. Companies that feel that they have identified their best customers, but the understanding of this characterization differs across the company.

In a recent audit completed with 17 of the top officers at a large, publicly held company, a question was asked, "Who is your best customer?" No two answers were the same. The leverage companies have because of Pareto's Law is available only to those that know their best customers and understand what motivates them.

The Signals. Is there a common articulation of "our best customer"? For example, see how a credit card issuer might describe its best customers:

- *In company terms:* The top deciles from our database of those who have outstanding balances in the last sixty days.
- *In customer terms:* Two-income households with children living at home, who believe that life is for living in the moment. Consequently, they make the occasional unplanned, and sometimes large, purchase to make life feel easier, even if it is not in the budget.

The leading marketing companies are able to not only describe their customers, but do so in a rich and textured fashion. When Saturn invited its very loyal constituency of early adopters to come to Tennessee to the first celebration of Saturn, firm representatives met with these "ambassadors" for the car. Does Saturn have access to all the data on everyone who has bought one of its cars? Yes, and so do all the rest of their competitors; but with a focus on customer satisfaction as keen as Saturn's and events such as these celebrations, it has more than the data—it has knowledge about its best customers. In fact, Saturn's people have met many of those customers.

Stage 3: Value Your Best Customers

What is this special group of people worth? Is there a valuation that can be used to actually support resource allocation decisions? There is typically an intuitive appreciation for this concept, but best practices illustrate the ability to assign numbers in assessing *lifetime value* (LTV).

Credit card issuers aggressively solicit college students for cards, understanding that their monetary value to the company will be modest, at best, in the first several years of card ownership. The companies also know that the likelihood of creating a loyal customer is great with this group, as they seek to formulate professional relationships with banks, often for the first time.

Visa BUXX is a newly introduced prepaid card designed for parents of teenage kids, one that enables parents to introduce their teen to the lessons of managing credit and, in the process, give the teen his or her first credit experience. What is the likelihood that Visa will continue to be the card of choice for these teens in years to come?

Diaper companies have discovered that if they attract expectant mothers to their brands through Web sites and off-line information, they increase the likelihood that when the baby arrives, preference for the brand will be higher.

The very blunt guidelines for reaching customers effectively and with rigor include:

- Understand the revenue value for the targeted group.
- Understand the profit value for this group, independent of marketing costs.
- Understand the correlation or relationship between the value of this segment and the overall value of the current customer base.
- Agree on a timetable for the valuation that drives resource allocation decisions. In other words, if LTV calculations can really help shape the investment decisions made against this segment, LTV is an extremely valuable tool.
- Understand the pattern of value over time; for example: When do college students become profitable to a credit card company? When does an insurance company likely enjoy profit from a customer on whom it has spent aggressively to attract?

The Signals. Is the term *LTV* used at the company being assessed? If so, is it used by more than the analysts? Do marketers use the term to make resource allocation choices? Is customer valuation seen as a function of only immediate- to near-term value, such as the projected profit over the next 90 days? Are new customers monitored to identify their purchase patterns over the early stages of the relationship?

Stage 4: Set Goals

Alignment First. With a clear understanding of the "best customer segment," valuation in terms of customer segment, and overall business impact, goals can be set. Setting these goals typically determines where the issues of organizational alignment emerge.

More companies are organizing their marketing groups around markets or even market segments. Doing this makes it easier to set goals aligned with the strategic intent of increasing customer loyalty.

The FedEx marketing group is organized around market segments. The marketing managers typically "own" the segment all the way down to having each customer segment's database accessible on their desktops for analysis and decision making.

Early in 2000, Microsoft shifted from being a brand or product development structure to reflect a strategy similar to that of FedEx, in which it would seek to understand and market to segments.

Scholastic is a large, highly successful media organization that specializes in educational and developmental learning products. Like so many other companies that have built successful brands, Scholastic is in the midst of analyzing these marketing issues. Currently, the firm is organized around its very successful products, such as its Junior Scholastic Program and Grolier Book Club, in strategic business units (SBU). Scholastic understands that SBUs sometimes market to the very same targets independently, and it seeks to understand the risks and rewards associated with this approach.

Aligned with market segments, a company can design goals by customer groups that directly connect to overall revenue and profit goals. As Peter Drucker has recently reminded us, only customers actually pay for things, so only they (not products) are the ones able to generate revenue.[8] Table 3.3 contains a list of sample goals that a firm may wish to examine in creating its own loyalty strategies.

Revenue or Profit: Pick One. Marketers have been encouraged to set goals based on either increasing revenue or increasing profit, because doing both simultaneously has been a strategic challenge rarely accomplished. Lane Supermarkets, a small grocery store chain, claims to have succeeded in growing both, using a strategy that focuses on "best customers."[9] In 1999, this company analyzed the results of its weekly advertised sales, only to learn that its card-carrying frequent shoppers did not alter their behavior because of these sales. Rather, the low-price promotions were attracting the cherry-picking group of price-sensitive shoppers who would move to Lane's to take advantage of the heavily discounted milk and bananas but not return again until the next sale.

Mass-media publicized events were thus driving revenue growth at the expense of profit margin(s), which lead the firm to further analysis and research on its best customer segment. Many in this segment were time-pressed, two-income households with little leisure to grocery shop—people who actually would prefer to do this after the children are in bed, but typically after Lane's closed its stores. Therefore, Lane's communicated to these folks that it would keep the stores open later and offer delivery as well. The

Table 3.3
Sample Goals in Enhancing Customer Loyalty

Shall we grow the size of the segment? If so, by how much?
Shall we grow the value of the customers currently in the segment? If so, by how much?
Shall we seek to maintain the current value of this segment due to increased competition?
Shall we identify a group of "look-alike" best customers from our database, and seek to migrate them to the next level of value? How much is this move? For example, can a catalogue company move a customer segment from $150 in annual value to $200?

chain diverted funds from the heavily advertised sales attracting the non-loyal group to add more value to this special best-customer segment. The goal, increased profits, was achieved, but revenues grew as well because of the increased purchase frequency from Lane's (already) best customers.

Stage 5: Determine the Attributes Most Important to Best Customers

The prevailing wisdom on customer loyalty confirms that while price is often an important component of the customer shopping experience, it becomes decreasingly important as customer loyalty increases. While this fact is encouraging to marketers because it confirms the fundamental belief that the customer is connected for "value," not "price," it doesn't tell marketers what is truly important: If not price, is it points? miles? free delivery? better information?

The customer experience is multifaceted and dynamic; and any serious attempt to turn this magical blend of cognitive, psychological, and sociological influences into a simple model is a fool's errand. However, it is not entirely without predictability. There are, of course, tools that marketers use to put the right mix of levers and triggers in place in hopes of better connecting with the consumer. Yet, many of these prevent an iterative process from emerging. Ethnographic research is a wonderful tool to observe behavior, but even if it is done once a year, can it be used to alter a frequent buyer program?

What we can do is to decompose the customer experience enough to be able to analyze what might be of greatest importance to customers in hopes of then delivering on it and using a framework that can be revisited as regularly as needed. So, consider the framework presented in Table 3.4 as a way to understand the variable motivations of customer experience.

The value of this framework increases as it is fed with customer-directed input. It can be improved on as a marketing tool when it is informed with customer behavior, insight, and motivations. The methodologies for getting the input differs across organizations, but a single questionnaire-based approach yields a simplistic view. Rich data, typically coming in disparate forms, will be the most valuable tools to inform this framework.

An Illustration: How Stage 5 Can Work. For purposes of illustration, I have identified a credit card issuer or consumer bank as the marketer.

First, identify the customer experience, starting with the so-called best customer segment from the firm's view; and catalogue all the ways in which

Table 3.4
Drivers of Customer Satisfaction

For purposes of focusing on the most salient drivers to loyalty, the customer experience can be decomposed to reflect six attributes, all of which affects the customer value exchange. These six attributes are:

1. *Product performance:* the customer's Base Level of Expectation for what they pay for the product or service; *"Does this do what I expect it to do?"*
2. *Price:* the price for the product or service; *"What are (all the) costs for this?"*
3. *Information:* the intellectual property and communications that aid in the process of shopping and buying and using the product or service; *"I can see why and how to buy/use this."*
4. *Privileges:* the stated benefits of buying or using the product, over and above product performance expectations; *"If I buy, I get ______________, and the more I buy, the more I get."*
5. *Surprises and delights:* the unexpected and un-promised benefits that enhance the product or service; *"I never expected (them) to do this for me."*
6. *Delivery Systems:* the method of providing the product or service; *"It's how I transact with the company to have the product or service."*

A caveat for using the Framework: Use multiple sources of customer information.

products, services, benefits, and features are delivered within the framework. Build this into a comprehensive list of all the benefits the best customer sees in each of these six attributes:

1. For *product performance,* the benefits may be a plastic card that reliably allows credit transactions, a monthly bill that is accurate and on time, 24/7 customer service to resolve complaints, a competitive rate of interest on borrowed funds, universal acceptance, credit line, credit line increase availability.
2. For *price,* the benefits may be the available credit line, annual percentage rate to borrow funds, balance transfer rate, late charges or fees, annual fee for ownership.
3. For *information,* the benefits may include the how-to-use credit brochure, offers mailed along with the bill and separately, offers made by phone, national brand advertising, permission-based e-mail(s) containing relevant offers, privacy policy statements, notification in service establishments confirming acceptance of the card.
4. The *privileges* benefits might include frequent flyer miles for dollars spent on the card, cash-back bonus for dollars spent on the card, ability

to donate a portion of the charges to a charity, a dedicated 800 number reserved for "best customers," access to truly unique offers not made to non-credit card holders.

5. For *surprises and delights,* the benefits in the words of the customers might include these: "The call I got from the credit card company to ask if I might have lost my card because the pattern of my card usage had changed recently"; "the time I was out of town, unable to pay the bill on time, but the company waived the late fee because I'm a special (long-time) customer in good standing"; "the time I was told I could skip a payment one month because I was a special customer in good standing"; "the time I called in and didn't have to wait for even twenty seconds to speak to a live customer service representative."
6. Finally, benefits of the *delivery systems,* might include the process of using the card online and off-line, the way information from the company arrives, and all the ways to access the company.

Next, perform research in which selected members of this segment are invited to review, and add to the list, from their perspective. Rank order the six attributes in relative order of importance from the customer perspective, supplemented by research and analysis as needed.

Last, rank order the benefits in each attribute in relative order of importance, again driven by customer-supplemented research and analysis. Table 3.5 demonstrates a simplification of these steps and ways the information can be used to drive decisions.

Table 3.5
Rating Our Performance on Important Customer Attributes

Six Attributes	*Attribute Rating 1–6*	*Attribute Benefits Prioritized*	*Our Rating 1–10*	*Gap Index*
1. Product				
2. Price				
3. Information				
4. Privilege				
5. Surprise or Delight				
6. Delivery System				

Stage 6: Make a Communications Plan

In a wholly aligned organization, the individuals with marketing communications functions are working in a cross-functional environment with those in product development, so that the insights gained about customer needs are converted to product and service enhancements. In this environment, the opportunities to then communicate these enhancements and changes within the organization to "internal customers" and beyond the organization to "external customers" are more likely to be better leveraged.

Use the Data to Know What Works. In early 2000, Next Card, the online credit card issuer, gained a customer base of more than one million card holders in three years and admitted to having run 200,000 market tests in search of optimizing customer acquisition and retention efforts. Admittedly, this extraordinary number is facilitated by the exclusive Web-based environment in which Next Card operates, and the sheer number is imposing. Nevertheless, consider the significant advantage of knowing what is working and what is not. Consider how much more effective a firm can be in using customer feedback to continuously improve its business.

Consider, too, the Lane's supermarket case. This company used its analysis in its decision to divert funds from mass advertising to a more focused and directed program designed to enhance the current best customer's experience.

Historically, media planning has been done with a priority based on the media that gets the largest share of the communications budget, which, for many advertisers, means mass media, either television or print media. This tradition is becoming less often the case, however. Today, for example, Carat, one of the world's largest media-buying companies, refers to its approach as the "360 degree" view of the customer as the driver to their planning.

Or consider FTD.com, which launched its business using a healthy budget (over $3 million) in television advertising designed to reach the largest audience possible. Yet, with the power of data, the firm learned that the cost per customer acquired can be managed down with a far more targeted approach. In short, it now boasts a communications strategy that first focuses on the costs to earn additional purchases from current customers and then looks at the costs to acquire new customers.

This notion inverts the media planning model by first investing in those customers for whom the return on investment is greatest. Consequently, a different model, like that in Table 3.6, emerges.

Table 3.6
A Marketer's Knowledge of Customers' Important Attributes Drives Marketing and Communications

Who:	*Best Customers*	*Next Best Customers*	*Prospects*
	↓	↓	↓
What attributes matter	Surprises and delights, product performance, privileges	Product performance, privileges, price	Price, product information
	↓	↓	↓
Marketing goal	?	?	?
Communications goal	?	?	?
Communications plan	?	?	?

Stage 7: Measure and Evaluate

Today, with data emerging as a byproduct of practically every so-called marketing and sales practice, the challenge is less about having the ability to measure and evaluate the effect of an effort and more about what to measure and why. The presence of frequency-based loyalty programs ensures that hotels, airlines, supermarkets, bookstores, and so on have purchase behavior captured in a database. Add to this the explosion of information Web sites, and marketers are swimming in opportunity. This opportunity has caused an interesting new set of challenges within organizations. There are two, in particular, that I have seen emerge.

First, if "I" know it, shouldn't "we" know it? The single most frustrating, even maddening, practice I hear in workshops is the lack of information sharing within an organization. Companies waste significant amounts of time and money replicating findings already known or testing concepts already tested.

Procter & Gamble (P&G) is still credited with bringing so much science to the practice of marketing that it measures its risks, some argue, better than most. In 2001, the firm launched a worldwide intranet in which it committed to ensure that "what anyone at P&G knows, everyone can know." Through a Web-based environment, it has challenged everyone in the organization to share any learning by posting the information for all to see.

Imagine being hired as an assistant brand manager on the Luvs Diapers brand in the P&G office in Mexico City and being able to read the marketing plans, new product development initiatives, market tests, advertising research, advertising tests, and so on, on this brand, from dozens of offices all around the world, before beginning to solve the challenges that the Luvs brand faces in Mexico.

Now imagine competing with a company that has this ability. Today, it is a competitive advantage. Tomorrow, it may well become a "cost of entry." The lessons from this initiative require all marketers to capture the data, interpret the data, and convert it to insight and learning, and then, finally, to share it.

Second, which metrics really matter? The sheer volume of data is the second challenge and opportunity that has emerged in organizations. In the presence of so much to measure, the greatest challenge is to know what to measure.

How important is the knowledge of what to measure? It can be argued that this is among the more important strategic decisions to be made. As one of my faculty peers, Dr. Frank Mulhern (who wrote a chapter for this volume), likes to say, "What gets measured is what gets done." In the fall of 2000, a group of students in the Integrated Marketing Communications program at Northwestern University endeavored to answer the question, "What are the drivers to 'stickiness' in a business-to-consumer e-commerce environment?" Their research caused them first to understand what the term *stickiness* meant. How was it used? What did it tend to mean to users? The term was not universally accepted and it had different meanings. Consequently, the metrics used to describe stickiness were similarly lacking in consistency.

Most of the literature, however, suggested that stickiness was achieved when consumers came to a Web site frequently and stayed at the site longer than they would have for a competitor's site. When students compared this observation from customer-based learning, they came to believe that the metric to measure stickiness, *length of time at the Web site,* actually had an inverse correlation to repeat purchases because purchasers want ease of ordering, which, if inhibited, causes dissatisfaction and a lack of loyalty.

Therefore, which metric mattered? In the case of stickiness, repeat purchase behavior, not time spent at the site, was the metric to watch. Imagine if the strategic goal for the Web developers was to increase the length of time the consumer spent on the site. Surely, the measurement could be done, and this measure could demonstrate how well the goals were being met. Yet, though everything might be perfectly measured, the determination to measure the wrong metric might well hasten the demise of the business.

SUMMARY

Marketers have forever sought to increase customer loyalty. This goal is not new, and yet, the challenges to do so have increased. The customer is in greater control, and the fragile basis on which loyalty is built forces companies to consistently do better to earn it.

I believe no single tool or tactic serves to build loyalty. I do not believe that the consumer votes for products and services that are simply enhanced by unrelated benefits and privileges. Rather, it is the marketing organization that takes a systematic and strategic approach—actually a process driven by customer insight to earning loyalty—that I would bet on for a sustainable future growth.

The stakes are high, and consumers are only going to continue to demand that they get *My Brand, My Way.*

Notes

1. Frederick Reichheld, *The Loyalty Effect* (Boston: Harvard Business School Press, 1996).
2. Heidrick & Struggles surveys can be found at www.heidrick.com (see CEO Survey '99).
3. Patrick Barta, "Web Firms Underwhelm: Survey Finds Customer Satisfaction in U.S. Is Moderate and Spotty—There Are Stars, but Others Might Not Make It," *Wall Street Journal* (November 28, 2000), p. 25.
4. Brann Worldwide surveys on buyers' experiences can be found at www.buyers-experience.com (see Survey Results).
5. See Polk.com.
6. See Note 4.

7. Susan Kuchinskas, "The End of Marketing: Regis McKenna," *Business 2.0* (October 2000), (see business2.com). More of Regis McKenna's opinions may be found at www.mckenna-group.com.
8. Peter Drucker, *Management Challenges for the 21st Century* (San Francisco: Harper Business, 2001).
9. Scott Kirsner, "Dorothy Lane Loves Its Customers," *Fast Company* (June 1999), vol. 25, p. 76 (see fastcompany.com).

CHAPTER 4

USING INTERACTION MAPS TO CREATE BRAND EXPERIENCES AND RELATIONSHIPS

ANDREW J. RAZEGHI and BOBBY J. CALDER

The hallmark of an integrated approach to marketing is the translation of a brand concept, not just into advertising messages and other coordinated marketing mix decisions, but into specific contacts or touchpoints with the consumer. The goal is to create an experience that flows from the guiding brand idea. Here we describe a tool that is very useful in this regard, the *interaction map*. The tool was first developed in service industries as an aide to designing service systems. We find it to be much more broadly valuable as a tool for designing brand contacts.

The interaction map is a method for helping to design a brand experience. A brand experience is based on the specific set of contacts—both implicit and explicit—that defines the interaction occurring between a company and its target consumer or customer. The interaction map allows marketers to visualize what that interaction is now and the experience it gives rise to. The goal is to create an experience more in keeping with the brand.

Before describing interaction mapping methods, it may be helpful to make a further distinction between customer experience and experience innovation.

DIFFERENCE BETWEEN CUSTOMER EXPERIENCE AND EXPERIENCE INNOVATION

Interaction mapping gives managers a tool for thinking beyond service or operational improvements to identifying new routes to growth. Historically, interaction mapping has been the domain of customer service and service companies. Today, interaction mapping goes far beyond customer service to have implications for strategy development. In fact, service is no longer just the domain of customer service departments, much less service companies. There are two reasons for this: convergence and marketing noise. Strategy convergence is rampant in today's business world. In an MCI/Gallup Poll, when asked if the strategies of the four to five competitors in their industry were getting more alike, the same, or more dissimilar, more than 50 percent of respondents claimed likeness of strategy.

Add to strategy convergence the proliferation of marketing noise. Consider the facts. People *like* you. I mean, they *really* like you. In fact, they like you so much that they are adamant on reaching you—day or night. Today, you will be assaulted with more than 1,300 marketing messages. By 2003, online marketers will send more than 200 billion marketing messages via e-mail and text messaging. Let's do some simple math. That's 67 billion e-mails per year for three consecutive years; about 5.5 billion per month; 18 million per day; 750,000 per hour; 12,500 per minute; 208 per second. Given the proliferation of marketing noise and strategy convergence, it is not enough to tell a good brand story and to deliver good service. The brand must actually be expressed in service, and service must be broadly construed to include all contacts with consumers. Moreover, the experience arising from these contacts must be seen as a source of potential brand innovation.

As indicated, existing methods and techniques for mapping customer behavior have been designed primarily to improve service delivery systems. But think about the great experience brands, names such as Nordstrom's, The Ritz-Carlton, and Charlie Trotter's. These organizations have gone beyond making advances in how service is delivered in their respective industries. They have made significant improvements to the ways in which consumers interact with their brands.

Interaction mapping methods can be used by managers to think in innovative ways about brand experience. The strength of interaction mapping is not merely in its ability to improve service experience delivery systems per se. Interaction mapping has the potential to radically change the industry rules of the game when applied appropriately. Before explaining the details of the interaction map tool, we introduce a case situation that illustrates the innovative possibilities of the tool.

WALT DISNEY AND EXPERIENCE INNOVATION

The Walt Disney Company is an example of the potential of the interaction map tool. Disney obviously excels at translating brands into well-designed contacts that allow people to interact with the brand. They are a great example of the power of brand experience even in a world of strategy convergence and marketing noise. One element for which they are justly famous is what they call *"staging the guest experience."* You have only to think of visiting Disney World to realize the power of this brand experience.

Now what if the Walt Disney Company were to go into the hospital business? And what if it were to apply its brand experience expertise in "staging the guest experience" to a hospital environment? In short, what if Disney were to become a hospital? We are asking, in effect, if Disney could create a unique brand experience in health care by rewriting the rules of engagement, redesigning customer interactions, and creating new relationships with patients, family, and the community. The objective would certainly be to improve the existing health care service delivery model. However, the major goal would be to create new rules for interacting with health care customers. These rules would, no doubt, overturn conventional norms of hospital service. The result should be a brand of hospital experience like no other.

Disney is in fact doing this. Together with the Florida Hospital system, it has successfully identified, augmented, deleted, created, and overturned the conventional interactions between patients and hospitals through a brand experience known as Celebration Health. The Celebration Health case illustrates how you can use the principles and methods of interaction mapping to leverage your existing brand as well as create an innovative new brand experience.

THIS ISN'T MICKEY MOUSE HEALTH CARE: THE CELEBRATION HEALTH CARE BRAND

The Florida town of Celebration is tucked away on 4,900 acres in northwest Osceola County, five minutes south of Walt Disney World. At its core, the town is the manifestation of the brand values of Walt Disney himself, who said, "I don't believe there's a challenge anywhere in the world that's more important to people everywhere than finding solutions to the problems of our communities."

Despite its evolution from Walt Disney's 1960s dream of an Experimental Prototype Community of Tomorrow (also known as EPCOT Center), Celebration does not look futuristic at all. There are no monolithic buildings, no hovercraft, monorails, or people movers. Instead, the town is designed in a pre-World War II setting, from the $500 per month "above-the-store" apartments to the large homes around the golf course. Home designs include styles such as Victorian, Greek Revival, and Country French. When compared to the modern American subdivision, the differences are striking. The plots of land for homes are small, with home plots a mere 40 feet across and townhouse plots only 25 feet. The streets are intentionally narrow, leading to slower traffic, a greater sense of intimacy in neighborhoods, and the promotion of walking over driving. The houses have broad porches designed for warm summer evenings. All houses have alleys behind them to keep cars and trashcans hidden away. The town plan is strewn with walkways, bike paths, and pocket parks. According to Celebration's manager of community business development, "We think of them more as shared front yards. Our assumption is that people crave community." The downtown is small, clustered around a lakefront, with a main street only 25 feet across.

Resting just above the treetops in the comfortable confines of Celebration is Celebration Health, a 265,000-square foot modern health care facility. The center includes physicians' offices, general and emergency surgery, as well as rehabilitation and fitness centers. Celebration Health originated from the realization that health arises not just from medicine but from the way people live, from the health of the community, of families, and the environment. These lifestyle attributes, versus illnesses, are the brand anchors on which service innovation would be designed.

In 1992, Dr. Trevor Hancock described a vision of the ideal healthy community. It was the reflection of the dreams of thousands of people interviewed by Dr. Hancock and the World Health Organization. The ideal healthy community that emerged from his studies was to be:

> . . . small and compact. There are no high-rise buildings, and all the activities of daily life are located physically close to each other . . . people walk, bicycle . . . The center of the community has a square, a green, a market, or community garden. It is a social center, with outdoor cafes, lots of street life and activity, and different age and ethnic groups living together harmoniously. The place is green, with lots of trees and flowers . . . There is water—a river, lake, or fountains—and the water is always clean and accessible for recreational activities, including walks along the

bank, swimming, fishing, and boating. It is an environmentally friendly place as well . . . recycling and pollution control are routine . . . the industry is nonpolluting . . .

We describe the origins, vision, and mission of Celebration to make it clear that the guiding corporate strategy clearly fits with the brand as described next. This sort of link between strategy and brand is a critical aspect of any integrated marketing plan.

We now turn to the guiding brand idea for Celebration. It can be described in terms of eight brand principles:

1. *Choice* is the first step toward an improved health care experience. Research has shown that people who believe they have more control over their lives tend to be healthier and live longer. The implication of this principle is simple. When designing interactions in the provision of health care, product and service offerings must empower and provide choice to the patient and family.

2. *Rest,* the second principle of the Celebration Health brand experience, is important both in a good night's sleep and during the day. Again, research indicates that relaxation techniques can lower blood pressure and counteract the effects of stress over the course of a day. This principle can be witnessed through education programs and facilities designed for private and quiet resting.

3. *Environment* is the third principle. All of our senses—sight, smell, sound, touch, and taste—can influence our health. Recent research illustrates the importance of air, water, light, aroma, sound, and touch to health. Celebration Health has borrowed elements of Disney's brand experience in "staging the guest experience" by designing a set of interactions in an environment that appeals to all senses.

4. *Activity,* the fourth principle, includes stretching, muscle development, and aerobic activity. This may be obvious, but many hospitals do not have exercise facilities onsite nor are most hospitals designed to promote preventative wellness in this way.

5. *Trust* is the fifth principle. Through its relationship with Florida Hospital, part of the Adventist Health System, Celebration Health promotes the importance of spirituality in the healing process.

6. *Interpersonal relationships* is the sixth principle. Research indicates that knowing you have the support of others can fortify your resolve and contribute to your well-being. This principle is translated into a set of

interactions including support groups and programs for family to assist in the recovery process.

7. *Outlook* is the seventh principle. Attitude influences health. Celebration works to promote positive attitudes and foster an environment that supports the mind-body relationship.

8. *Nutrition,* the eighth principle, is the fuel for the whole system. Gone are the traditional hospital meal trays. Enter well-managed nutrition programs designed to promote overall energy and nutrient levels.

What is important to understand is that Disney and Florida Hospital system first identified the principles of the brand and then developed products, services, and operational support systems. The goal from the start was to use the concept embodied in the brand principles to create, or stage, the hospital experience, and to deliver the experience through a series of selected contact points.

To deliver on the brand principle of *choice,* Celebration concierge staff provide visiting patients (guests) with personal communication devices as they enter the facility. With these devices, rather than sit in a waiting room, patients may walk through the lobby or shops until they are paged by their doctors. To deliver on the brand principle of *nutrition,* computer kiosks in the Celebration Health facility lobby allow patients to obtain nutrition information, contact the pharmacy, and schedule doctor appointments via touch-screen monitors.

In the spirit of *wellness,* a patient can go directly from his or her doctor to the workout center to set up an exercise program. After that, he or she can head to the information center to check out videos or sign up for a cooking class and then to the bookstore to buy a guidebook to his or her condition. After leaving the hospital, the patient can log onto the health information network to do continuing self-evaluation, ask the doctor a question, join a support group, or just compare notes with friends.

Eventually, it should be possible to perform many home-health services, including remote monitoring and even some diagnostics, over the town's information server. While the technological innovations required are interesting in and of themselves, the importance of these and other operational innovations is in their contribution to delivering a better brand experience.

The brand principle regarding *environment* extends beyond the walls of the health care facility itself. In fact, the Celebration Health brand experience starts at home where Celebration residents use telephones or computers to plug into the Celebration Health network, through which residents are able to ask a nurse questions, schedule appointments, or consult with personal health counselors. The network also allows patients to monitor medical conditions such as high blood pressure and diabetes from home. This is the way the Florida Hospital system and the Walt Disney Company have redefined how people interact with the hospital.

One objection to the logic of focusing on contacts with the end of creating an experience that follows from the brand concept is that it ignores operational realities. Certainly, the contacts described require operational changes, from new technology to new programs to new staffing models. At Celebration, these include a computer-based patient record system that, beyond just replicating paper patient records, allows multiple users in separate locations to access the information simultaneously. Wireless networks allow video, voice, and data to be distributed throughout the Celebration Health network—even to mobile users. Hand-held computers allow physicians to access medical histories, see X-rays, update electronic patient records remotely, and even transmit prescription orders to the Celebration Health pharmacy. These operational advances, however, are not the same as actually creating a new consumer experience. It is not that operational requirements are not important; it is important to view them as means and not as an end in themselves. The brand experience is the end, all else are means—including operational requirements and customer contacts.

INTERACTION MAP TOOL

How did Disney and Florida Hospital system arrive at improvements to the health care system when any number of other sophisticated organizations have failed at this? They did it by identifying opportunities to revolutionize the patient-provider experience. They did it through a process of interaction mapping.

Interaction mapping is a technique for designing customer contact points from a brand point of view. At its core, interaction mapping is a tool that enables innovation by starting with the premise of working from the customer interaction of the future back to the present.

Consider the case of Celebration Health. Imagine you were Disney at the outset; now think about the conventional hospital experience. Recall the last time you visited a hospital. The interactions you had were probably less than enjoyable. For example, you suffered a fall. You stumbled into the emergency room with a broken arm and intense back pain. On entering the emergency room, you were probably first asked to wait and fill out a lengthy questionnaire. You proceeded to answer questions including name, address, and insurance provider while writing with your opposite writing hand. You were probably then escorted into a triage environment and immediately cloaked in a hospital gown that proudly highlighted your rear end. You were then asked to sit on a cold table and await the doctor's examination. In the meantime, your loved ones were being held hostage to a sterile, cold, and clinical waiting room with a 1987 edition of the *New England Journal of Medicine* as their only reading material. Depending on your insurance coverage, you may or may not have been admitted to the hospital after your examination. In short, it probably wasn't a walk in the park. It is certainly not an original thought, whether you were the patient or were visiting a loved one, that the health care system is not designed with you in mind; it's designed with the ailment in mind. Hospitals have traditionally been designed to treat illnesses, not people, and certainly not family. The process begins by mapping current interactions such as the ones mentioned. It is crucial to take the point of view of the target customer in the same vein as we have just pictured your own hospital experience.

Think of the daunting task of changing this harsh reality. Where would you have started in your search for a new brand experience?

Mapping current interactions begins by sketching out all of the current contact points from end to end. A helpful hint: Use large wall charts or butcher paper to sketch the interaction. A typical layout scheme for an interaction map is provided in Figure 4.1. It shows the contact occurring around the emergency room visit. The map makes clear the flow of contacts that constitute the interaction. Another useful device is to go back through the contacts after they are laid out and summarize the consumer's experience at each point. These are shown in the circles in Figure 4.1.

It is not essential to map the contact points at a super micro level. It is not even necessary to include them all in some sort of exhaustive inventory. It is more important to spend time identifying the experience at each point and capturing it in a succinct way. At the end of the process, it is useful to summarize the experience at a higher level, as shown in the bottom portion of Figure 4.1.

As you plot the contact points, keep a tally of those areas ripe for innovation. What are the implications of the customer experience for your brand? In addition, how can we change the rules? After you have the wall charts in place, ask yourself a number of questions and plot symbols according to your responses. There should be a team discussion around the map. Questions should be asked and answered from the customer's perspective. For example, after a patient provides information, how does he or she proceed through the triage process? What messages do the interactions send to the customer?

Figure 4.1
Interaction Map of Present Hospital Emergency Room Contacts

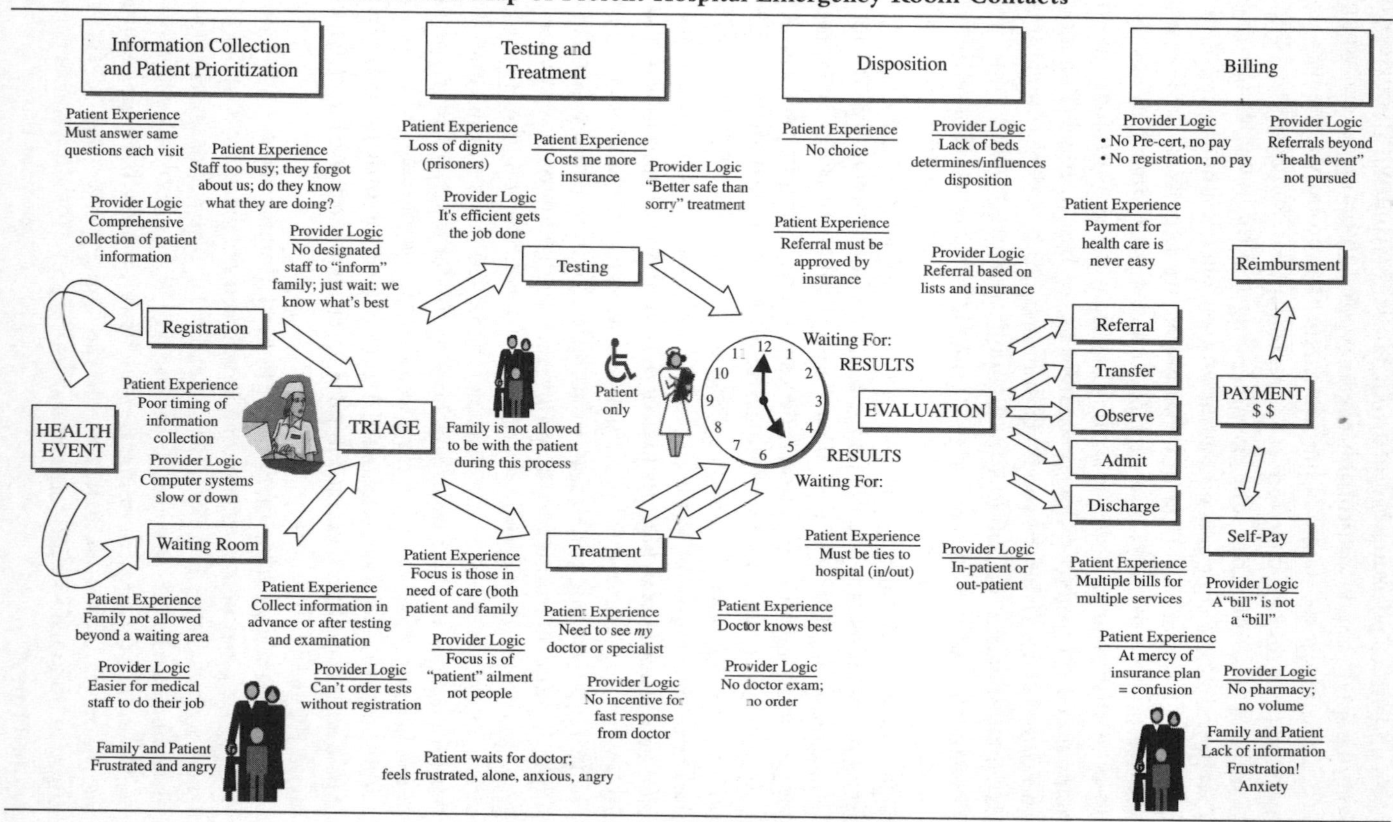

Use call-outs to illustrate how customers are interpreting the experience. For example, how do you think patients typically respond to providing insurance information before being admitted? Next, what are the pain points in the current relationship? Use call-outs to capture the disruptive elements of the current experience. For example, long waiting times, bareback hospital gowns, and billing procedures may cause concern among patients. Capture these interactions. Finally, what points are perceived to be uniquely positive by the customer? Use exclamation points or other symbols to note these. Perhaps the emergency room physician has an outstanding bedside manner and is revered by the community as the best in town. Patients love him or her. These contacts should be highlighted and later elaborated as internal benchmarks for building the brand experience.

In the case of the emergency room contacts in Figure 4.1, we have also classified the contacts into Collection, Testing, Disposition, and Billing. After you have classified contacts in this way, you can begin to assess each set of interactions individually and as a group. To create a classification system, keep in mind that it is vital to create the classifications based on customer needs, not on operational necessity. For example, in a traditional hospital setting, patients are often carted from floor to floor depending on their needs. For example, they may have to go to the second floor for X-ray, the third floor for blood work, and the fourth floor for a CT scan. Is the hospital designed this way because patients like to move around or is it designed for operational efficiency? For each phase, what is common about the phase? For instance, waiting time creates frustration, billing processes create confusion, or the environment is imposing and cold. Moreover, study the progression of contacts carefully. In other words, do the activities occur in the most convenient order for the customer? Does the fact that information collection precedes medical treatment help or hinder a patient's interpretation of the brand?

The next major step is to use the Interaction Map of Present Hospital Emergency Room Contacts (Figure 4.1) to map future contacts that improve the brand experience.

The Interaction Map of Future Hospital Emergency Room Contacts (Figure 4.2) can be constructed and analyzed on the same map, or a new map can be started if it would be clearer, or if it is predetermined that there will be drastic changes to the current experience. The key is to go back through the present contacts to identify points where the experience can be made to better reflect the brand concept. We like to flag these points with starburst call-outs and use this activity as a vehicle for team brainstorming.

Figure 4.2
Interaction Map of Future Hospital Emergency Room Contacts

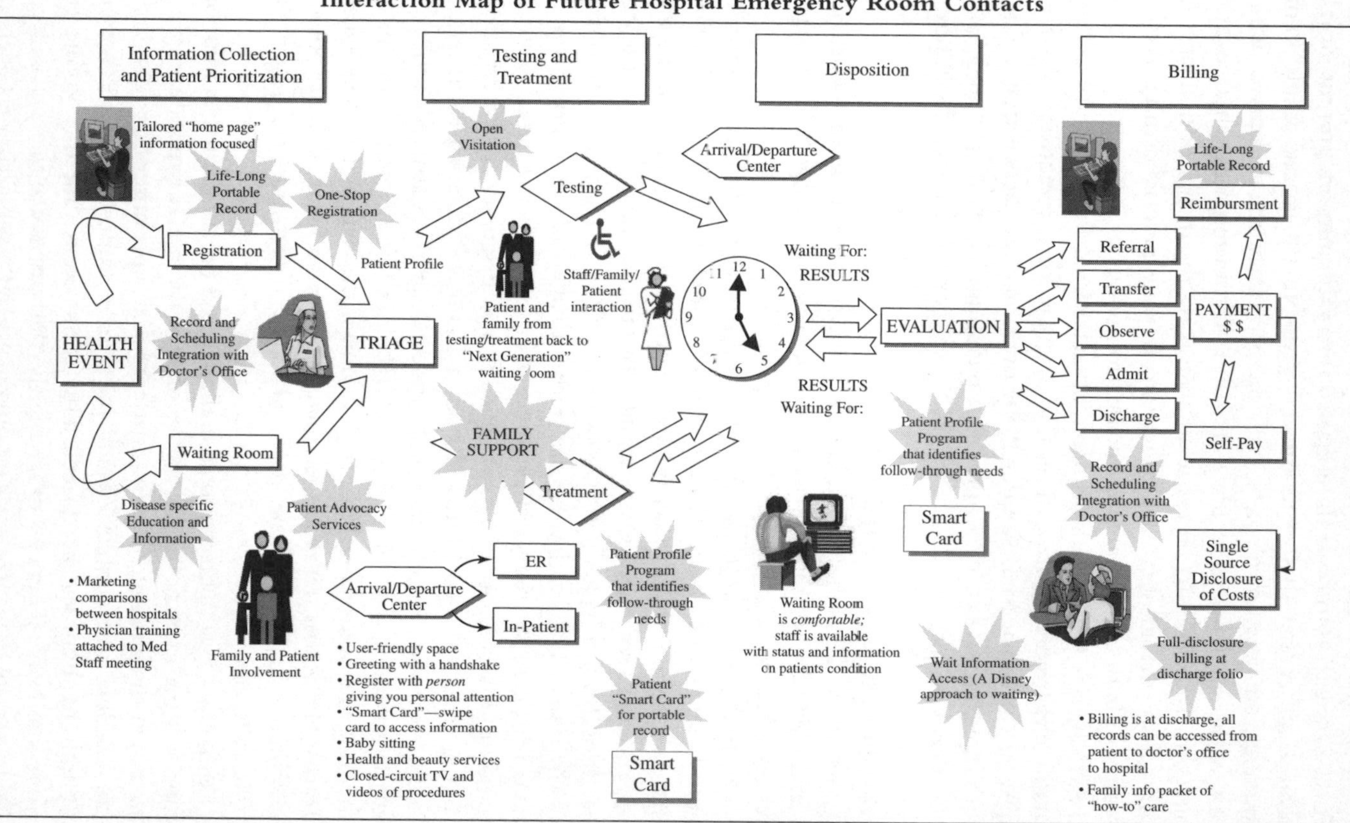

Recall that an important part of the Celebration brand concept is support through *interpersonal relationships.* Our map of present contacts clearly shows that this experience is problematic. For example, family members are not allowed to be with the patient during treatment. We flag this with a starburst in Figure 4.2, calling for more family support at this point in the process. The team discussion results in the notion of a new contact involving a "Next Generation Waiting Room," which connects family to both the patient and the staff.

Often, it is not the addition of contacts that helps to create a desired brand experience; rather, it is the deletion of interactions. As famed Chicago architect Mies van der Rohe pontificated, "Less is more."

Simplification can be a home run technique in creating brand experiences. For example, at Celebration Health, gone are conventional hospital food, waiting rooms, and departments such as the ICU, PCU, or other separate units. Gone are the overexposed hospital gowns. Patients remain in one room throughout their stay, regardless of the type of care they receive. You have the same nurse at your bedside when you have cardiac arrest as when you're discharged.

A number of contacts may be either impossible to eliminate and/or may not warrant being eliminated completely. For example, waiting is a fact of life in many environments. Whether you are waiting for your airline to depart or a movie to start, you spend a lot of time practicing a virtue called *patience.* Ironically, patience is a necessity of life in a hospital environment. In the case of Celebration Health, rather than eliminate waiting, the hospital has borrowed a technique used at Disney's theme parks. Instead of standing in a two-hour line waiting for a ride, guests are entertained by roving musicians, costumed characters, and, in some cases, interactive kiosks. Likewise, at Celebration Health, the pagers mentioned earlier allow guests to browse the many shops and restaurants of the facility. In this case, the wait time interaction may not be shorter. In fact, in some cases, it may be that the wait time is longer than the average hospital visit; however, Celebration has reduced the unarticulated need of its guests: *Make the wait time more enjoyable.*

Important as simplification and redesign can be, new contacts most often represent the most powerful way to change the brand experience. For example, in the emergency room, patients must encounter busy doctors and nurses. But these contacts would have more impact if the patient knew something about the personnel. This could be as simple as giving them more impressive nametags or having the staff introduce themselves according to a script. The primary care physicians and psychiatrists at Celebration are direct employees of Celebration Health, giving the center the ability to ensure they relate to patients in this way.

The interaction map is thus a tool for innovative thinking. It should be approached as a chance to rewrite the rules. We strongly suggest you unleash the creativity of the entire organization in pursuit of this—for innovation is truly everyone's job. In this spirit, Celebration Health has created many more contacts. When taken together, these lead to an even more positive brand experience. These new contacts include everything from a kids' gym, to classes on how to cook and eat better, to the patient's awaiting an appointment while enjoying an organic and healthy meal from the mesquite brick oven of The Seasons Café.

Although these are only a few of the many innovations introduced by the efforts of Florida Hospital system and the Walt Disney Company, they are indicative of the opportunities. In fact, the brand's principles translate so well that they have not stopped at hospitals. Celebration has extended its experience beyond patients to family members and loved ones.

The question became this: What other experiences could benefit from a version of the brand principles designed for Celebration Health? What other experiences are similar to patient-provider contacts? Perhaps student-teacher? In fact, Celebration has founded its own department of education to develop ways of integrating wellness into the life of the Celebration school. Wellness training is offered to patients, adults, and children of Celebration as Celebration's brand dictates.

Perhaps nothing better reflects the brand's attention to contacts than the inscription on a sign at Celebration: "A 60,000-square-foot Health Activities Center, 100 health care professionals, and a doctor who knows all the words to 'Itsy Bitsy Spider.' "

BEYOND EXPERIENCE TO RELATIONSHIPS

There are many benefits to using the interaction mapping process in the creation of contact points that reflect core brand principles. The next step is in translating those brand experiences into loyal brand relationships.

Much has been written about customer relationships. The general notion is that it is important for consumers to feel a sense of personal contact with products or companies. The consumer should feel that a company is dealing with him or her as an individual and, at least to some extent, is customizing its responses to him or her or to people in the same situation. If the consumer calls to place an order, for instance, the company should recognize that the consumer is a returning customer or a new customer. This recognition could take many forms but could be as simple as an acknowledgment that the customer has done business with the company before. And this is possible with today's automated customer relationship management (CRM) systems that facilitate just this sort of contact with sophisticated software and hardware.

Beyond the general notion of personalizing and customizing interactions with consumers and using CRM systems to facilitate this, the concept of *relationship marketing* can be very fuzzy. The interaction map tool can be very helpful in making clear the opportunities for directly addressing consumers in a way that takes who they are into account.

Relationships of any kind are created through interaction. If you think of your relationship with a friend or coworker, you immediately see that your relationship with that person is defined by the person's actions toward you and your reactions. Suppose you meet a person at a party. The person seems very active; he or she travels frequently. The person tells you a story about a recent vacation trip. A few days later, you send the person an e-mail with an article you saw about the same place. The relationship that evolves from this pattern of interaction is that of "friendly acquaintances who share interests." Marketing relationships are of the same kind.

For a marketing relationship to be developed, a brand must behave in a way that is consistent with the brand and that leads to a reaction from the consumer that establishes a pattern of behavior. For example, a sports television network, such as ESPN, wants to engage in relationship marketing. The network could advertise that it is your sports partner. They team up with you to give you sports coverage wherever and whenever you want it. Is there a marketing relationship in what we have described? We think not. With whom is the consumer having the relationship? There is no experience to define a relationship. Nor is there any behavior flowing from that experience for the consumer to react to. Let's fix the problem.

The experience of the brand is for a type of fan (the target segment or subsegment), a sophisticated fan who doesn't just root blindly for teams but is knowledgeable and a bit of an insider about sports. Now the brand opens a sports bar in the downtown area of your city or a nearby city. Let's map it out. You go to the bar. Is there just someone to take your order and banks of television set with different games? No, the bar should treat you as a fellow insider. Maybe there is a device at your table that allows you to predict the winner of the game and this prediction is displayed on a television screen. Perhaps there is a tape of a special interview with a star that is played only in the bar and addresses customers in a way that acknowledges their sophistication (as opposed to the usual homilies of sports interviews). In short, the relationship is one of "hanging out with insider fans." The brand has interacted with you in a way that is consistent with the brand's concept and added a sense of relationship to the experience.

With this in mind, we suggest the following interaction map approach to creating a marketing relationship. We find that it is usually useful to work backwards from the current situation to a more desirable situation.

- First, consider the interaction with the consumer. What are you doing, actually *doing,* that the consumer has to respond to?
- Does this define a relationship such that the consumer sees that there is a brand experience that leads to what you are doing in the interaction?
- If the answer is no, there is no current relationship with the consumer. Any talk of being the consumer's partner, or anything of the like, is simply that, empty rhetoric.
- If the answer to the relationship question is yes, what is the relationship and brand experience that you are delivering? What is the set of actions that creates the experience?
- Last, is this the relationship that is intended given your brand's experience, and does the brand experience need to be changed to define a more positive relationship?

A CALL TO ACTION

Interaction mapping is a great way to make concrete the task of building brand experience and relationships. Too many organizations get sidetracked from this task by internal operational issues. It is easy to pay lip service to the brand without really trying to affect the experience of the brand. So, the question now is how can you use interaction mapping and the insights from Celebration to design innovative contacts that allow consumers to experience your brand and to feel a sense of relationship with it?

CHAPTER 5

INTEGRATED MARKETING AND THE CONSUMER EXPERIENCE

LISA FORTINI-CAMPBELL

This book began with the premise that marketers are most successful if they can develop an integrated and comprehensive approach to their consumers or customers. Such an approach begins with a focus on a specific consumer target—the group of people with whom it will be most valuable for the company to develop a relationship. Then, after consumer research and analysis and a study of the company's goals, strengths, and opportunities, a strategy for developing a brand relationship with that target is developed.

The focus of this chapter is on how to turn that strategy into a meaningful consumer experience with the brand. In keeping with the theme of the rest of this book, we focus on how to develop the experience from the consumer's point of view, analyzing how consumers experience the brand, and how they make judgments about it. If we can take into account the way a consumer experiences and judges the brand, we have the information we need to design and implement a compelling brand experience.

WHERE DO BRANDS COME FROM?

Marketers have been explicitly focused on building compelling, relevant, and competitively distinguished brands for more than a century. A look at classic advertising posters from the 1890s shows some of the considerable creative energy that was devoted to that purpose well before today's broadcast, narrowcast, and Internet media even existed. And helping to create a strong brand is still considered a marketer's greatest achievement. It would be hard to find a company that did not want what brands give them—loyal current consumers, an irresistible attractiveness to prospects, the ability to charge a premium price, and the ability to extend itself into other products or even lines of business, as David Aaker has thoroughly documented.[1]

The popular marketing literature is full of stories about the brands everyone loves to admire—Coca-Cola, Marlboro, Apple Computer, Harley-Davidson, Mercedes-Benz, and Sony. We eagerly read about them, hoping to adopt their best practices to help us duplicate their success. We are spurred on our pursuit to build compelling brands by companies whose research helps us to compare our brand's performance with others, inside and outside our industries. Whether it is through Interbrand or Landor or any of the other firms researching and documenting brand performance, we know where our brands stack up in terms of awareness, desirability, and personality.

But in our eagerness to have great brands, we give one question too little attention. That question is: Where do great brands come from?

This question gets so little attention because we think the answer is obvious. Great brands come from great advertising. Marlboro is the perfect case in point. A simple cigarette with few, if any, functional differences from other cigarettes is one of the world's most valuable brands. What has made it so? Advertising that has been evocative and consistent for fifty years. The same might be said for Coke. A simple, brown, sugared, carbonated beverage is sought for what it represents, not what it is. And what it represents comes from the power of its advertising.

Some people take issue with giving the credit for creating powerful brands to advertising alone. They would have a point if they were to argue that other forms of marketing communication should be added to the hall of fame. After all, Budweiser's success owes something to its sports sponsorships, as does Amazon's to its direct marketing, as does The Body Shop's to its public relations. But, even if we extend the credit for creating powerful brands to all of marketing communications, we still make an unspoken assumption—that marketers create brands and that the tools the marketer controls are the ones that truly do the job.

It is the purpose of this chapter to question that assumption and to show how consumers build brands, gathering the information to do so from sources that go far beyond what we marketers call *brand communication*. Let's start with a few examples.

Imagine that we know nothing about two mobile phones except their sizes and designs. Brand A is a hotdog-bun-sized, rather heavy phone with a shell of gray plastic. Brand B is a smaller, thinner, lighter phone with a shell of burnished metal. Now imagine you have been given a branding survey, asking you to rate each phone brand on an attribute such as "advanced technology." How would you rate each phone, knowing nothing else? Which phone do you assume is made with a more advanced technology?

Most likely, you say the second phone—the small, light, metallic one. Notice that you have been given no information directly about the phone's technology. Nonetheless, you have interpreted something about it based on product design alone. Your interpretation is not without foundation—in most of our experience with technology products, from desktop computers to phones to laptops, we have learned that as technology advances, products tend to get smaller (e.g., recall the suitcase-sized laptop computers when those products were first introduced, or the first heavy, ungainly mobile phones). The point is that we can draw a conclusion about a dimension of a brand's character or offering without being told something directly about it.

Consider another example. Imagine that a new brand of beer is being introduced. You know nothing about it except its price—$8 for a six-pack. Do you have some expectation of what that beer will be like? Is it being offered in bottles or cans? Dark bottles or clear ones? Was it made in the United States or somewhere else? Do you expect a strong, rich flavor or a light, thin one? Do you expect to see men or women drinking it; older adults or younger ones?

Again, most likely, it was not difficult to answer these questions. You have probably decided that the beer is being offered in dark glass bottles, that it was probably imported from somewhere in Europe—most likely Germany, that it is strongly flavored, and the most likely consumer would be an older man. Notice how many dimensions of this brand's attributes and personality you have interpreted knowing nothing more than price.

Consider still another example. Imagine that you are planning to have an addition made to your house and you are shopping for an architect. You have a referral to an architectural firm in a downtown location in a major city. You arrive at the new 40-storied building that houses the firm and take the elevator to the 26th floor. The doors open into a lobby with a marble floor, crystal wall sconces, and a rare wood reception desk behind which is seated a beautiful receptionist wearing an Italian designer suit. What is the first thought that runs through your mind?

The architect who greets you might be surprised when you give voice to that thought and ask immediately about the price of the firm's projects and wonder whether you can really afford so expensive a firm. Once again, you have had no direct information about the price of services; instead, you have interpreted something about the brand's offering by drawing conclusions from the opulence of the décor.

The point here is obvious, so obvious, in fact, that it is easy to fail to see its importance. Human beings are sponges for information. We gather it anywhere and everywhere, and everything we notice, we interpret. We do not just see a small mobile phone, or notice the price of a beer, or see the decoration of a room and stop there. We interpret. We make it mean something. Those meanings gradually weave their way into the idea we call a *brand*. Stephen King, a retired executive from the WPP Group in London, said it best, "People build brands the way birds build nests, from the scraps and twigs they chance upon."

Typically, however, brands are not designed or managed with this principle in mind. If we look at the typical division of labor represented by the classic 4Ps marketing mix (Product, Price, Place, and Promotion), it is easy to see the problem. In most marketing organizations, brand managers are usually members of a marketing communications function with responsibility for that fourth P—promotion. Yet, we have just seen how important the brand messages are that can come from the product, price, and place as well.

That theme is this chapter's overriding point: Brand information comes from the entire product or service offering. The entire marketing mix is a brand communications mix. From a consumer's point of view, brand information can come from a thousand different places, not just from things marketers call *communication* and directly control—activities such as advertising, direct marketing, promotion, and public relations. Perhaps it comes from things we do not even designate as *communication* at all—such as the way we design a product or service, or the way it is priced or distributed. Perhaps it comes from the people who represent the product in the sales force or customer service areas or in its retail distribution outlets. Perhaps it comes from things that independent dealers, distributors, or resellers do or say in the course of selling the product. Perhaps it comes from things that we are not even aware are affecting the consumer's idea of the brand.

Here is an illustration of just how small a piece of brand communication can be. Imagine that you have received a catalog in the mail from a company you have never done business with. You page through it and find that you like some of the items you see. After thinking it over, you decide you are going to make a purchase; and as someone who has bought from catalogs before, you get ready to make the phone call. You circle the item number in the catalog. You find the phone number to order. You look for a customer number on the back of the catalog and get your credit card ready. Now you dial the phone and it begins to ring . . . once . . . twice . . . three times . . . four times. As it begins its fifth ring, what are you thinking?

I have asked that question in executive classes hundreds of times all around the world, and here are the things people say to me: "It makes me wonder whether anyone is there. Maybe it is just a small, understaffed company operating out of someone's home instead of a legitimate business." "I start to question whether I'm going to have trouble with the order. If it's this hard to get someone to answer the phone, how hard will it be to return the product if I don't like it?" "I begin to have second thoughts about the products and the company. Do I really want to buy something from a company that's so unresponsive?" "I just start to feel uncertain about the whole transaction. With all the credit card fraud out there, maybe I just shouldn't take a chance on this company." "I wonder if they even are in business!"

Think about what has happened here. In just five rings of the telephone, we began to question product quality, customer service, credit security, and even business legitimacy—all dimensions of any viable brand. All of this from five rings of the telephone.

Brand information comes in a multitude of forms. It is what the consumer, not the marketer, says it is. The notion that marketers create brands primarily with the tools of promotion, advertising, direct marketing, and public relations hinders us from exerting the influence we could have over the totality of brand communication. Only when we realize that consumers create brands and that we must manage the entire range of things from which they take brand information will our chances for success increase.

Brand Contact Points

To help clarify this entire range of things from which consumers get brand information, I introduce a phrase to refer to them—*brand contact points*. This phrase is meant to highlight the idea that any time a consumer comes into contact with any dimension of the product's or service's total offering, there is potential for the consumer to notice, and then assess and interpret information about the brand (also called *touch points, moments of truth*). Information about the brand is being conveyed every time the consumer encounters the offering. Any element that the customer notices and attributes to the product or service is one of those brand contact points.

It is important to underscore that the brand is what the consumer thinks it is, even if the contact point is not under the direct control of the marketer. An airline meal is a good example. Airline meals are aspects of an airline experience that customers notice and that factor into the reaction they have to their trips. If you have a bad meal on an airline, one that is not your first choice, is badly prepared or poor tasting, you like the experience of flying with that brand of airline less. Now comes the interesting question: Whose fault do you think that bad meal was? Most likely, you would say it was the airline's fault, and your negative judgment about the quality of the food will likely fuel an assessment that the airline brand is not very customer-oriented in some small way. Yet, whose fault is the poor meal really? Actually, it was not prepared by the airline at all, but by a subcontracted caterer. But, from our point of view as a badly fed passenger, we blame the airline and hold it responsible. It is the airline that chooses the subcontractor, after all.

A brand contact is any element of the consumer's experience that the consumer attributes to the brand. Here is an easy test to decide whether something is or is not a brand contact. If a particular element of the consumer's experience goes well, who gets the credit? If that element goes poorly, who gets the blame? If the consumer gives credit to or blames your brand for something, that thing is a brand contact. Whether that is fair or not, the consumer's verdict is final. The customer gets to decide what the brand contacts are; we marketers really do not have much of a say in the matter.

Notice that we could rephrase everything we are saying about brands and talk instead of taking the consumer's view of the whole product or service offering. It should be obvious that if you accept the consumer as arbiter of what is and is not an element of your brand, then you must also accept the consumer as arbiter of what is and is not an element of your product or service. The ideal frame of mind for a marketer is that of the wise chef who orchestrates a diner's whole experience, starting with the reservation system and ending with the parking valet's smile at the end of the evening. The chef knows the entrée has to be good, but he also knows the entrée simply cannot generate the warm glow of a memorable evening all by itself. The entrée is a meaningful part of the experience and it contributes a noticeable bit to the restaurant's brand, but it is one of many elements and the consumer is experiencing the whole lot of them, not just a bit of meat on a strange plate. Failing to appreciate the consumer's point of view about the brand contacts (or about the elements of the whole product and service experience) can lead to disaster—delicious food served by snarling waiters, in ugly rooms, accompanied by loud, obnoxious music. So, we can say that the consumer decides what makes up the restaurant's brand, or we can say the consumer decides what makes up the restaurant's product and service offering—these are just two ways of talking about the same important principle.

We continue with the main theme, which is the primacy of the consumer's point of view. We have just discussed the importance of knowing what the consumer holds your brand responsible for so that you can find and manage as many of the important brand contacts as possible. Now we consider the other side of the coin, because it is also important to know what the consumer does *not* hold your brand responsible for. The reason is simple economics: A marketer who knows what does not matter to consumers can shift scarce time and money away from those things and allocate the resources to managing the real brand contacts instead.

Imagine that a consumer goes to a store to shop for a new computer and finds that the merchandise is disorganized and the sales associates do not understand the products' features. In that case, the consumer probably would blame the store, rather than the manufacturer, for the disorganization and for the ignorance of the sales associates. This unequal division of blame is a plausible outcome of the scenario even though the manufacturer chose to distribute its computers in that outlet. The retail outlet's brand will be hurt by the sloppiness and the unhelpful staff, but the manufacturer's probably will not be. The implication for the manufacturer is that there probably are other brand contacts that deserve more of its attention than any attempt to fix the store's problems.

We should not take this simple story for more than it is worth. After all, consumers can arrange and assess brand contacts in subtle and finely nuanced ways; and they can form complex webs of associations, so the boundaries between brands are not always sharp and clear. The consumer who finds the computer in a disheveled store might think a little less of the manufacturer for being in such a questionable place and a tiny bit better of the store for stocking surprisingly good merchandise, while still blaming the store for its disorganization and ignorant staff. Therefore, we can talk of the store's brand as interacting with the computer manufacturer's brand because the consumer attributes some brand contacts to them jointly or because the consumer considers the store to be a brand contact for the manufacturer and the manufacturer's inventory to be a brand contact for the store.

Sometimes consumers do hold manufacturers substantially responsible for the sins of their distribution channel and then the consumer's experience with the channel gives rise to significant brand contacts—often very negative ones—for the manufacturer. Automotive dealerships are classic examples. A consumer who has a bad experience at a dealership ("These people took advantage of me!") is likely to think worse of the car maker's brand ("These cars aren't so great; I'll never buy another one"), even though the dealership is independently owned and operated and the manufacturer has no control over it.

The same is true for certain restaurant franchises. Few consumers distinguish, for example, between a company-owned McDonald's restaurant and a franchised one. And why should they? Both display the same architecture, menu, crew uniforms, kitchen equipment, names, posters, and logos; and they both cook with the same ingredients. As a result, a bad experience with a meal at a franchised store damages the consumer's perception of that store ("This is a bad McDonald's!") and it damages McDonald's brand in general ("McDonald's isn't what it used to be"), just as a good experience helps the store and the brand in general. McDonald's rational response is to control the operations of franchisees as tightly as possible to protect the overall brand (in ways car makers can only dream of).

Similarly, a consumer's good (or bad) experience with a disputed charge on a Visa card issued by a particular bank becomes a brand contact for Visa in general, and, to the degree that the card holder distinguishes the issuing bank from the association, it becomes a brand contact for the issuing bank as well. And if a Premier Executive consumer's trip on a United flight operated by British Midlands goes sour, United's brand suffers—and the passenger might give United more blame than the code-share partner. Affinity marketing works both ways, for better or worse.

MEANING IS IN THE MIND OF THE CONSUMER

It should be obvious that the interpretation a consumer makes of a contact point is the one that affects the brand, regardless of the intention of the person who designed the experience at the point of contact in the first place. For example, if you intend to create a restaurant with a reputation for friendly, attentive service, you may instruct your wait staff to visit each table several times between courses, and particularly during dessert to inquire whether everything is satisfactory, or whether anyone would like anything else. However, if a diner interprets that behavior to mean the waiter is trying to rush him or her out the door so that a new table of guests can be seated, the consumer becomes irritated even though that was the opposite of the restaurant's intention. According to the principle we have set forth, the consumer's interpretation of the brand contact point is the only relevant one, and the brand experience needs to be managed from that point of view. The consumer's interpretation is the real brand; the restaurant's intention is just the aspirational brand.

It is important to have a clear idea of who the target consumer is before a brand can be either understood or managed. Sometimes different segments of consumers interpret the same element of experience in completely different ways, drawing very different conclusions about the brand. If it is not possible to delight all sets of consumers with the same experience, the company must decide which set of consumers is most important to achieving its business objectives and design its brand with them in mind. Southwest Airlines is a good example. Southwest wants its brand to stand for inexpensive, efficient, no-frills transportation—its tagline is "Freedom to Fly." Its planes fly frequently on short hops, often from a city's secondary, rather than primary, airport. There is no meal service or movies. There are no seat assignments. The crew is dressed casually and often behaves that way, too, singing songs, playing games, and telling jokes.

It is easy to see how different people might react very differently to this experience. Typical frequent business travelers accustomed to a more serious full-service experience on a major international carrier might find this experience overly familiar and too plebian. They want an experience that acknowledges their status as elite travelers and offers expedited check-in, preferential seating, as well as meals and entertainment. They often complain that Southwest is "like a cattle car." They come to a negative conclusion about the Southwest Airlines brand.

Yet, for leisure travelers making a discretionary trip, the low fares and frequent service that Southwest's spartan operations make possible are delightful. They may find meals on an airplane trip of less than two hours unnecessary, especially when they could bring something on board they would prefer to eat. And, the friendly, relaxed behavior of the flight attendants may make the flight a much more pleasant experience. For them, the same experience is fun and happy, rather like a trip to camp on a bus. They have positive associations with the brand.

So, what does a company like Southwest do about such a problem when two different segments of consumers have very different interpretations of exactly the same experience? In this case, it is not possible to delight both sets of consumers simultaneously. The high-service experience that would delight the more frequent business traveler would raise Southwest's operational costs to a point where the discretionary leisure traveler would be unhappy with the prices. The company must choose its most strategically valuable consumers and make sure the consumer experience is most delightful to them, and, consequently, that the brand is most compelling to them first. In this case, Southwest has clearly chosen to delight the discretionary traveler, even if it means disappointing the high-service-oriented business traveler.

Weaving Brand Contact Experiences into a Brand

It is easy to see that even in a simple consumer experience such as one might have with a packaged food product, there might be several dozen brand contact points as the consumer reacts to things such as shelf placement, number of facings, shelf detailing, package design, package graphics, pricing, promotional offerings, and advertising. There will be more contact points as the consumer uses the product at home and reacts to the way it opens and closes, dispenses, looks, smells, and tastes, and how it is disposed of.

In a more complex consumer experience, such as one might have with an automobile, a computer product, a financial services offering, or a professional service such as an architect, lawyer, or accountant, there may be literally hundreds of small elements of experience the consumer notices. At each point of contact, the consumer interprets his or her impression, creating one of those "scraps and twigs" out of which a brand image is woven.

No matter the complexity of the experience, the consumer's reactions to various elements of experience are diverse. For example, with a shampoo product, the consumer may react positively to the brand name, package design, and graphics, thinking they look feminine and sophisticated. But, the difficulty of finding the product in the store or the placement of the product on the highest shelf not in easy reach may suggest that it is not a very popular brand. An extraordinarily low promotional price may make the consumer wonder why such a sophisticated-looking product is so cheap and may corroborate the impression that the brand is not very popular. The smell and appearance of the product when the consumer uses it may reinforce the image of sophistication, but a dispenser that breaks after just a few uses can leave the impression that the manufacturing has been cheaply and poorly done. When it comes time to dispose of the product and the consumer finds the package is made from a material that cannot be recycled, he or she may be left with an impression that the company is not very environmentally friendly.

So, what is the consumer's impression of the shampoo brand after all this? Assuming for a moment that the consumer puts equal weight on each one of these brand contact points, we can only say that this consumer's impression of the brand is mixed. That is not to say the consumer is confused. It is more likely that the consumer has a very clear idea that the brand is confused and inconsistent. A perception of sophistication conflicts with an impression of cheapness, poor quality, and environmental unfriendliness. The brand perception is not clear, coherent, consistent, and compelling—all things that the strongest brands should be. In the next section, we consider how consumers actually weave together all of the impressions they process, as they place more importance on certain brand contact points, creating their idea of a brand.

To summarize:

- Any element of the entire product or service offering the consumer notices has the potential to convey information to the consumer, whether the marketer intends it to or not, and whether the marketer directly controls it or not.
- The consumer interprets each point of contact and makes a judgment about some aspect of the product or service brand. In that sense, each of these points of contact is a *brand contact*.
- The consumer integrates all of these interpretations and judgments into the large idea we call the *brand*. The brand the consumer has created influences the way the consumer purchases.

DIAGNOSING A CURRENT BRAND

The concepts we have discussed can help marketers design and plan for new brands, but they can just as easily be used to help marketers understand brands that already exist and make them more compelling to their target consumers.

If you have a brand, which is to say that consumers have an image of your products or services now, the question we should try to answer is: How did the image form? How did the brand develop? If we know how consumers constructed it from all of the "scraps and twigs they chanced upon," we have the information we need to consider how to make the brand more coherent and stronger. To answer this large question, we have to answer three subordinate questions:

1. What are all of the contact points that consumers notice in the course of their experience with our product or service offering?
2. How do they interpret these contact points, and which ones are most important to them?
3. How do these interpretations weave together to become the consumer's idea of the brand?

We answer these questions by discussing an example. Imagine that you are the marketing manager of a bank offering a wide array of commercial and retail services such as checking accounts, savings accounts, personal and retail loans, mortgages, and investment services. You've recently completed a branding study among a segment of customers you've determined to be especially valuable—small- to medium-sized business owners whose companies have annual sales of $2 million to $50 million.

Your company has decided this segment of customers is valuable for a variety of reasons. The small to medium business's corporate accounts are valuable and profitable. The owners and officers are likely to be high net worth individuals whose personal accounts and investment accounts are also valuable and profitable. Because businesses in this segment are trying to grow, there is the opportunity to sell business loans to help them fund their growth. There is also potential to handle the company's profit sharing and retirement accounts, and perhaps even long-term investment opportunities, such as estate planning for the owners. To increase the chances of capturing this lucrative business, you want to make sure that you have the strongest and most compelling brand image possible in the minds of these customers.

The brand awareness and image studies done by your marketing research department show that your brand is recognized by 80 percent of the customers in this market segment. It enjoys about the same level of awareness as most of your national and regional competitors. These customers are aware of your advertising, and a sizeable portion of them can correctly recognize your tagline—"The professional bank for business." Nevertheless, a closer examination of the brand's image attributes reveals some worrying data. Compared to your key competition, your brand is relatively weak on attributes such as "professional," "business-like," and "responsive," although you do get higher than average scores on dimensions such as "has a full range of services," "offers competitive pricing," and "has convenient locations close to my business." This data confuses you, especially because you can see that awareness of your brand name, advertising, and tagline is very high. If people understand that yours is the "professional bank for business," then why are ratings on the key brand image dimensions "professional," "business-like," and "responsive" so low?

According to the principles previously discussed, an even better question to ask is: Where do impressions of professionalism, business-orientation, and responsiveness come from? If we can understand the elements of the customer experience that give rise to those impressions, we can understand how to correct these negative impressions.

Fortunately, you have the transcripts of some customer experience interviews, and you decide to examine them for clues. One example, taken from an interview with the owner of the largest school photography business in the Midwest, follows. The company takes student pictures in local primary and secondary schools, as well as identification cards for local colleges. It prepares yearbooks for these schools and commemorative photo albums for community groups. Recently, it has expanded into sports photography services in the secondary and college markets. Revenue for the business is $5 million annually, and 60 people are employed as photographers, photo developers, graphic artists, producers, printers, binders, and shippers.

> I've lived and worked in this town for 30 years and have built the business from just a two-person operation to the 60-person firm it is today. The size of the business and the scope of our services have changed a lot over the years, but our values have always remained the same—to give our customers the most professional personal service possible. We pride ourselves on our deep relationships with long-term customers and in being as flexible as we can be with their particular requests. Every school is different, and you have to treat each one as if it were your only customer.
>
> I'd been banking with Bank A for a number of years, but with all of the consolidation going on in the banking industry, a national bank I wasn't familiar with took over our local branch, and I decided to look elsewhere. Bank B—"The Professional Bank for Business"—was the logical choice. They're right downtown close to our offices, in a modern building. When I first went in to visit, I was really impressed. The offices looked sharp and professional. The employees were well groomed and behaved in a very business-like way—no chatting around the water cooler and ignoring customers when they came in through the door. I met with one of the vice presidents and explained our business and needs to her, and she was really sharp and understood immediately. The process of moving our accounts was smooth and easy, except for a couple of small paperwork mistakes. But, those things happen and they were easily corrected.
>
> Once our accounts were set up, the trouble started. I needed to change the signatories on several of our corporate accounts and went to talk to them about it. But, when I arrived, I learned that the vice president I'd worked with had quit and a new person had taken her place. Even though we had an appointment, it was clear he hadn't prepared for the meeting and asked me a lot of obvious questions about our business that I'd already answered and were documented in our file. It was a huge waste of time. After a lot of waiting and paper shuffling, he produced the signature change cards and they were duly filled out. But when a check to one of our major suppliers was sent back as invalid because it had the "wrong" signature, I

was really mad. It was even worse that the bank enclosed a note with the returned check saying that this service was "one of the many ways we protect your business." Ha!

That was the last big problem. Now there are lots of little ones that add up to a big headache. There have been mistakes on our last three statements. There are charges for services that aren't itemized or explained and don't conform to the fees I've agreed to pay. Now we've started to have problems with our employees' retirement accounts. There's nothing major, but with this history of problems, I'm starting to get worried. One of my employees came in this morning to tell me she'd tried to check her account balance on the bank's automated phone system, and when it confirmed her password, it told her the balance in the account was zero. Fortunately, she didn't panic, but tried calling again, and this time the system gave her a balance that sounded right.

If this doesn't all get straightened out, we're going to switch banks. But regardless, every time I see one of their signs that says, "The professional bank for business," I just shake my head.

This is a bank with a serious customer service problem that has led to a serious brand problem. This customer has had a variety of experiences, both good and bad, from the encounter with the original vice president to the process of moving accounts, to the encounter with the second vice president, to the mistakes on the statements and the unclear charges, to the employee's experience with the automated account balance system. None of these experiences were under the control of the bank's "brand managers," nor in the typical organizational structure would anyone imagine they should be. However, each one of these "scraps and twigs" had been noticed by the customer, interpreted by the customer, and the customer had reached the conclusion that the brand did not meet a standard of professionalism, business-like practices, or responsiveness. We see the results on the brand survey.

An analysis such as this begins to document the elements of consumer experience—the brand contact points—that result in the meaning of the brand. A similar analysis can be completed for any existing brand by gathering accounts of key customers' experiences with the entire product or service offering.

ANALYZING CUSTOMER EXPERIENCE

The first step is to identify all of the elements of experience that the customer notices as they appear in the interview. If the customer interprets and draws a conclusion about the things he or she has noticed, then we have a brand contact point. In the previous short example, we can easily identify 17 different contact points. The phrase that corresponds to each one is pulled out of the text and listed here:

1. Close to our office.
2. Modern building.
3. Offices looked sharp and professional.
4. Employees were well groomed.
5. Behaved in a very business-like way.
6. She was really sharp and understood immediately.
7. Process of moving our accounts was smooth and easy.
8. Couple of small paperwork mistakes.
9. New person had taken her place.
10. Asked me many obvious questions.
11. A lot of waiting and paper shuffling.
12. Check to one of our major suppliers was sent back as invalid.
13. Note with the returned check saying that this service was "one of the many ways we protect your business."
14. Mistakes on our last three statements.
15. Charges for services that aren't itemized or explained and don't conform to the fees I've agreed to pay.
16. Bank's automated phone system, and when it confirmed her password, it told her the balance in the account was zero.
17. This time the system gave her a balance that sounded right.

You could reread the transcript to see whether you agree with this list. Identifying and stating brand contacts is not an exact science; you might make a reasonable case for adding something else to the list. In addition, the brand contacts can be divided or combined to make the total come out to more or less than 17. Some thoughtful analysis at this stage to understand what customers meant when they said what they said will pay big dividends later. It is more important to understand what customers *meant* than to preserve their quotations.

If we were really analyzing a commercial bank's brand contacts, rather than as an exercise, we almost certainly would find hundreds of significant brand contacts in the experience of a particular customer, and the sum of the significant brand contacts for a good sample of customers would be some multiple of the number for any one customer.

Sometimes marketers flinch at the sight of so many brand contacts and retreat to a few more general attributes of customer experience such as "responsiveness" or "breadth of product line," or "friendliness of staff," or "quality." Such general attributes are not bad as such, and organizing the hundreds of detailed brand contacts in terms of a manageable number of more general dimensions or factors can make it much easier to understand and talk about the mass of data. However, we must either preserve the fundamental level of detail along with the summary attributes or lose the power to manage the brand. If a brand were a house, then one level of summary variables could be the rooms; another level of summary variables could be the walls, windows, and roof; and the brand contacts could be the beams, studs, insulation, bricks, drywall, muntins, staples, and nails. Good architects and builders know the details as well as the overall structure, and good marketers must know the brand contacts as well as the summary attributes. For a marketer, the test of whether brand contacts are stated at the right level of detail is one of utility—they should be expressed in a way that helps marketers (and other managers) to bring the real brand into synchronized orbit with the aspirational brand.

After we have a good list of brand contacts, the next step is to analyze them so they can be used to make decisions for the brand. A good start is to consider the brand contacts one at a time and to answer the following two questions for each of them:

1. How important does the consumer think it is?
2. How good or bad does the consumer think it is?

These two dimensions give rise to a grid with four quadrants. We call this a *Brand Contact Priority Grid* (see Figure 5.1) because the location of brand contacts in particular contacts has implications for what the marketer should do to bring the real brand into conformity with the aspirational brand.

The Brand Contact Priority Grid shows the elements that make up the real brand. It reveals the ones consumers think are good and the ones they think are bad, and it can be a shock to see such a grid for the first time. The names of the quadrants are significant. A marketer should focus on the *delighters* and *disgusters* because they are the brand contacts that are doing the most to shape the brand in the consumer's mind. Think of your brand as a medical patient for a moment. *Delighters* might be things like having excellent muscle tone, good blood pressure, and low cholesterol. A *disguster* might be a separated shoulder. *Annoyances* might be having a receding hairline and uneven teeth. *Frills* might be having a superior sense of smell and great night vision. Faced with this patient, a doctor would immediately

Figure 5.1
Brand Contact Priority Grid

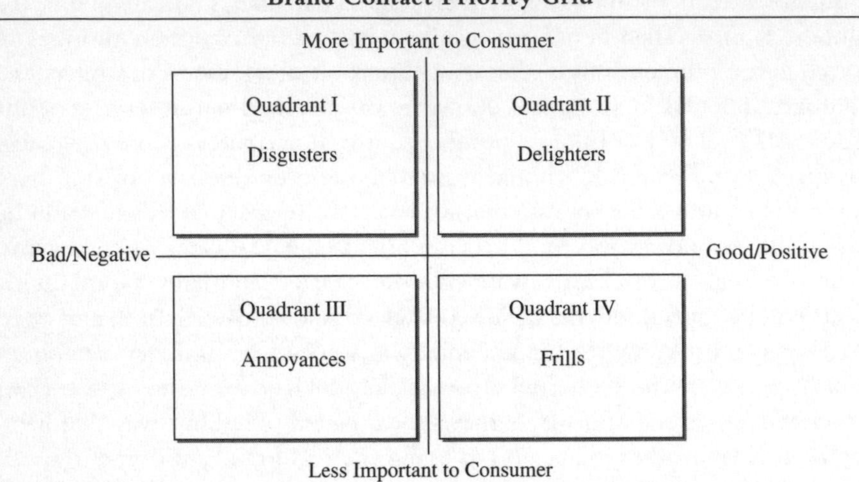

address the separated shoulder. And marketers who want to help their brand the most should try first and hardest to fix the disgusters in quadrant I, because those are the important things that consumers think are broken.

Notice that consumers do not care that the disgusters might be very hard for the marketer to fix. That is the marketer's problem, not the consumers'. And the hard truth is that a marketer who shies away from the disgusters because they are too hard to fix simply will not be able to rescue the brand. Of course, there are no free lunches and the marketer must find the resources needed to fix the disgusters somewhere. The grid can even help the search for resources. If the company was actually incurring costs to disgust or annoy consumers ("But we thought you liked stale rolls with your dinner—we've been drying them out especially for you!"), then it should be able to free up some resources simply by ceasing to do whatever it was that consumers found disgusting or annoying. This is rare, fortunately. But it is quite common for marketers to incur costs to create frills—the things that customers notice and like, but which are not important to them. If any resources are being used to create frills, the marketer should shift them to fix the disgusters and the annoyances instead. And if the disgusters and annoyances are all gone, the marketer should make sure the delighters are becoming more so.

In filling out a Brand Contact Priority Grid, it is good to start by applying a nominal scale to the dimensions. That means we merely try to distinguish important brand contacts from less important ones without worrying about whether one is twice as important as another. And we try to distinguish good brand contacts from bad ones without worrying about whether one is half as good as another. If, after doing that much, we are able to draw some conclusions about the relative importance or the relative merits of brand contacts to customers, we can try to show that information by means of where we plot brand contacts within the quadrants. If we are able to do that, we can prioritize elements within quadrants and, for example, fix the worst disgusters before we fix the milder ones.

We can practice applying this technique by completing a Brand Contact Priority Grid for our banking customer. We have classified the brand contacts one-by-one in a sort of quick and dirty way.

Delight	1.	The bank is close to the customer's office.
Frill	2.	The bank is in a modern building (this is a little mysterious and we would like to know more about what the age or style of the building meant to the customer).
Frill	3.	The offices looked sharp and professional. (We would like to understand this a little better. In the absence of experience, the customer seems to treat the bank's appearance as a surrogate for its competence. Ultimately, competence is more important to the customer than appearance, so we call this a frill.)
Frill	4.	The bank employees were well groomed.
Delight	5.	Vice president X was business-like.
Delight	6.	She understood us easily.
Delight	7.	Moving our accounts was easy.
Annoyance	8.	There were a couple of small mistakes on paperwork.
Annoyance	9.	Vice president Y replaced vice president X (we would like to know more about how the customer experienced the transition from one contact person to another).
Disguster	10.	Vice president Y asked questions the customer had answered already.
Annoyance	11.	There was a lot of waiting and paper-shuffling.

Disguster 12. The bank failed to honor a valid check. (The customer thinks paying valid checks goes to the heart of the bank's competence.)

Annoyance 13. The bank said dishonoring the check was a valuable service.

Disguster 14. The bank made mistakes on three statements.

Disguster 15. Unexplained and invalid charges.

Disguster 16. Automated phone system gave employee the wrong balance.

Frill 17. Automated phone system gave employee the right balance. (Items 16 and 17 are interesting because they both deal with the accuracy of responses by the automated phone system. It would be reasonable to combine these brand contacts and to conclude that the customer thinks that overall, the automated phone system is a disguster because it is untrustworthy—sometimes it's right, sometimes it's wrong. Alternatively, we've called "getting the answer right" a frill because being right doesn't make up for being wrong.)

Plotting the Brand Contact Priority Grid would show that we have something in each of the four quadrants. Even without knowing what the elements are, we can conclude that this bank's brand is incoherent. The delighters are telling the customer that the bank is competent, caring, and solicitous. The frills are just that—pleasant but unimportant—but the customer takes them as reassuring signs ("Surely a bank that spends money to have sharp, modern offices and such well-groomed employees must have all the important things under good control"); therefore, they intensify the impact of the annoyances and disgusters. The annoyances simply remind the customer that the bank is, after all, only a bank, and banks think nothing of wasting customers' time. The disgusters shout the message that the bank doesn't care about embarrassing the customer in front of suppliers and employees and that it doesn't know how to perform basic banking functions.

This brand is in serious trouble and no amount of pure marketing communication can save it. Just as obviously, fixing the brand requires concerted effort involving every functional area and department of the bank. The real brand grows from brand contacts that come from myriad aspects of the whole enterprise, and real marketers have to follow the brand contacts to their source. That entails educating everyone in the enterprise about the marketing issue and engaging him or her in the big process of bringing the real brand into conformity with the aspirational brand.

Gathering Customer Experiences

There are two things to consider as you plan to gather customer experiences: Determine which customers you ought to seek the information from, and determine how to get the information you seek from a customer. (We are using *customer* as a convenient form of shorthand; everything we say could also apply to prospective customers or lapsed customers.) We start with the issue of how to gather information at the right level of detail from a customer and then take up the question of which customer to investigate.

The problem of getting the right sort of information raises a closely related question: Once we figure out how to get the information we need from a customer, how do we get some assurance that we have not gotten all of our information from customers who do not represent anyone else in the market at all? The great temptation is to spend so much of the information budget on studying many customers that we are forced to study each of them in a relatively superficial way. Doing so gives us comfort about the representativeness of the data, but, unfortunately, the data are too general and superficial to reveal many true brand contacts. We learn things like "customers care about quality and reliability," for example, without learning how customers draw particular inferences about quality or reliability. *Quality* simply is not detailed enough to be useful as a brand contact. A better approach is to study a customer in sufficient depth and then to do that with as many customers as the budget will tolerate. At the end of the day, the marketer has to apply some business judgment in assessing the risk that the customers who have been studied might be unrepresentative of the market, but at least the marketer knows about someone's brand contacts.

The best information about brand contacts is comprehensive, detailed, fresh, and unfiltered. In the ideal world, we would capture the full sensory impressions of customers—sight, sound, smell, feel, and taste—as they experienced our product or service, starting with the first moment they became aware of it and finishing only when it dropped out of their awareness and they turned to something else. In such a perfect world, we would be sophisticated enough to capture the customer's memories as they were triggered by real-time experience with our product or service, and we would capture the formation of new memories based on the real-time experience.

This sort of research is expensive with today's level of technology and it is not done very often. Fortunately, there are some more practical approximations to the perfect research technique.

All of the approximations are based on in-depth interviews. Getting the right sort of information requires a customer to concentrate on his or her experience and the interviewer to concentrate on what the customer is saying; the necessary level of concentration is very hard to achieve in a focus group setting where several customers are having a conversation.

Not all in-depth interviews are equally effective. It is a great help—almost a necessity—to work with introspective, articulate, and willing customers in the effort to get the microscopically detailed accounts of experience that reveal the richest and most complete set of brand contacts. A customer has to cooperate with the marketer's effort to peel back the superficial conclusions and look under the hood of the generalities and platitudes that make up most introductory conversations between strangers. For example, an interview with a stockbroker about the brand contacts of a mutual fund family is likely to start out with the broker saying he likes (or does not like) the commission structure and the retail name recognition of the fund family. The broker is busy and tries to help the interviewer and save his or her own time by expressing summary conclusions in conventional business terms. However well meant it might be, this is useless for the purpose at hand. What begins to be more helpful is to find out that the broker is turned off by a parade of young wholesalers, none of whom bother to learn anything at all about the broker's history with the fund family or his or her current book of clients, before launching into a canned sales pitch. And from there, a skillful interviewer and a willing broker might uncover ten or a dozen specific things from which the broker infers that a wholesaler is credible and helpful, as well as explore how much influence the wholesaler has over the broker's decision to sell the funds.

If we designed a technique to discover everything that a customer could tell us about contacts with a particular brand, we probably would have several interviews over an extended period. That would give the customer a chance to relax and warm up to the task of searching for the detailed impressions behind the general conclusions. The process would be more like customer psychoanalysis than a typical one-shot marketing interview. A customer might well have a less extensive set of contacts with one brand than another; and once the right level of rapport and introspection is reached, the customer could tell us everything there is to learn about the less significant brand in less time. Test this at dinner parties: Most people can talk much longer and with far greater depth and nuance about their own favorite hobby than about their spouse's favorite hobby.

Fortunately, even a one-shot interview can yield useful results if it is done well. Doing it well requires that the interviewer, at least, be adept enough at introspection to lead the customer through the process. I like to train my graduate marketing students to do this sort of work by first practicing their own introspection skills. I require them to behave as if they were the customer, to go interact with some product or service, and to reflect on their introspections about their experience as they do. Then they have to write down their impressions. In a first exercise, my goal is for them to capture impressions at a sufficient level of detail and to record them with some precision. That is a necessary starting point for any sort of analysis and drawing of conclusions, and it is important to get it right.

Many students use coffee houses for their exercises, and most of them are able to generate a list of brand contacts that surprises them with its length and level of detail. The brand contacts go far beyond the coffee itself, and they begin well outside the store. For example, the scruffy panhandler in front of the store is a brand contact (and a management challenge for the store owner). The student-customers make inferences that affect their decision to enter and buy coffee based on how the panhandler behaves and how close he or she stands to the doorway. Once in the store, they assess the length of the line, the presence or absence of an empty stool or table, the song playing over the sound system and the volume at which it is playing, whether the crowd at the tables are the regulars or parents in for the football weekend, whether the cigarette smoke is too heavy, whether the rack of newspapers is full, and a hundred other things in the instant between opening the door and taking a place in line. I know they have appreciated the point of the exercise when they get past telling me they do not like messy tables and they begin to distinguish their reaction to a few pastry crumbs on top from their reaction to the gummy residue of a spilled latte. It is pages and pages before they get to the mouth-feel of the rim of the paper coffee cup and the awkward placement of the handle on the ceramic mug. Some students are better at this than others, but the ones who can do it well are able to recognize when their customers are being introspective, and they are better at coaxing them past the superficial stage.

We could go on and on about nuances of technique and risks of misapplication, but we now consider the next branch of the issue: how to determine which customers to study, given that we cannot study all of them right away. One obvious consideration is that customers who actually have some experience—good or bad—with our brand can tell us far more about brand contacts than those who do not. Therefore, it's much easier to learn about the brand contacts of a product or service that is already being marketed than about one that has not been launched yet. If we are just in the planning stages, we must resort to studying customers of products or services that are very similar to the one we are planning. They can tell us about the brand contacts of those products or services, and we marketers have to extrapolate to our coming product or service. Whether we can do that effectively depends in part on the degree of similarity between what customers know about and what we are planning to offer them. It is easier and safer to extrapolate brand contacts for a simple line extension or a new package size than to extrapolate the brand contacts for cell phones and PDAs to a new combination PDA/phone.

Assuming that we are lucky enough to have customers for an existing product or service, we should give careful attention to the selection of the customers we use in our investigation of brand contacts. These customers must be self-aware, capable of introspection, articulate enough to tell us what they think, and willing to help us with the work. But what other characteristics should they have? Which market segment should they represent? This is a good opportunity for the marketers to ponder what sort of customer they would like to have if they could have only one. That "alpha customer" might be the one who is most representative of the largest market segment, or the one who is the heaviest consumer by unit volume, or the one who is the most profitable, or the one who is most sophisticated and demanding, or the one who is not distinguished yet but who is likely to become one of the other types in the future.

BRAND ANALYSIS: CASE INSTRUCTIONS

Step I: Brand Contact Inventory

Inventory all of the brand contacts that affect this target, affecting the customers' satisfaction with the "whole" product and, therefore, their impression of the brand.

1. Start by going through the case and finding the *brand contacts* that are part of their stories. Remember that brand contacts are the "moments of truth," where impressions about the product and brand are made on this person throughout the purchase and ownership processes. Think about the entire experience of buying and owning some generic "ACME" product from the consumer's point of view. What

are all the points from which the consumer gets information and makes a judgment about the ACME brand (even if they are very tiny)?

2. List these contacts in column I of the Brand Contact Inventory (see Table 5.1).

Step II: Importance Evaluation

Now that you have identified the brand contacts, evaluate whether the contact is highly important or less important to the person's impression of the ACME brand. The temptation is to label them all as highly important; however, they are not all equally important. As you make a qualitative judgment about their importance, remember to evaluate them from the consumer's perspective.

Label those contacts that are relatively important to the person's impression of the brand as *higher,* and those that are relatively less important as *lower.* Write these labels in column II of the Brand Contact Inventory.

Step III: Impression Evaluation

Next, evaluate whether the contact is currently leaving a positive or negative impression on the consumer. Again, remember to evaluate them from

Table 5.1
Brand Contact Inventory: Importance and Impression

Brand Contact Column I	*Importance to Target (Higher/Lower)Impression Column II*	*Positive or Negative Impression Column III*

the consumer's perspective. Write a *yes* for positive or a *no* for a negative impression in column III of the Brand Contact Inventory.

Step IV: Agreement and Placement on Priority Grid

Review your list of brand contacts. Using your analysis of the Brand Contact Inventory (Table 5.1), consolidate your findings to the Brand Contact Priority Grid (Figure 5.1). Begin by identifying all brand contacts you have labeled as having a *higher importance* and leaving a *negative impression.* List these contacts in quadrant I on the Brand Contact Priority Grid. Place all contacts identified as having a *higher importance* and leaving a *positive impression* in quadrant II. All contacts labeled as having a *lower importance* and leaving a *negative impression* go in quadrant III, and *lower importance* and *positive impression* contacts belong in quadrant IV.

Step V: Customer Expectations and Experiences at Each Contact

Now that we have an idea of how and where consumers think the ACME is contacting them, we need to step back and look at those contact points from their perspective. Begin by writing the contacts from quadrant I in the first column of the Brand Contact Inventory (Table 5.2). Taking the contacts in quadrant I only, ask yourself these types of questions:

1. What does the consumer *expect* at each contact point? What information is he or she seeking? What are his or her wants and needs at this particular point? (List your ideas in column II of the Brand Contact Inventory in Table 5.2.)
2. What does the consumer *experience* at this contact point? What actually happens? If the consumer had to describe exactly how he or she felt at this moment of the experience, what do you think he or she would say aloud? If able to tell ACME how he or she felt about it at this moment, what would he or she say? (List your ideas in column III of the Brand Contact Inventory in Table 5.2.)

Step VI: Messages Sent

Before you know what "message" *you want to send* to your consumers, you have to know what messages those contacts in quadrant I are *currently*

Table 5.2
Brand Contact Inventory: Expectations and Experiences

Brand Contact (Those Found in Quadrant I) Column I	*Consumer Expectation Column II*	*Current Consumer Experience Column III*	*Message Sent Column IV*

sending. Based on the consumer's expectation and actual experience, what messages is the brand sending?

Describe the message ACME is sending *from the consumer's point-of-view* in column IV of the Brand Contact Inventory. As you look at the difference between the consumer's expectation and experience, what impression is he or she taking away about ACME? What have you learned about where the "brand image" of ACME comes from?

HOME COMPUTER AND PRINTER CONSUMER CASE STUDY—ACME BRAND

In this final section of the chapter, we illustrate the techniques we have discussed. The consumer verbatim responses follow. Tables 5.3 and 5.4 contain the brand contact inventories, and Figure 5.2 represents this consumer's priorities.

> Hi! My name is Debbie and I'm a chef at an Italian restaurant downtown. I've been there about three years and really enjoy it, but I'm planning on opening my own restaurant sometime next year. My husband, Tom, and

Table 5.3
Example Brand Contact Inventory

Brand Contact Column I	*Importance to Target (Higher/Lower) Column II*	*Positive or Negative Impression Column III*
Computer/printer advertising	Lower	Negative
Price of computer/printer system	Higher	Positive
Word of mouth recommendation	Higher	Positive
Computer jargon	Lower	Negative
"Smart Friend" advice and recommendation	Higher	Positive
Product features	Lower	Positive
Brand name	Lower	Positive
Computer/software bundling offer	Higher	Positive
Consumer report recommendation	Higher	Positive
Brand displays in retail store	Higher	Negative
Availability	Higher	Positive
Personal past experience with product	Higher	Positive
Product industrial design	Higher	Positive
Demonstration units	Higher	Negative
Parts not included (cable)	Lower	Negative
Printer set-up	Lower	Positive
Availability of ink cartridge	Higher	Positive
Out-of-ink notification	Higher	Negative
Ink cartridge design	Lower	Negative
Retail experience for ink cartridge	Higher	Negative
Ink cartridge price	Higher	Negative
Ink cartridge package design	Higher	Negative
Manual	Lower	Positive
Ink fading on photo	Higher	Negative
Technical support (not a toll-free number, "phone maze"	Lower	Negative
Technical support operator (helpfulness, resolution tip)	Higher	Positive

Table 5.4
Example Brand Contact Inventory with Customer Responses

Brand Contact (Those Found in Quadrant I) Column I	*Consumer Expectation Column II*	*Current Consumer Experience Column III*	*Message Sent Column IV*
Product displays in the retail store	"The computer display set up should be friendly, easy to understand, and should help me decide which computer or printer I want to buy."	"The displays are disorganized, and everything is described with a lot of jargon. They put me off."	"If I can't figure it out in the store, I worry that I won't be able to figure it out at home. Maybe they don't really want customers like me."
Performance of demonstration units in the store	"I expect to be able to see a print sample from the color printer before I buy it. Print quality is important to me and the only way I know it produces the quality is by seeing it."	"There are times when the print demonstrations don't work."	"If the printer doesn't work in the store, how do I know that it will work at home at what quality it will print? It makes me think that ACME's print quality may not be as good as I thought.
Out-of-ink notification	"I am sure that the printer will tell me when it is about to run out of ink. It's probably like a copier that will start fading before it runs out completely."	"There is no warning that the ink is going to run out. The printer even keeps on printing when one of the colors runs out, ruining many sheets of paper if I don't catch it."	"ACME is supposed to be a technology company, and so they should be able to create something to let me know the ink is going to run out. Maybe they're not as technologically advanced as I thought."
Retail experience for ink cartridge	"The right ink cartridges have to be easier to find than the right printer was for me. I bet that I will find the cartridges next to my printer's display at the store."	"The supplies are displayed differently in each store. Some are mixed in bins and others are hanging on shelves. Some stores don't even have the cartridges on the shelf."	"The cartridges were even harder to find than I thought. Just one more reason for me to feel uncomfortable in these stores. Why can't ACME get their cartridges organized so that their customers can find them no matter what store they go to?"

Table 5.4 (*Continued*)

Brand Contact (Those Found in Quadrant I) Column I	*Consumer Expectation Column II*	*Current Consumer Experience Column III*	*Message Sent Column IV*
Ink cartridge price	"A small cartridge like this should cost $10–$12. Each cartridge should last about six months."	"The cartridges are priced between $25–$30. ACME cartridges are on a par with other manufacturer's prices, but refills that fit ACME printers look like a better value."	"I was not expecting the ink cartridges to be so expensive, and that I would have to change them so frequently. I didn't even think to price them when I bought them. I wish ACME had let me know what to expect, or were they worried that if I knew, I wouldn't have bought the printer. Are they trying to cheat me"?
Ink cartridge package design	"I will bring my old cartridge with me to match it with the ones on the shelf. This will help me find what I need. I will also look for my cartridge's model number and my printer's model number."	"Some of the displays are very hard to navigate. The ink cartridge model numbers are on the back of the packages. The printer model numbers are confusing, and my printer is hard to locate."	"I had to track down a salesperson to make sure I had the right cartridge. This is a huge waste of my time when I ought to be able to just pick these things up. Why does ACME have to make this so hard"?
Ink fading on photograph	"When I buy a printer that says it prints photo-quality prints, and when it sells photo paper, and encourages me to print my photos, then I expect the photos I print will behave just like the photos I get at the photo shop. They ought to last in good condition for years."	"The photos I print start to fade after just a few months, especially when they're displayed in a frame."	"This is the most aggravating thing I've ever experienced, and I feel ACME deliberately lied to me about what to expect. I'm only going to use the printer for photos I think people are going to throw away after a short time, and never for anything I expect to last. The whole experience makes me really wary of trusting them."

Figure 5.2
Example Brand Contact Priority Grid

More Important to Consumer

Brand displays in retail store Performance of demonstration units Out-of-ink notification Retail experience of ink cartridge Ink cartridge price Ink cartridge package design Ink fading on photograph	Price of computer system Word of mouth recommendation "Smart Friend" advice and recommendation Software bundling offer Consumer Report recommendation Availability Past personal experience brand Printer industrial design Availability of ink cartridge Technical support operator
Computer/printer advertising Computer jargon Cable not included Ink cartridge design Technical support toll number Technical support phone maze	Product features Reputable brand name Ease of printer set up Manual

Less Important to Consumer

I have been married for 12 years and we have three boys: Kevin's 9, Kyle is 5, and Spencer is almost 2.

This was a big year for us. Kevin was MVP of his baseball team, Kyle won the Science Award at school, and we finally got Spencer to sleep in a "big boy's bed!" Small stuff to the rest of the world, I know, but important to us. This was a big year for another reason—we finally bought a computer! I know we are a little behind the times, but it is a big step.

We'd been "seriously" thinking about it for a while but had to unexpectedly use some extra cash to repair a leak in our roof. As December rolled around, I felt like all we saw were ads for computers. They're a lot of money, but not as bad as I thought. So, we decided to take the plunge!

I was really anxious to buy a computer—a little nervous too—but very excited. I also wanted to look at something called a scanner. The woman who takes reservations at our restaurant showed me invitations to her dad's 60th birthday party that she had made. She included this precious baby picture of him on the front of the invitation. It looked so great! But I have hardly any computer experience, and I will have to see if putting pictures into stuff is way over my head. One of our main motivations for buying a computer system was the kids. As parents, we feel responsible for providing them with opportunities that will give them an edge in life, and we believe a computer really makes a difference. In the back of my mind, I was also hoping that I could use this computer to get my business off the ground. We also wanted to make sure we bought a color printer. To the kids, it's more "fun" to see things in color. But I believe it makes them stay on the computer and work a little harder. A color printer meets both our goals!

I was nervous about buying computing equipment for our home. It's an expensive mistake to have to live with, if you don't buy the "right" system. I've overheard people at work saying they love their home computer and some others saying they wish they had bought a different model. I was afraid we'd make a big expensive mistake.

We were having Jeff, Tom's brother, over that night for dinner. He is a sales rep for a manufacturing company and carries one of those portable computers with him on the road. Besides that, he is a real "techno guy." I used to poke fun at Jeff for being a "nerd," but not anymore. He's a lifesaver. Tom and I would have been lost without him, and I honestly don't think we could've made our best decision without his help.

During dinner, I told Jeff about my experience with the ads in the paper. He wasn't very surprised and actually said it was pretty typical. That was discouraging. He said the only way to combat confusion is to really know what you want before you look at ads or even go into the stores.

He asked us a lot of questions about how we planned to use the system. Although Tom and I had played around on computers, we had no idea what all the terms meant. So Jeff explained some that I had seen in the paper and, more importantly, how they would affect what we wanted to do. After dinner, he helped us make a list of the features we needed to ask the salesperson about. He was terrific and covered everything we needed. Some of what he said surprised me. I thought all this stuff came together. His list made sure we got everything we would need, from the "monitor" (who knew you had to buy that separately?) to a cable we needed for the printer (wouldn't that be included?).

He suggested we look at the ACME and BASIC. ACME! Finally, a name I recognized! We also asked his opinion about the ACME color printer that Sue from work had used to do her invitations and he said that would be fine. He also told us to look at QUATTRO and said they make a good photo-quality printer for the home.

One day the following week, I had to take the kids to the library to return some books. Just to satisfy my own curiosity, I looked at the most recent edition of *Consumer Reports* that reviewed different computers and printers. I always consult it whenever we make a "significant" purchase. To me, it's a credible, non-biased source of information, and I've never been dissatisfied with a decision I've made based on their recommendation. Luckily, that issue reviewed the ACME and BASIC computers and the ACME and QUATTRO printers we were thinking about and highly rated them. Their review made me feel even better. Having done what we felt was enough homework, Tom and I decided that the "big day" had come.

The mall nearest to our home has an Electronics World store, and armed with the sheet Jeff had given us, we entered the store. The place was really loud and seemed disorganized. We were sort of overwhelmed, but still optimistic that we'd be bringing home our computer and printer that day. We maneuvered our way to the computer aisle.

Tom called me over to the ACME. The complicated terms that Jeff warned us about were everywhere. As we were looking, I heard a voice ask "Can I help you with something?" He seemed fairly knowledgeable, but he kept on talking about the product and all the bells and whistles that I did not understand or care about.

I realized that I had to ask specific questions to get him to use words that I could understand. I asked him a lot of questions such as "What do you think about this computer?"; "Would you personally buy it?"; "Do you recommend we look at anything else?" Once I starting asking the questions, he seemed to catch on that I was not very knowledgeable about computers and that I needed his help.

The ACME seemed perfect for our family because it came with something for all of us-an encyclopedia and something called "Jump Start Kindergarten" for the kids and a financial planning program and something to do your taxes with for us. Plus, it had a three-year warranty and an 800 number to call if we had any problems. Although the ACME wasn't the least expensive by far; overall, it seemed like the best value.

I asked the salesperson what he had heard about the BASIC, and he said they were good, too. However, we were more familiar with the ACME name, so we went with them. We asked the salesperson to show us the color printers. The woman at work who had done her own invitations had an ACME 725C, and Jeff had agreed that it was a good brand.

I had also heard of ACME; in fact, I think some of our printers in the office are ACME. I wanted to be sure we bought a brand we had heard of. It not only reassures me that the company will be around for a while, but it makes me think they make high quality products. But the salesperson insisted that QUATTRO was the best printer for us and showed us what they had available.

I know it sounds silly, but I didn't like how the QUATTRO printer looked. It was small, which is good because it's going to "live" in our family room but it didn't look like a normal printer. It was longer than it was wide and you put the paper in through the top. Also, it looked cheap and with three boys, I can't take the chance that it will break easily. I wanted to see how both of them worked, so I asked the salesperson to show us.

The salesperson got the QUATTRO to print out an actual sample while we were there, but the ACME did not work for some reason. How could I have been sure that it would work at home if it didn't work in the store? I felt torn. We were ready to consider the QUATTRO. When the salesperson saw that we were upset and confused, he showed us how the ACME 891C printed.

He said the other printer must have been out of paper or something. Nonetheless, the 891C looked great! The salesperson assured us that the 725C worked just as well. That made up our mind once and for all. The ACME 725C was the one we wanted. We were finally done shopping. As we took the printer box off the shelf, I noticed some words on the side of the box that said "Printer cable not included." I remembered Jeff had told us this and asked the salesperson. He gave us what we needed and apologized—"I usually remember to tell my customers they need that, too. Glad you caught it!"

As we were heading toward the counter, the scanners caught my eye. The salesperson saw me stop and said that the MICRO scanners were at an unbeatable price. He said that the ACME scanners run for around $500 and the MICRO scanner was on sale for under $100. The MICRO seemed more compact than the ACME. That was a must for us, and it was much cheaper for seemingly the same thing. The salesperson even said that the MICRO was easier to hook up than the ACME. He said something about it being "plug and play." He explained that the ACME required you to open the computer up. That made up my mind right there. I was not going to mess around with this very expensive piece of equipment. I asked how long the sale would last. The salesperson thought that it was ending that weekend. I just kept on thinking about the great cards that the woman at work made and all the fun I could have and how much it could help with Tom's and my business ventures. Tom knew what I was thinking and said, "You want it. It is at a good price. How hard can it be? Just get it." I was thankful that he said that without my needing to make a strong case for it.

We went to the counter and paid for our purchases. We were a little over our budget, but that was okay, because we had got what we wanted and were confident in our decision.

We took it all home and were so excited we started to hook everything up right away. It took the whole afternoon to set up the computer—there were so many things to plug in. Tom even had to go back out and get one of those strips that have a lot of outlets in them and a bunch of floppy disks to back up software on. After we had the computer set up, we took a break before hooking up the printer and scanner, thinking they would take just as long.

But you know what? They were pretty easy to set up. You put disks in the computer and follow the instructions on the screen. I am thankful that the ink cartridges came with the printer, because I did not think to ask at the store.

Over the past couple of months, we've been using the computer like crazy. The kids print out everything in color—from their school reports to their "works of art." About four months after we had purchased the computer, printer, and scanner, Kevin was printing an assignment for school and he yelled "Mom, the printer is broken." My stomach sank to the floor. I looked and saw that half of his page was blank where there should have been a picture of Florida he scanned from the encyclopedia.

When I saw this, I assumed that the ink needed to be replaced rather than the whole printer. I thought that there would be some warning, like a couple of pages with faded lettering, a buzzer, or something, like you'd see on a copier. I guess I had never really thought about the ink running out, but I just assumed that it would have lasted longer than it did. But, we had been printing a lot of photos and stuff. I looked at the manual and found out what I needed to do.

Taking the cartridge out was as easy as putting it in the first time. This did not cause much of a problem, because Kevin could wait until tomorrow to print out his paper. So when Tom got home, I headed to Electronics World with the used cartridge in hand. I had almost forgotten how confusing the store was. The aisles were not marked, so I went by where we saw our printer displayed thinking that supplies would be by my printer. No such luck. I ended up going aisle-by-aisle until I bumped into a salesperson, who pointed me in the right direction.

Once I found the right aisle, finding a cartridge that looked like the one in my hand was a challenge. I found the ACME section. I glanced at the rack of boxes and prices, and I noticed that they were around $30. That seemed like a lot, but I guess for four months of learning, it wasn't too bad.

Then I noticed that there were boxes that said ACME, but were less than half the price. That sounded even better, but what was the catch? After looking at it closer, I found that they were not ACME products. They were generic brands. I took the two boxes to a salesperson to ask about the difference. He explained that one was a new cartridge and the less expensive one was a refill.

I then remembered that the manual specifically said to not use refills. They don't work as well. I told him that I wanted to buy a new cartridge and showed him my old one to make sure that I picked up the correct one. He said that I had the right model, but I had a used color cartridge in my hand but picked a black ink cartridge off the shelf.

I misread the box. I just read the word "color" and did not pay attention that it had a black dot next to the word. I am glad that I asked or I would have left with the wrong cartridge. It would have made me mad if I had to come all the way back to the store after all of this. When I got home, I just threw the old cartridge away and popped the new one in. It worked as good as new as soon as I put it in.

A few months later, I received a frantic call from my mother. She said that the picture that I scanned and printed for her of the boys had faded terribly. I was as shocked and disappointed as she was. For the past six months, I had stopped getting double prints and just sent printed copies to friends and family across the globe. I had no idea what to do.

Of course, I couldn't find the manual. I need to tell Tom to make a list of "help" phone numbers of all the products we had bought and tape it inside the top drawer of the desk. I ended up calling 800 directory to get ACME's number. The operator asked me which department I needed. I replied, "Technical Support."

She explained that she had a listing for general information and product information. I chose the general information number by default. I called the number she gave to me, 1-800-555-5555, only to be given a toll number when I indicated I needed help with service. I thought all companies had 800 number help lines. I couldn't believe ACME would make me pay for the call. Didn't we spend enough on the printer?

I then dialed the third number anyway and went through the "phone maze" until I finally reached a live person. Tim was very helpful. He confirmed I had used the right number and politely listened to my complaint that it wasn't toll-free. He explained that photographs printed on a printer would only last about three months out in a frame and a few years if they were in a photo album. I explained to him that because ACME said that it was a photo-quality printer and the box and manuals suggested that I use the printer to make photographs, that I was under the impression that the printouts would last as long as photographs last. And, in my mind, that is about three generations! He told me that I shouldn't be so upset because I have electronic copies of all of the pictures I have printed. He must have been crazy to think that I was going to print out a new picture for my mother and everyone else I send photographs to every three months!

While I was so upset, I decided that for my own satisfaction, I needed to tell him that I thought the price of the ink cartridges was a little too high. He then asked me what I used the printer for. I said that the kids used it a lot of the time. He explained to me that I could set the printer to print in draft mode, which would use up less ink, for less important things like their drawings. He said that this would make the cartridges last longer. With that bit of advice, Tim made things a little better.

I have since stopped using my printer to reprint my photos. If I need a duplicate, I go back to the processor. Now I just put photos into letters. I wanted to make all the members of my family a photo calendar for the holidays, but I am afraid that the pictures would fade before the calendar would be thrown away.

All in all, I don't know how we lived without a computer in our home. This year I made our own Christmas cards. Someone at work actually asked me how I did them. Boy did I feel proud! Sounds impressive, but the truth is, I only know the "tip of the iceberg" about how to use our system. But that's okay—the way I use them works just fine for me. I figure I'll always have Jeff to help me if I ever get "stuck" and, to be honest, I don't really care how it works.

Hopefully this illustration gives the reader a sense of the richness of discovery of consumer information that the approaches described in this chapter can achieve. The relationship you have with your consumers can inform and be strengthened by this interchange of ideas.

Notes

1. For example, David A. Aaker, *Building Strong Brands* (New York: Free Press, 1995).

CHAPTER 6

STRATEGIES FOR VIRAL MARKETING

MARIA FLORES LETELIER, CHARLES SPINOSA, and
BOBBY J. CALDER

It has been around forever, but as a marketing strategy, it goes back only about 50 years. How do you sell a line of kitchen containers without advertising and even without distribution? The answer: Have women hold parties and talk about them to their friends. The Tupperware Party strategy was based on a simple premise that is as valid today as it was then. Consumer-to-consumer contacts are powerful! When one consumer says something to another, the message is likely to be immediate, personal, credible, and relevant. For a while, this sort of communication—one consumer contacting another—was called *word-of-mouth,* or WOM. Currently, it is most often called *buzz.*

The impetus for thinking about WOM or buzz from a strategic point of view originated with the work of Elihu Katz and Paul Lazarfeld, again, almost 50 years ago. In their book, *Personal Influence,* they contrasted the power of consumer-to-consumer contacts with that of advertising and other types of mass communication and postulated that the process operated through a "two-step flow." Certain individuals, termed *influentials,* took in information and passed it on to others with whom they were in contact. The key idea was that influentials were influential because of their links to a community of other people who would not otherwise be exposed to or absorb the information. In a well-known example of the two-step flow model, Pfizer had Katz, Herbert Menzel, and James S. Coleman identify the characteristics of physician opinion leaders who spread word-of-mouth about tetracycline among physicians.[1] Gradually, the notion was added that as information "diffuses" through a community, consumers pass through stages from just being aware of the information initially to finally being persuaded to adopt a product.[2]

The marketing strategy that emerged was to focus on reaching influentials or early adopters, who would then transmit information that eventually would cause others in a community composed of targeted consumers to buy the product. Marketers in the recording industry were attracted early to this strategy. In one instance, they grouped class presidents, cheerleaders, and sports team captains from certain cities into an expert panel to review records. Although these influentials, or opinion leaders, owned very few records, their word-of-mouth was able to pull certain of the records into the top ten in their cities without any radio play.[3]

Ford Motor Company gave the original Mustangs to airline employees who were then called *stewardesses.* The stewardesses used the cars in towns where they had flight layovers. People in these communities would talk to or at least see glamorous young women driving the cars, and this WOM had more impact than a television ad. According to a recent *Business Week* article titled "Buzz Marketing" (thereby confirming the status of *buzz* as the buzzword today for *word-of-mouth*), Ford continues to pursue the strategy.[4]

Rather than blitzing the airways with 30-second television commercials for its new subcompact, Ford Motor Company recruited just a handful of trendsetters in a few markets and gave them each a Focus to drive for six months. What were their duties? Simply to be seen with the car and to hand out Focus-themed trinkets to anyone who expressed interest in it. "We weren't looking for celebrities. We were looking for the assistants to celebrities, party planners, disk jockeys—the people who really seem to influence what was cool. . . ."

So, buzz marketing is alive and well. As Renee Dye points out in a *Harvard Business Review* article titled "The Buzz on Buzz," the strategy is now thought to be widely applicable:[5]

- Not just to edgy products, but to products as routine as prescription drugs.
- Not just something to be left to chance, but a strategy to be used consciously and deliberately.
- Not just for current customers, but for nonusers because countercultures can create buzz.
- Not just for new products or first-mover advantage, but for products anywhere in the life cycle.
- Not just as an extension of advertising or as a replacement for advertising, but as something that is different in kind and that might even be harmed by advertising.

Emanuel Rosen, in his book *The Anatomy of Buzz,* emphasizes the point that buzz marketing must be strategic. Natural contagion, in which a few people are exposed and buzz is left to take care of itself, is not enough. "To get buzz going, a heroic push—*beyond natural contagion*—is usually called for" (p. 123).[6] Rosen points to the early days of Federal Express in which it proved necessary to send a team to designated cities to get potential customers to give the team a sample package, which they would ship for free to someone in a distant city. In this way, Federal Express actually forced the contact from one customer to the next to the point that buzz was created.

FROM BUZZ TO VIRAL MARKETING

In the last few years, there have been further advances in the strategic use of buzz. The key insight is that buzz can be more than just a matter of actively stimulating the transmission of information from some consumers to others in a community. This insight is most often conveyed in the analogy of viral marketing.

The "viral" analogy views buzz as spreading by "infection." The consumer is infected by buzz, catches it as someone catches a cold, and passes it on in the same way unless he or she takes actions to stop it. In wired communities, the infection is just a click away. Buzz can cause "epidemics" much more quickly than the traditional two-step flow or diffusion implies. Rather than getting the word to a few opinion leaders or influentials and waiting for them to spread the word, a strategy of viral marketing gets users to pass the word almost involuntarily. Beyond this, what is passed is not mere information. It is something more akin to a virus—something that takes over and alters the consumer's thinking. That it is readily accepted is as much a consequence of the process of person-to-person contact as the information itself.

Steve Jurvetson, the venture capitalist behind Hotmail, coined the term *viral marketing* to describe the principle behind Hotmail's growth. Each time a Hotmail user sent someone an e-mail, the e-mail had at the bottom an implicitly user-endorsed solicitation to "Get your free e-mail with Hotmail now." The technology of the Web enhanced the scripting, passing, and responding to word-of-mouth. More than this, what was being virally "caught" was the idea that Hotmail was the right way to use e-mail.

The insight is that ideas or ways of thinking can be propagated through a community. Ideas "network" through the community and become the *de facto* way the community thinks about something.

Malcolm Gladwell in *The Tipping Point* uses the viral analogy to underscore the speed at which buzz can spread.[7] Once buzz reaches a critical "tipping point" in a community, it simply takes over. Like the flu, it reaches large numbers of people in the community very quickly. But the substance of the buzz needs to be, in Gladwell's phrase, "sticky," and it needs to fit the context of community. The buzz must be about an idea that is inherently important to the community and that fits the time and place. Gladwell gives as an example the case of Hush Puppies, a dying brand of shoes, in the mid-1990s. The company, Wolverine, learned that the shoes were, improbably, still being sold in small stores in the East Village in New York City. It turned out that kids were buying the shoes, probably with just the thought in mind that the shoes were so different as to be stylishly counterculture. Suddenly this idea of Hush Puppies reached a tipping point, with the assist of some New York designers, and spread like an epidemic. It went on to infect large numbers of young men's thinking about shoes.[8]

So what is a viral marketing strategy? Like all buzz, viral marketing is about the power of consumer-to-consumer contacts. But it is more than this. It is about the rapid, almost involuntary, spread of a way of thinking about a product and what it means in the context of a community.

UNDERSTANDING BUZZ BETTER

The viral analogy is useful. It certainly helps marketers to see that the power of buzz goes beyond the diffusion of information. Information may be part of buzz, but, typically, buzz is also about what information means. It is *about* information, about ways of seeing and thinking about things. In short, it is about the evolution of shared culture in a community.

Buzz causes people to think differently. In the case of Hush Puppies, it was not just that the young males learned about a new shoe. In fact, they probably learned very little new about the shoe. What was new was the way they came to see the shoe and its significance in their community. Buzz is subjective. It is about the intersubjectivity of a community of people. Objective information can be part of buzz, but to grasp the true power of buzz, marketers must understand the role it plays in making things culturally relevant.

Actually, there is a better analogy than that of a virus. It was created by the biologist Richard Dawkins in his book *The Selfish Gene.*[9] Dawkins used the term *memes* as a contrast to "genes." Genes are passed from person to person and produce biological replication. Memes are cultural ideas that produce cultural replication as they are passed from one person to another. Susan Blackmore, in *The Meme Machine,* argues specifically that evolution applies to memes in the same way as to genes.[10] While there is debate over the scientific status of memes,[11] the concept seems useful to us as a metaphor for thinking about buzz.

Viruses are destructive and essentially corrupt their hosts. Memes are constructive and enabling. Memes program people to be more effective, or they do not survive. We think the notion of memes provides a better conceptual understanding of the way in which buzz works.

Take baskets for example. Baskets are useful devices for carrying things (e.g., picnic supplies), and they no doubt have their objective features and intricacies of construction. But how would you like to be selling baskets? It is safe to say the basket industry would not be your first choice. One company, the Longaberger Company of Newark, Ohio, however, does quite well at selling baskets.[12] It does so with a viral marketing strategy that is instructive.

Taking a cue from Tupperware, Longaberger associates get women throughout the United States to host basket parties in their homes. At these parties, women who have bought baskets tell other women about how they have used them in their lives. What is being transmitted is the idea that baskets can fit into your life to provide a sense of relaxing simplicity, authenticity, and personal creativity. The *New Yorker* magazine ran a cartoon that gets the buzz just right. Two women are sitting side-by-side on a couch in a living room. Covering their heads is a large, upside down basket. It is the idea of the basket as it replicates from one person to the next that is the power of buzz. And it's not just parties; the Internet figures in, and there is the founder's book. It is all about the cultural meaning of baskets in the targeted consumer community that has been networked together by the company.

So, understand that viral marketing is more about memes than about viruses. A good viral marketing strategy is one that uses buzz to replicate shared cultural meaning across a community of consumers. Another way of saying this is that the brand itself must become a meme that is conveyed by buzz.

One final thought on understanding buzz—it has not been lost on many observers that viral marketing is right now enjoying considerable buzz in the marketing community. Once you get the idea, you see it everywhere. Seth Godin (*Unleashing the Ideavirus*) even sees the "Mona Lisa" in the Louvre as a nice job of viral marketing.[13] This can be debated. What cannot be debated is that cultural meaning is everywhere. The key idea for viral marketing is not that brands can be culturally relevant, but that buzz can be used to spread cultural meaning in a self-replicating way.

NETWORKING IN TARGETED COMMUNITIES

A viral marketing strategy calls for creating buzz and networking in an existing community or creating a new community of consumers. Many of the cases we review later involve electronic communities, where networking is greatly facilitated by the speed of communication. However, remember the case of Tupperware—networking is the key, not electronic communication per se.

We now present our ideas for developing different viral strategies that fit different kinds of communities. First, however, we should describe what we mean by *communities* in more detail. We begin by exploring the nature of communal, networked behavior and the new challenges they present for marketers. We then present the four basic types of networked behavior and corresponding network marketing strategies. In examining the opportunities associated with each strategy, we look at various cases of how viral network marketing strategies have been orchestrated or coordinated with more traditional strategies. Because marketers tend to believe that viral network strategies work only for e-networked communities, we include one case of a highly networked, traditional community in Mexico. It is also worth remembering that business to business (B2B) marketers regularly work with highly networked business communities that may or may not be electronically linked.

There are four general principles of highly networked environments that marketers must take into account. Understanding and acting in accordance with these principles is a matter of basic viral network marketing hygiene.

1. Networked communities are frequently formed without a company's support and maintain their autonomy no matter how much support they get. This is clear for industry groups but also true for people who care deeply and talk to each other about cars, music, wines, high-tech equipment, and so forth.
2. Networked communities have network leaders who regard themselves and who are regarded by others as experts. Palm gives us an exemplary case of how to treat such experts. When the Palm Pilot was launched at Demo, an invitation-only event for influentials in the high-tech field, it supplied attendants with the product for the course of the show and then offered it to them at a discount at the end of the event. The product was such a hit that attendants showed the Palm to others on their flights home, and they signed purchase orders for Palms once they reached home. It is frequently difficult for B2C marketers, who know products and their creators intimately, to treat the customers as the brand and product experts. However, within a network, the product and brand live in the customers' discussion and shared experience of it.

3. Network leaders frequently promote products and brands in the name of social values that often seem irrelevant to marketers. Network leaders see products and brands standing with them for the kinds of lives they care about. Birkenstock sandals are a famous case. Because the U.S. distributor, Margot Fraser, could not sell them through conventional shoe stores, she came up with the idea of trying to sell them through health food stores. It worked, but the product and the brand have never been able to leave behind their association with the values of the health-food store owners, who were the first network leaders to talk about the sandals in the United States.
4. Because network leaders frequently promote products in the name of values they care about and associate with the brand, they love categories and products in a category for their own reasons, which must be respected, indeed, often endorsed. Sylvestor Stallone, for instance, knew that his file *Driven* was not only an action, racecar film that would appeal to core Stallone fans but also a teen film. He thought that teens would care about it for their own reasons. Since the film was going to be marketed conventionally as an action, racecar film, Stallone asked for help from Marc Schiller of Electric Artists, a company that specializes in developing and deploying communications strategies for talking with people in online communities to create positive word of mouth. Schiller has been particularly successful with teen communities as well as working with a variety of other communities. The point is to "put the products into contexts relevant to people talking in those communities so that they can continue talking about the products to their friends and coworkers." For Stallone, Electric Artists developed, tested, and deployed a strategy that included talking online about *Driven*'s young actors such as Estella Warren. It turned out that Stallone and Electric Artists were right. Teens talked about the younger actors, not the action, not Stallone, not the conventional or expected values or concerns. The Electric Artists campaign correlated closely with increased ticket sales.

These principles show that intervening in discussions over a product and the brand can no longer focus on conveying the benefit of a few product attributes. There must be a memic quality. Here is an example of a failed intervention into a bulletin board at fashion.alt.

> Hi, I've noticed a lot of talk about *Glamour* on this site. I know some of you are saying the magazine isn't into serious issues anymore. Well, I work at the magazine and there's plenty of substantial stuff in here! Did you check out the

> June issue? There's a story on women who've been jailed unjustly, a fascinating report on "Is Your Body Aging Faster than You Are?" and a health investigation on what happened to a young woman whose savings were wiped out when she became ill with a chronic disease. Yes, we cover fashion and beauty and sex and love, but those topics are part of life—why wouldn't we cover them? We're dying to know more about what you think of these articles, and the rest of what's in the magazine. So please write us directly!

A flurry of harsh responses followed. Here is a shortened version of a typical one:

> I assure you that everyone here, like me, who has complained about the way *Glamour* has gone down hill, and everyone, like me, who has cancelled her subscription, is able to read and can easily see that the magazine has not in any way changed from a disappointing *Cosmo*-wanna be. Telling us that it is not something that we know very well it is will not magically make it so. If *Glamour* is serious about winning subscribers back, there are other, less annoying and insulting ways to do this than telling us we are wrong. Since I am not being paid to improve the magazine, I do not feel like listing what these things are.

The women who are speaking about these fashion magazines love them. They are genuinely disappointed by the direction of *Glamour*. They would not be spending time talking to each other about it if this were not the case. The conversations are not casual. The women who are most vocal on this bulletin board see themselves as experts. And telling an expert that she is wrong in some simple way will not do. A marketer has to *ask* experts. Why did the article on unjustly jailed woman fail to change their view? These experts, moreover, saw some small changes in some of the attributes—a little more "fashion and beauty and sex and love"—as having shifted the whole memic meaning of *Glamour* and the social values they see the magazine standing for. To these experts, *Glamour* had changed the values it stood for. It had declined into a "*Cosmo*-wanna be," which roughly translates, for these networked experts, into a product that values sexual voraciousness and ignorance. The editor's reason for writing about "fashion and beauty and sex and love," because "those topics are part of life" insults these readers because it does not take into account their reasons for reading the magazine. The reasons were there to see in their exchanges. (They cared about certain accessible and economically reasonable fashions.) These women are well networked and they are not going to be swayed from their conversational experience of the brand by cute and upbeat notes written by an editor. Both the reading experience and the conversation must change.

In summary, networked communities have their own lives. They have their own vocal brand and product experts, who focus attention on the way products and brands support cultural values. These leaders, therefore, promote the product and brand more for reasons having to do with their connection to the social values than for clear and easily communicable benefits backed by attributes. In such a setting, the dynamics of communicating to such groups are different from those of more broad-based mass communication. As we see later, broad-based communication plays a critical role in any promotional campaign, but it cannot be the center of network marketing. All interventions in networks succeed best when they follow the guidelines that we now set forth for setting the principles into action. Again, these guidelines are basic. Viral networking strategies can be deployed only after the basic network marketing is mastered.

GUIDELINES FOR COMMUNICATION WITHIN NETWORKED COMMUNITIES

Approach members of networked communities, particularly their vocal leaders, with a genuinely questioning attitude and with questions. Members of networked communities often begin conversations with questions among themselves. Here are two examples, the first from Jack B. of autos.alt, in which he is asking about what happened to BMW and the kind of cars it stands for.

> Is there anyone out there that produces cars that have the "spirit" of the old 2002, 320i (which I remember being hotly debated upon arrival), the 533i, and first-generation M3? Cars that are light but not flimsy-feeling, fun to drive, and not priced well above their competition?

The following is from Martha Stewart's online community:

> I really miss Thanksgiving now that I live in England and my husband is Australian. But, I still want to celebrate. Does anyone have a suggestion for a turkey substitute (I am only cooking for two, so I can't make a whole turkey)?

It is necessary to begin with questions because in the face of complex subject and group dynamics, respect must be shown—respect for expertise, the way the subject matter matters, and the informal roles that exist in the group. Even though some conversations may look as though infobits or other snippets are being exchanged, these small exchanges can have highly charged content. People are writing because they love the topic or product category. They are interested in talking only to others who also love the category.

Indeed, this point about respecting the love of the conversants for their subject is so crucial for network strategies that Christopher Locke makes it the foundation of *Gonzo Marketing*. In his book on the subject, he suggest that businesses subsidize sites where their products are discussed and allow and incent only their own employees who have the same interests as members of the site make comments there. Otherwise, the "industry insiders" will come across as phonies who are only trying to get money and will thereby injure the company's reputation.[14]

Intervening in a group requires showing your personal connection and love of the category—show your personal bona fides. To see this, we return to the same two conversations, first the one about BMWs.

> Fourteen years ago I worked in the parts department of a BMW dealership in Columbus, Ohio. I would occasionally have the chance to drive the cars. My parents also had a 733i and a 325e, so I was definitely well-exposed to the "BMW mentality." I remember the first time I drove a 533i—it was unbelievable, a light-footed, tail-swinging beast (at the time).

Those in the Martha Stewart group who respond to the question about England show as a matter of good form their personal connection to the question.

> When my husband and I were in grad school, we were poorer than poor and couldn't afford to buy a huge turkey for just two of us. Several years ago my husband, parents, and I were in the Cotswolds for Thanksgiving. We landed up cooking Thanksgiving dinner in our little Cotswold stone cottage that we had rented for the year.

Assume that every conversation takes up cherished memories and hard-won insights. For this reason, personal and social values are confidently mixed together with attributes in evaluations of the product.

Conversational interventions take up both attributes and personal and social values seriously and fluently. One of the responses shows how seamless the combination of attributes and values is:

> I believe that the BMW is good for what it does best. It makes small sedans that make you smile when you drive. It's what BMW did best then, and I

> personally believe what BMW does now. Head to head, a new 325 or 330 is a generation or two past a 2002 when all fond memories are put aside. It's like remembering that old IBM PC with 256K of memory and the 5Mb hard drive. It did a great job when I needed it most, but now my watch is a hair more powerful.

The respondent responds with a claim about attributes: The technology of the new 325 is two generations ahead of the 2002. He speaks of benefits. You smile when you drive. And he puts the values of having self-knowledge and tough-mindedness ahead of sentimentalizing the past. In an unquoted section, he explains why, given the past competition to BMW, it seemed like more of a step up. The Martha Stewart writers do the same. One, for instance, talks not only about what to cook but also about how to invite the English to the dinner so that it does not have to be only for two. Obviously, she is promoting the value of a large celebratory feast. That brings out the point of the complicated social dynamics of any networked community.

Interventions are complicated actions of personal positioning and positioning of others. Networked community members use their knowledge of products constantly to promote themselves and their values. Networked community members are intensely aware of their value inside the community. They are not just trying to win points in conversations but to gain followings. That is why the best name for them is probably *colloquists*. They are speaking to each other but also need to be heard by a much larger, quiet audience. They speak and act as though their value increases by about the square of the number of people listening to or citing them. Thus, they constantly, carefully, and craftily position themselves and others. The respondent we have already cited in the BMW conversation actively positions himself as young and nonsentimental while positioning the initial questioner as an over-the-hill, romantic baby boomer whose past makes him hyper-subtle.

The new BMWs are superior cars. Perhaps those who have not experienced the dramatic difference (that used to exist between BMWs and other brands) cannot appreciate some subtle ones. Perhaps those who have experienced the dramatic difference give it too much credence. It is a generational thing.

A following response neatly repositions both earlier comments:

> I sold my BMW and bought a Honda, and it's the best car I've ever had. The Honda is far superior in design to a BMW and never breaks down.

> Further, my Honda dealer never screws up and doesn't charge an arm and a leg for routine maintenance. Though I remain Teutonic at heart, the smart money no longer buys BMWs.

Though this respondent loves the value of German engineering and longs, as does the first colloquist, for the BMW of the past, he values even more being smart. Being smart is better than suffering the indignities that go with smiling while you drive.

Interventions must deepen and modulate the developing memic understanding of product and brand internal to the conversation of the networked community rather than simply return it to the brand's basic positioning. As people interested in product categories and making purchases are increasingly listening in on and taking part in conversations like the one on BMWs, an important part of the meaning of the brand and product involves these reflections. Marketers can no longer assume that brand equity lives in the hearts and minds of individual consumers. Instead, brands are increasingly coming to live in networked communities' conversations. And as conversations in these communities develop, the meaning of the brand and product develops as well.

When, for instance, the "smart" colloquist says that he sold his BMW and purchased a Honda, suddenly this community sees Honda as a relevant contrast to BMW. That is one surprise for a BMW marketer. Then the colloquist reports, "My old rear-wheel drive BMW spun out many times on rainy roads; my front-wheel drive is sure-footed in the worst New England snow storms." This comment requires a deepening of the "ultimate driving machine" brand. To say that the new BMWs would not spin out only puts them on a par with the new Hondas. What is the new driving experience that fills out the sense of the "ultimate driving machine" in such a way as to put it out of reach of a Honda? These are no longer questions inside the BMW R&D facility. They are not questions that BMW's marketers are anticipating for the new year. They are not even the questions that a few, very savvy customers ask. These are the questions that are absorbing a networked community with many lurkers.

In networked communities, the brand is undergoing constant development. This development gives marketers enormous opportunities for constant brand testing and sharpening, as long as they accept the ways of networked communities.

The new electronic media brings about a general change in the social behavior by reclaiming the networking of industry, hobbyist or special interest, and traditional communities. Instead of commercial conversations that are primarily between vendor and customer, conversations now include opinion leaders, particularly leading-edge, specialist users rather than public personalities like Michael Jordan and Oprah Winfrey. Influential leading-edge users themselves find the Internet makes it easier for them to get together either through group e-mailings or through one or another kind of conferencing site (bulletin boards, chat rooms, and so forth). In September 1997, there were approximately 96,000 online, topic-based discussion boards. By April 2000, there were more than 300,000.[15] Now, Vanchau Nguyen, founder and CEO of ezboard, says his site hosts more than 500,000 communities, with 10 million unique users and 500 million page views per month.[16] The growth has been entirely through grass-roots word of mouth, and it continues to be double digit.[17] Of course, as online communities become more popular, potential network leaders, particularly leading-edge product users, increasingly seek to build their online stature by successfully promoting products.

While the new communications media reclaim past or specialist networked behavior, it also brings about two changes in networking. As people increasingly communicate in the new media's hybrid of speech and writing that is both transient and lasting, people are increasingly getting in on influential leading-edge users' conversations that were previously heard only at trade shows or by people who were "connected" in the old sense of the word. The Internet remains open 24/7 and holds for years reviews written by influential lead users and, again new, reviews of these reviewers. Amazon, for instance, carries reviews of books, CDs, videos, and electronic equipment. Epinions has reviews on arts and entertainment, autos and motorsports, business and technology, computers and Internet, electronics, home and garden, hotels and travel, children and family, personal finance, restaurants and gourmet, sports and outdoor, and wellness and beauty. Planetfeedback has shared letters on a similar set of categories. Although still in its infancy, WebMD has patient reviews of physicians. Increasingly, customers are checking the accumulated reviews before they make purchase decisions.

Because these network leaders tend to be widely dispersed demographically, psychographically, and geographically, working with them in the context of an online community is one of the most practical ways to proceed. Just as importantly, well-designed communities give the network leaders an important place where they can speak. It gives marketers a primary place where they can monitor and influence the conversations. Online communities also give sympathetic network leaders—normally network leaders to whom marketers have listened—a forum for promoting the product. By listening to these conversations, marketers can learn how to support the network leaders' claims and how to extend the brand with new products. Forward-looking companies are building online communities, using bulletin boards, forums, and chat rooms to cultivate relations with network leaders. CNN, Disney, Shell, Pentax, Martha Stewart, REI, and Amazon are some examples. Heineken and Nescafé allow their site users to open virtual bars and cafés. WebMD and Weight Watches have support group communities.

Success with network communities requires forming focused strategies for building or enhancing them and for creating buzz. Building or enhancing a networked community requires understanding the different kinds of communities that develop and focusing on those that are best suited to the brand and product line. Each type of community supports a certain type of strategy and disables others. Consequently, we first present a framework for understanding the main types of community. Then we turn to the strategies suited to each. We give some examples of how these viral network strategies can usefully be leveraged in a fully orchestrated campaign and give a framework for this.

COMMUNITY FRAMEWORK AND FOUR TYPICAL KINDS OF COMMUNITY

To work with networked communities, it is critical to understand network behavior and the role that products play in them. This understanding reveals to marketers the distinct levers for strengthening the communities and what they can ask network leaders to do to create buzz. The critical factors for understanding community membership and leadership can be usefully sorted along two dimensions that help us understand the behavior of different types of communities. The first dimension has to do with how networked community members view the role that brands play in their networks. This dimension is a continuum that runs from communities that treat brands as playing an authoritative role in their lives (Apple, Grateful Dead, Harvard, Martha Stewart, the *New York Times*) to communities of people who see brands as critical tools—cool things—for self promotion. Cases in point include Palm, Christina Aguilera, Ferrari, Williams Sonoma, and "Sex in the City." In other words, the dimension ranges from *loving the brand* and giving it a sacred place in the community members' lives to *loving the promotion* of the brand and the meaning that promotion provides network members.

Therefore, at one end of the continuum, we find most religious and political communities—communities that are focused on certain figures, parties, issues, and the values they stand for. In contrast, at the other end of the continuum lie communities devoted to fashion, the popular, or progress. Most are concerned with promoting new figures, new products, new ideas, and new achievements for the sake of promoting something new. (Note that the new is sometimes the old, like Hush Puppies.) The possibilities for promotion and the relationships that occur because of it are what makes the product interesting to people.

Sports clubs and other sports communities tend to be in the middle of this continuum. They revere the ancient constitutive rules of the sport and some of the historic performers. But they focus on promoting the current season, the newest achievements, newest players, newest plays, newest venues, and so forth. As we move along this continuum, the drivers to join start with reverence and end with innovation.

The second dimension that helps us understand the behavior of types of communities concerns the "texture of recognition" in the community. At one end of the continuum lie communities in which what each member says and the way each member acts matter enormously to others in the community. Differences of opinion seem to require resolution. An inability to appear at a nearby event requires an explanation. Members of such communities seek recognition for an accomplishment only in the name of some common cherished value, as is the case with the Weight Watchers community. These are high recognition or *we-focused* communities.

If you are a Deadhead, it matters which concert you think was the best. Likewise, if you are a Palm promoter, it matters if you were among the *first* users to be given a Palm at a conference or if you were the one who got all your friends to purchase them. It matters, too, if you were a member of the team who recognized Christina Aguilera first and helped get her to the top of the charts. If someone says you did not play that role, then you have to settle the issue.

In networks at the other end of this continuum, the texture of recognition is much looser. In these networks, "I" stay up on what is going on. "I" contribute when "I" feel moved to or can lend a hand. I certainly appreciate it when other members of the community recognize my contributions. But I do not lose sleep over a lost opportunity for recognition or sharing. These are low-recognition or *I-focused* communities, networks of people who join the networks for self-improvement more than for mutual recognition.

Consider the communities around Martha Stewart. Community membership is driven more by the personal benefit that people derive from the products than from the recognition they receive. Similarly, the networks of reviewers at Amazon or Epinions are composed of people developing their own sensibilities and testing them against the views of others. Amateur sports clubs are again an interesting middle ground in which members can sometimes get caught up in huge arguments over who was a better player or which past team was better as though the fate of the nation were at stake. But sometimes the same members can come and go equally well as the club suits their individual participation and viewing of sporting events.

We put these dimensions together in the matrix in Table 6.1, with authority on the horizontal dimension and recognition as "we-focused" or "I-focused" on the vertical. The upper left-hand box describes solidarity groups that are most like traditional community groups such as churches, and as we move from brand- to self- and from we- to I, we move toward maven networks in the lower right-hand corner. Thus, each cell represents a different type of community that is either already networked or can be networked. We refer to these communities as *networked communities* or more simply as *networks* because their affiliations may be much looser than those that might be associated with the word *communities*.

As depicted in the matrix in Table 6.1, *mavens* are people who are happy when they are informally educating us in the domains of their expertise. You are bound to know a wine, music, electronic equipment, fashion, or car maven. Before the Internet, mavens generally had small groups of friends who came to them for advice. They knew other mavens but did not track them closely. The Web has had a great effect on them, enabling them to track one another and to give their refined advice to larger groups.

Taste-maker communities form around intense taste-makers who are heavily promoting some new or cool thing. Everything can matter for a while to these networked communities, as everything is about creating a

Table 6.1
Types of Networked Communities and the Networked Behavior Typical of Each

	Brand as Authority	*Self as Authority*
We-Focus	*Solidarity Community* Networking by sharing experencies with products and brands and the social values they imply	*Taste-Maker Community* Networking by self-promotion in the name of being the first or coolest
I-Focus	*Appreciator Community* Networking by emulating other appreciators and the brand personality	*Maven Network* Networking by educating and broadening horizons

success. However, most of these communities are shorter lived than traditional communities. Appreciator communities, in contrast, can last for a very long time, but the level of ongoing engagement tends to rise and fall.

We now describe each of these networked communities in more detail and describe the kind of viral marketing strategy that is most appropriate to each one.

Solidarity-Networked Communities

A solidarity network forms around a brand that stands for certain social values. Members of the community see the brand as a symbol of the values they love and gather to celebrate a shared sense of purpose. Fans of the Grateful Dead and Apple enthusiasts understand well the values these brands stand for. Deadheads love the laid-back, lyrical, faintly drugged mood of Dead concerts. Being laid-back, lyrical, and having a faintly druggy good mood were values, keys to a way of life. Likewise, Apple enthusiasts see themselves as a band of renegades who were introducing a form of technology that would increase liberty—of the creative, doing what you please sort—in the world. Again, social values, not technical performance features, matter most in these networks. Weight Watchers celebrates certain values of discipline, accomplishment, and good health. In Mexico, CEMEX's *Patrimonio Hoy* clubs, in which low-income, do-it-yourself builders gather for saving and purchasing cement and other building materials, stand for the value of patrimony. They stick together through the tough regimes of saving and building to be able to leave their children a patrimony. Online, Christian rock bands, or those with Christian rock roots, like Creed, have active value-based solidarity communities.

The principle networking action in these communities amounts to attending events that celebrate the values the brand stands for and deepening the experience through interaction. Apple has conventions. MacWorld is part of a viral marketing strategy. Rock groups have concerts. Harley-Davidson and Saturn have celebratory events. Saturn says: "Come visit the factory in Tennessee." After these morally and emotionally intense events, networked community members have to debrief together, either online or in follow-up meetings.

How do you determine whether your brand could gather a networked community in this way? The first step is to find out how brand users are engaging with each other already. What kinds of networks have they formed? Have they formed tightly knit groups on the Web? Are their conversations oriented by a love of the social values they see promoted by the brand? Are events like conferences, seminars, new releases, new issues, and so forth key parts of their discussion? Do they take pride in reporting to each other what they learned and whom they met?

Look also at the nature of your brand. Does the brand stand for values that serve as a call to action? Compare them with Apple's value of liberation or Saturn's value of small-town caring. Are their values ones around which events have already been developed? If the answers to these last two questions are mostly affirmative, a marketer has reason to engage in viral strategies appropriate to a solidarity-networked community.

Appreciator-Networked Communities

An appreciator network forms around a brand with a strong personality, one with whom people want to identify themselves. Usually, the personality is a human, but it can be some other kind of figure. In the arts, culture, and sports worlds, many individual performers and teams attract networks of appreciators. So do fashion designers, other kinds of designers, chefs, and star CEOs. High-service brands such as the Four Seasons and high-quality brands such as Saab can attract networks of appreciators.

Appreciators are clearly different from members of solidarity communities in that they revel in knowledge of technical details and facts about the brand and emulate each other in being a better exemplar of the brand. For this reason, their conversations include much one-upmanship and many unresolved disputes. People become members of such communities to sharpen their ability to be exemplary.

While Martha Stewart's online community members are in the dead center of appreciator-emulative behavior, as are David Bowie's and Meredith Brooks's fans, others can slip off in the direction of other categories. A Four Seasons' aficionado who delights in the way the hotel wraps underwear is an appreciator. A Four Seasons' aficionado who goes on and on about the number of Four Seasons hotels he or she has stayed at and why they are better than any other hotels is moving away from being an appreciator toward being a taste-maker who is promoting himself by means of the hotel. So how do you tell whether to start a network of appreciators?

As always, start by examining how your brand is being talked about. Find out if people see your brand as a stable, interesting feature of their lives: Do you find discussions where people like to show off their knowledge of your products or company? Are there good-natured, emulative disagreements about the value of this or that product? Do people talk more about your product line's technical features than about how your brand fits into their lives?

Also, find out if there is already a hidden star. Do people talk about your CEO or some other company figure? Do they spend time wondering what your company will do next? Do environmental, social, or financial concerns regularly surface that would ordinarily be addressed only by Investor Relations or Corporate Communications?

Look at your brand. Appreciators experience their love of the product alone in a more or less romantic solitude, like Wordsworth appreciating nature. Are your products ones that enable individuals to experience themselves as solitary individuals with particular tastes? Are they artistic products like jewelry, poetic (as opposed to dance or party) music, and the kind of high-performance product that solicits individual testing? Is the nature of your product, as with culinary products and even some appliances, such that it would make sense to attach a "designer" personality? Is there a tradition of service that makes people feel special individually, as at the Four Seasons? Last, is there a fascinating intricacy in using the product? Is something particularly ingenious about your product line or company that could be leveraged into making a founder, C-level officer, or someone else into a genuine star like Steve Jobs or Jack Welch?

Positive answers to these questions show that your company is positioned to build or join a networked community of appreciators.

Taste-Maker Communities

Taste-makers are opinion leaders who simply love being imitated or persuading others. Malcolm Gladwell, in his book *The Tipping Point,* calls them a sales force.[18] These are people who are driven by the new. They are always finding something that they think is cool or neat and getting others to go along with them.[19] They are admired for the way they carry themselves through life and are trusted for the same reason. They are not experts. The pharmaceutical industry early found that taste-makers among physicians were different from technical or expert opinion leaders. Experts do not carry the same level of trust. Taste-makers draw others to them. They have contagious moods.

Some celebrities such as Oprah Winfrey are taste-makers. Certain disc jockeys count as well, although it is not always clear which are taste-makers by force of admirable personality and which by expertise. But the professional taste-makers are not the interesting ones for viral marketers. Better to find the nonprofessionals who can be enlisted to produce word-of-mouth successes.

Taste-makers network with each other and with their followers by talking about and promoting the new and cool. Their credibility with people is determined by their spotting and promoting brands that become popular. They talk about what is cool, why it is cool, and what people can do to make it cooler, to get it better known.

Marc Schiller's Electric Artists (mentioned earlier as specializing in building online networked communities for companies and stimulating the networks to promote brands) emphasizes that taste-makers have an uncanny knack for telling people what is cool and then challenging them to do something achievable to make it cooler. "Let's call the radio station to get the song played." "Let's tell retailers how cool the product is and ask them to stock it." Taste-makers and those who join with them in taste-making want to be in on the action, and that almost always means being first in their social circle to promote something cool.[20]

In most cases, searching the Web shows whether a company has taste-makers promoting it or its brand. Taste-makers create sites focused on your brand or company. Taste-makers identify what is cool about your company. The company's product need not be trendy. A utility company that tries out a few new environmental programs can come under the eye of taste-makers.

Look also at your products. Do they come in new releases, in new updates? Are the differences between your products and your competition matters of design more than function? Do your designs delight people more than raise their curiosity? Can your designs be broadly appreciated without requiring much special education?

Look at your company's actions. Are you first in cleaning the environment, in making the world better, in ESOPs, in producing something that could be delightful and a cool trend? (It cannot be too complicated.) You will not find taste-makers promoting a new and valuable but arcane engineering standard, even if it does make the earth a better place. However, if your company is buying up and preserving the Rain Forest, that could be a source for taste-making viral activity.

Look also at the channels by which taste-makers could expand in the appreciation of your brand. Can they call retailers and talk shows? What can they do after they have enticed their friends to buy more? Taste-makers have to have a channel for action! If your product is updated regularly, has a design that produces delight of some sort, and is distributed in a way that taste-makers can affect, then building a taste-making community may make sense.

Maven-Networked Communities

Mavens have recently received much recognition. Nick Hornby celebrated music mavens in his novel (later turned into a movie) *High Fidelity* (1996).

Malcolm Gladwell stressed them in *The Tipping Point.*[21] While taste-makers celebrate and promote the cool and neat, mavens educate us about what is admirable. Mavens study electronics, cars, fashions, music, real estate, finance, wines, or whatever subject they happen to have a strong interest in. They are generally not professionals but rather enthusiasts—car buffs, stereo buffs, and so forth.

Normally, mavens are like teachers who want to educate others to appreciate something that they understand deeply; and like teachers, they gear the lesson according to the student. In music, they recommend not simply what they currently find interesting but music that their interlocutors will like and that will also refine their tastes. Mavens generally do this with the simple hope of more conversation. Mavens tend to build networks of friends or acquaintances whom they advise most often one on one or in small groups.

Businesses like Hear Music and REI have developed maven viral strategies that include hiring mavens as their sales staffs. They gain the maven's enthusiasm and product knowledge but cannot control the maven's fierce independence and his or her own brand building. Commonly, though certainly not always, mavens are charming, witty, and warm when talking about their preoccupation; and that is why the Internet is an extraordinary boon for them. On the Web, they can form relationships focused mainly on what they love.

Epinions, Amazon, Uplister, and, to a lesser extent, REI are creating online maven networks. They are providing a forum for mavens to take positions, review products, and give their accounts of brands. Remember that mavens are educators. Like professional educators, the best of them seek to find the best way to bring their students to the next level of sophistication or refinement. Mavens stand for designing better and more erudite lives. Their currency is their love of their domain. That love builds trust in their followers. Mavens cannot be bought. Their autonomy is their gold.

How do you know whether you want to attract and facilitate mavens? Do your brands or the brands you sell, if you are a retailer or distributor, require developed tastes or skills? If the answer is yes, then you very likely already have mavens commenting on your product. You certainly want to cultivate them. Research the Internet to see what you can find.

To an untrained ear, the difference between taste-makers and mavens can seem slight. The simplest way to tell the difference is to note that taste-makers promote the delightfully cool, the pop; mavens take us beyond it. Mavens try to teach. Retailers have been best at recognizing and cultivating mavens. This is so because mavens are attracted to whoever gives them the best, most honest inside knowledge. But you may very well want to cultivate mavens for early product design and draw on taste-makers for promotion. We now turn to developing viral marketing strategies appropriate to each type of networked community.

VIRAL MARKETING STRATEGIES FOR EACH TYPE OF NETWORKED COMMUNITY

Viral strategies for building networks should be based on the kind of interaction that takes place in a networked community. Thus, the appropriate strategy for a solidarity community is one that builds allegiance and drives promotions as a matter of celebrating the community. Likewise, a community of appreciators is enhanced and mobilized by strategies designed to increase emulation. Taste-maker communities should be driven by strategies that build excitement over promotional goals. And networks of mavens call for strategies designed to expand their educational influence. Individual mavens are gathered into maven universities like that at Epinions. We must focus on developing the best strategy for each community. When communities and strategies are mismatched, network development is stunted.

The four basic viral strategies called for by each type of networked community are summarized in Table 6.2 on page 112. Descriptions of each strategy and illustrative case studies are given in the following sections.

Allegiance-Building Strategies for Solidarity Communities

The goal of an allegiance-building viral strategy in a solidarity-networked community is to encourage members of the community to make, and incite others to make, product purchases as a display of their commitment to perpetuate and enlarge the community. Solidarity communities are unique in that perpetuation of the community becomes the focus of buzz.

Organizing a Solidarity Community. Solidarity communities are usually organized by grass-roots means with offline events used to familiarize people with the community (whether it is online or off). In the music industry, the concerts of values-based bands such as Christian Rock or Alternative Hip Hop are ideal for introducing fans to the online community. Photographs of the audience and backstage accounts of the concert draw people to the site.

Table 6.2
Viral Strategies by Networked Community Type

	Brand as Authority	*Promoter as Authority*
We-Focus	*Foster Allegiance Strategy* • *Organize:* Grassroots, shared meetings. • *Communications approach:* Solicit authentic voices, publish members' experiences with community. • *Reward for members:* Public recognition with testimonials. • *Brand role:* Symbol of community's shared social values.	*Build Excitement Strategy* • *Organize:* Suggest specific promotional goals. • *Communications approach:* Appeal to members as powerful tastemakers by giving them product previews and asking about what's cool and why. • *Reward for members:* Celebrate them as the ones who make products successful; celebrate their promotional successes. • *Brand role:* Next new thing, trend.
I-Focus	*Increase Emulation Strategy* • *Organize:* Official forums (offline and online). • *Communications approach:* Encourage emulation through questions that enable members to show how much they know and are like brand personality. • *Reward for members:* Exclusive technical information on product features. • *Brand Role:* Network personality who intervenes and acknowledges member likeness.	*Creating Dissemination Strategy* • *Organize:* Give mavens of product category tools to expand audience for their reviews. • *Communications Approach:* Ask mavens and their followers to review reviewers. • *Reward for Members:* Special events and special product editions, expand horizons. • *Brand Role:* Gives mavens and followers a way of feeling wiser, associating them with erudite brands.

Book tours can do the same, especially for books such as Rebecca Wells's *Divine Secrets of the Ya-Ya Sisterhood,* which stimulated communities of mothers and daughters. (Many books develop appreciators.) Events such as owners' barbecues, conventions, seminars, product demonstrations, and even, if done well, public product samplings can have the effect of drawing people to mix with others who are like them and with whom they would like to have further contact. Saturn managed it with its homecoming events. L.L.Bean organizes athletic nature lovers to participate in hiking, kayaking, and other events that they enjoy. This retailer has gone so far as to create an Outdoor Discovery School for budding nature lovers as a way of introducing them to the outdoors and making its products a part of potential customers' lives.

Companies that produce controversial products such as firearms can easily draw their users into a community that speaks for controversial values. Offline advocacy events remain critical for the solidarity community. The core experience of such embattled groups is sharing heightened experiences of expressing values they love in extremely high-trust, face-to-face venues.

Communications Approach. The heart of any viral strategy directed at networked communities lies in its approach to communications. Allegiance is built in solidarity networks as members feel increasingly an active part of the community. For that reason, the typical strategy is to develop a community bulletin board that functions as the community's daily Op-Ed page. Members of the community are encouraged to report on events they attended together, submit photographs, and write about their experiences living with the values they have. Seeing their reports appear and draw answers gives members the sense that they are recognized, critical members of the community. These bulletin boards have a number of different themes about which members regularly contribute. Members of solidarity networks that form around Christian rock bands obviously write about themes related to spiritual, ethical, and biblical matters. For example, the following is from the site of the Christian band P.O.D.:

> I think the cool thing with P.O.D. doing the worship stuff at their Cornerstone slot is not only cause it's worship music, but lately I've been meeting a lot of people who think they're sellouts. So if any people there thought P.O.D. sold out, I certainly hope they realized that P.O.D. is still playing for God. Later, peace out.
>
> Believe, Receive, Obtain, Withstand, Never die!!

Weight Watchers is also forming a large solidarity community. Weight Watchers—which stands for health, forming a team to succeed, designing your own life, and an attractive appearance that inspires self-confidence—has made publication of its members' experiences its key promotional strategy. People still give accounts of their struggles and successes with weight loss in their local meetings. But Weight Watchers has created a much broader international community, which contains more than 30 bulletin boards on its Web site. People discuss such themes as "stress and overeating," join "inspiration groups," and recount their aspirations toward losing 100, 200, or 300-plus pounds. Setting up such a forum is only half the battle. Members join such groups to be celebrated in their affection for the values the community stands for, and this must also occur.

Rewards for Members. One critical part of this allegiance-building strategy is to recruit leaders in the community to edit and write accounts of those who have achieved something important. Indeed, being identified as community leaders and being appointed to positions of responsibility in running the publication operation has to count as one of the highest rewards. Online community leaders write more than others, receive high levels of responses from people, are more articulate than the average writer, and exhibit high levels of passion for the values at the site. In addition to editing, these leaders must also celebrate other members for achievements. Being the subject of a leader's story or standing in the limelight as your own story is republished, as critical for everyone to note, is a second common form of recognition in solidarity groups.

Weight Watchers, for example, has network leaders interview others and publish their stories online. Communities live and die by how well the voices of the members are heightened while remaining authentic. Here are some excerpts from the story of Debbie Watts:

> "My sister Robyn was my inspiration for trying Weight Watchers meetings," explains Debbie Watts. Since joining in September 2000, this grateful sibling has lopped 34.8 pounds off her 5′5″ frame. Twenty-seven-year old Debbie is now a shapely 126 pounds.
>
> She has had lots of family help in her quest, as her parents, also inspired by Robyn, are Weight Watchers meeting members as well. Debbie says, "The problem to me was that 'diet' was a four-letter word." Weight Watchers, of course, eliminated that problem, as it's more a lifestyle plan than a diet."
>
> No woman is an island. Debbie stresses, "It's possible to succeed alone but it's so much easier with help. At meetings I get recipes, tips on how to handle myself at weddings, and so much more. And I have my built-in team with my parents and sister. They cheered me on when I got back into my old size-6 jeans."

Appearing in such a glowing column as this rewards Debbie and inspires others to equal achievements to receive similar recognition. Indeed, if the network leaders do a good job, many who have had similar achievements are willing to bask in the light of a Debbie.

Brand Role. Because the brand has to play the role of standing for social values that the community cares about, it must be established with a clear understanding of how members of the community express those values. Then it must give members a way to express their values. In the case of P.O.D., the band led concert-goers in prayer. Weight Watchers draws on the values of teamwork, family, shared meals, and honoring weddings and other festivals. Fitting into smaller sizes for a wedding is part of the celebration. For brands that focus on solidarity communities, the brand design has both to establish the connection between the branded product, the social value of which it is an expression, and to set up an enhanced practice of expressing and celebrating the value that includes using or purchasing the branded product.

A good example, and one drawn from the authors' own work, of how a company positions its brand with a social value and creates a new expression of this value around purchasing the branded product is the case of CEMEX's *Patrimonio Hoy.* In this case, the networked community was a traditional low-income community in Mexico. Yet, the same basic principles apply here as are potent in creating online solidarity communities among the wired, first-world affluent.

CEMEX, the third largest cement manufacturer in the world, discovered that its largest and most stable growing market, both in Mexico and internationally, consisted of low-income do-it-yourself homebuilders. In investigating these communities, CEMEX found that these Mexican do-it-yourselfers frequently got together in informal money-pooling associations to pay for materials to build homes they could leave to their children.

Most of the time, however, the money ended up going to unplanned celebrations or emergencies, not the home. Because patrimony mattered so much, CEMEX sought to establish its brand as the one that stood for patrimony. To do this, it developed a program called *Patrimonio Hoy.* In this program, do-it-yourselfers joined together to pool their money in a new version of the old practice. The pooled money was committed to building materials, and the pooling had to last long enough for each person to accumulate the materials for a nine-meter square room.

In this way, the group activity was both a celebration of patrimony and the purchase of branded cement. Hence, a practice was instituted for celebrating patrimony that involved purchasing the product. Weight Watchers groups do the same thing. They celebrate teams, life, life's events, managing weight and health, and do so as a prelude to purchasing more Weight Watchers' supplies.

Designing a brand to become strongly associated with a social value and to make the purchase of the branded product an expression of care for the value flows into the other elements of the allegiance-building strategy. Like Weight Watchers, CEMEX enhanced the basic money pooling, patrimony-building groups by including them in broader Patrimony clubs, which consisted of all the groups in a region. CEMEX identified the natural leaders in these clubs—usually the women who formed the old money-pooling groups—and gave them positions of leadership and offered them incentives to recruit and motivate members of the clubs. To keep motivation and customer loyalty high, CEMEX managers developed a publication strategy. Because more than 50 percent of consumers had less than a sixth-grade education, CEMEX turned to festive celebrations at the completion of each room. At each celebration, the builder would deliver a speech consisting of thanks and tips for how to do it better next time. Both members of Patrimony clubs and other members of the community attended these events. Thus, the events further enticed people to join *Patrimonio Hoy*.

Emulation Strategies for Appreciators Communities

Most companies fall into building sites with an emulation strategy dimly in view whether or not they have the appropriate brand personality. Appreciators are, after all, customers who write individual letters of appreciation or criticism to companies, performers, teachers, physicians, or lawyers. The stronger the personality of the brand and its primary disseminators—star CEO's like Disney's Michael Eisner or the people who have direct customer contact—the more likely appreciators are drawn to it. They write because they seek a response. Ultimately, they would love a response from the personality that they associate with the brand. Good direct marketers have learned how to maintain their loyalty and increase a company's share of the wallet of appreciators by putting them on mailing lists and sending them timely, useful promotions.

The strategy of increasing emulation among appreciators should have three specific goals. First, by stimulating emulation, appreciators develop reasons for purchasing more of the product. Second, as appreciators find increasing amounts of their interest being captured, they tell others about the brand. Well-managed appreciator Web sites are especially useful in converting people into community members following such recommendations. Third, encouraging emulation naturally brings community members to talk about themselves. They can even be solicited to write about themselves, and this enables marketers to learn more about members' preferences, their understanding of the brand, and how these types of people can best be reached. Such information helps marketers decide which alliances and cross-promotions can most profitably be developed.

In the music industry, product endorsements are as important as shared stages. Partly based on what he learns from his appreciators, David Bowie invites relevant artists to be interviewed or to perform on his site. In other industries, knowledge of such preferences can be used to determine where and how to promote—what rewards matter—as well as where alliances could be formed.

Organizing a Community of Appreciators. Appreciators are drawn to the official place or site. You can drive them by letting them know that there is a brand personality there who is going to speak, perform, or otherwise appear. Techniques include offering an exclusive, privileged look at one or another aspect of the product. What will the new release or generation look like? How will it perform? Do you want a free sample? Do you want to learn more? Offering to take up such questions, as we see every day on Netscape, AOL, and Yahoo, attracts appreciators. So do simple requests from the brand personality for evaluations of product or service. As much as possible, let appreciators know that the brand personality pays attention and will even sometimes respond.

Communications Approach. Emulation begins when appreciators are asked to respond, often to answer questions that they pride themselves on being able to answer. They find themselves empowered by answering the questions because they identify themselves with the brand personality.

David Bowie and Meredith Brooks (rock singer and guitar player) run effective appreciator Web sites as they solicit their appreciators for help in creating new albums, writing lyrics, choosing the single, programming the order, remixing, and so forth. David Bowie received more than 80,000 submissions of lyrics for a song he was composing with his fans. Both Brooks and Bowie frequently turn their questions to community members into contests with the reward of working with them to mix the album. Successful contests are effective in letting appreciators show their sophisticated skills, which are like those of the brand personality they admire.

Other sorts of responses can be used. Appreciators at Tori Amos' Web site compete with one another in telling Tori Amos about themselves in lyrical and considerable detail. Tori Amos' fans tell her about all the books, films, cars, trucks, tattoos, and so forth that they like. At the Plus 6 site (Plus 6 is a Christian rock group), the conversation on the bulletin board reveals that many Plus 6 appreciators have been home schooled or had parents who strongly considered it. They could be asked to describe this schooling.

Any innovative company can solicit ideas from appreciators. Usually marketers ask the questions, but members of R&D teams and other experts might well play that role. Commonly, a network of appreciators is built around events, conventions, seminars, or Webinars. Oracle and General Electric work with communities of appreciators this way. The key is for company leaders who speak to represent the core competence and basic personality of the company. C-level officers, if available, are ideal for this purpose.

It is critical to ask questions that appreciators can answer and that can make them feel good about answering. Asking other kinds of questions may provide valuable information or affect sales drivers, but it will not build a community of emulative appreciators. If the brand personality is strong enough, simply opening a bulletin board for appreciators to ask questions of one another can stimulate emulative conversation. Martha Stewart's site is constructed this way and is exemplary of the kind of emulative conversation sought.

At Stewart's site, a community member—perhaps one incited by a community leader—will ask a question about how to handle some matter of living a fulfilling life. Without guidelines, other community members help with advice written in tones that approach Martha Stewart's own. When a response finally comes in that sounds fully Martha Stewart-ish, the conversation ends by mutual consent. Here is a sample:

- *From: claradiaz.* "For the past few years 'Christmas-Eve' dinner has been at my house and every year I add to my table settings. This year, however, 'Thanksgiving' dinner will be at my house. For Christmas, my tablecloth and napkins have been a 'X-mas red.' What color should I buy my tablecloth and napkins for Thanksgiving? Thank you! Clara"
- *From: tmd523.* "Hi, my suggestion is it really depends on your own style; everyone is different. I always have Thanksgiving at home, and I'm cooking and setting a table for 20-plus people. I usually use a contemporary light green cloth, and I've purchased very cozy autumn napkins. I use a ring in which I insert a cinnamon stick with a small flower and a place card, which everyone loves. I usually have a turkey centerpiece made of chocolate. It really dresses everything up. It's all preference. Go with your own style, and I'm sure it will be a hit. Tracy good luck!"
- *From: nsadam.* "I always go with classic white tablecloth, and then I can use whatever colour I want for napkins, décor, etc. For Thanksgiving, I particularly like white with celadon green napkins with leaves on them. I have some turkey candles in an antique orange colour. Stems of soft green kale, hypericum berries, and fresh stems of oak leaves all seem to blend well."
- *From: linny7.* "Clara, I have Thanksgiving every year for over 25 people with Royal Dalton Lady Caryle (which has pink, blue, and

gold trim on it). In order to match fall colors, I include gold and use different colors of centerpieces and candles like butternut color or brown colors. I sometimes use a small cornucopia with fall chocolate kisses, or wreaths for favors. Also place cards with a bible verse or something to be thankful for at each setting for the guest to read. Napkins are gold or natural with matching tablecloth. I have one table with Turkey dishes and a Turkey centerpiece. Every year I get something special to surprise my guests like napkin holders. This is fun if you have children who like to create. Children make the best turkeys with their outlined fingers. Have fun! It is my favorite holiday. Start early and use Martha's suggestion about labeling bowls ahead of time so people can help. I wish Martha would put on her Thanksgiving TV show again. It was great. Blessings to you all. Linny"

Everyone who has written in response to Clara's question has enjoyed herself, shown off, will want to do it again, and probably does not want to get topped by Linny again. In the process, each respondent also gets better at gracious living and is thereby more attracted to the site. These responses give Martha Stewart corporate a cornucopia of products to endorse and promote on the same site.

Reward for Members. In these messages, Linny can be seen to ask for precisely what appreciators want. They want to be recognized by the brand personality. Linny wants Martha Stewart to drop her a note about the Thanksgiving special she is dreaming up. Recognition is reward.

Martha Stewart does not appear to monitor or drop in on exchanges at her site. Other appreciator sites have brand personalities who do. Meredith Brooks makes it a habit to respond to some of the comments on her bulletin board every Monday. Fans at her site turn toward the kinds of conversation that catch her eye. Brooks's appreciators care about the technical details of guitar playing and music production.

Generally, appreciators are different from solidarity group members in that they can glory in the technical details they learn about products without ever caring much about wider social, value-oriented considerations. They are attracted to the personality of the brand and to the branded products' technical success. Technical details matter. Getting together does not. Martha Stewart's appreciators need never meet one another to celebrate gracious living together. They need never talk about why gracious living is the best way to live. They are content to be the technicians of gracious living, admiring Martha Stewart as their ideal.

Brand Role. Many companies create costly appreciator events or sites that fail because they have not designed a strong enough brand personality. Obviously, the strongest brand personalities are professional performers or innovative entrepreneurs like Martha Stewart who have a public biography, have developed their business, and have created something new in the process. However, businesses can have corporate personalities as well. Appreciators are obviously willing to respond to a group that has a corporate passion. Shell's forum, for instance, continues to receive and publish a great deal of mail. Its correspondents are clearly seeking conversations. Many have gripes about Shell. Others are classic Shell appreciators who come to Shell's defense. But both show signs of deep disappointment whenever the Shell team answers in a way that sounds scripted or checked over by the lawyers. The brand personality that speaks on such sites, whether it is a marketing team, an R&D team, a corporate communications team, or some other, must exhibit six attributes that are taken for granted when the brand personality is, for instance, a Sam Walton. The six attributes are:

1. *Vision.* The brand personality must be able to answer in a way that would appeal to a diverse group of people: "Why would the world be a better place if the company magically achieved all its corporate goals?"
2. *Passion.* The brand personality must love the company's culture and have a story about why that culture will enable the company to succeed at making the world a better place.
3. *Details.* Because the brand personality has a vision and a passion, it must love to talk about the details of the business. That does not mean that it has to know all the details at once, but loving the business and believing the vision mean being interested in the details of how to do things, especially how to do them better.
4. *Reasons for listening and responding now.* The brand personality has to know what its particular goal is in listening today (not just in general). Teams need to be consistent on this.
5. *Commitment to act.* No matter what the corporate rank of the brand personality, it must be able to take action and speak about actions it has taken. That means making promises to appreciators. Announcing contests with prizes is the easy way of showing commitment. However, offering contests with prizes too often comes across as inauthentic.
6. *Honest evaluation and appreciation of valuable comments.* Appreciators want to be genuinely appreciated. They want to be told why a seemingly important comment cannot be made useful, and they want to be told when they are on to something important.

In short, for an appreciator viral strategy to work, the voice of the corporate brand has to have passion. It has to speak as though the corporation's business and its take on its business are among the best things in life. Appreciators are not value based. Passion need not be defended; it just needs to be enacted. Appreciators seek a response from someone they wish to emulate.

The next two networked community strategies draw even more powerfully on the change that is taking place as our society becomes more networked. Customers are explicitly taking for themselves large parts of the role that used to be the exclusive preserve of professional marketers. Especially among people born after the baby boomers, promoting particular products can be an important part of designing a life. Consequently, the overriding question for marketers in dealing with taste-makers and mavens is how to let them in on the act. These communities are fully conscious that they are creating buzz.

Excitement Strategies for Taste-Maker Communities

Building excitement is an element of virtually any viral strategy. But in dealing with a networked community of taste-makers, the goal is to turn *them* into critical excitement builders. We depend on them to reach on their own particular goals of getting increasing numbers of people talking, listening, and purchasing. Taste-makers are powerful even when their actions are not coordinated. Hush Puppies' sales, for instance, grew four times in one year, mostly by the uncoordinated activities of taste-makers (with some help from mavens).

Organizing Taste-Makers. For virtually any new and relatively simple product, taste-makers are already advocating it. Taste-makers talk to others, post on sites, and even set up their own Web sites for such promotion. According to Marc Schiller, the key to finding and cultivating taste-makers is adopting a new credo.

People, not marketing departments, break brands and artists. Taste-makers are in control and like to feel in control. No industry should rely on mass marketing techniques with taste-makers. You should avoid the appearance of mass marketing and bring them into the process of finding out and developing buzz for what is cool.

Based on this credo, a marketer like Schiller organizes taste-makers by going online and asking those engaged in relevant conversations what they think of this or that brand or artist. For those who answer positively, you escalate the conversation by giving a free and exclusive sample (or account) of what is to come. Ask whether it is cool. Get the taste-maker talking to you and, as a matter of technical ease, on your Web site if possible. Unlike appreciator sites, which have to be "official," the sites that organize taste-makers need no frills. The taste-makers find the product cool, mostly without much persuasion.

Many taste-maker organizers let the interested taste-makers know that they will make or break the product. A company sends some marketing material and challenges the potential taste-makers to show their ability to create buzz. If they succeed, they then get more samples and more marketing material. Promotional tests can be any of the basics of grass-roots marketing-telling friends, putting up posters, calling retailers, and so forth.

For example, when Marc Schiller's Electric Artists' team sought to locate Christina Aguilera taste-makers, they went to 25 teen sites and asked, "Does anyone remember Christina Aguilera—she sang the song 'Reflection' from 'Mulan'? Once the Electric Artists team located avid taste-makers, they were invited to get, as Schiller says, "a 'behind the scenes view' of the marketing machine behind Christina." An exclusive initiation into the marketing of the product, brand, or performer is a critical part of cultivating taste-makers. Taste-makers want to know what is going on before others know. They want to be in on what is happening. Schiller's team initiates them into the marketing process and gives them early knowledge. Only then could an Electric Artists marketer say, "Call your local station to request *Genie*. It is now 19 and we can make it number 1. Please help!"[22]

Communications Approach. Communicating with taste-makers is like communicating with prima donnas. You must constantly remind them that they are the ones who produce the success. Set exciting and achievable goals. Monitor and publish their progress toward reaching the goals. Taste-makers do best when they are brought inside the marketing process as much as possible. They thrive when they can develop their own ways of promoting the product to others. In addition, it is critical for them to understand why the goals, such as gaining a certain amount of retail space, matter for the product's success.

Taste-makers love to organize themselves and their friends to achieve goals. They love to be imitated. However, there are things a marketing department must do for them. It must enable them to coordinate in larger numbers than would otherwise be possible. The coordinated actions of even 150 taste-makers can produce amazing results. But the marketing department must monitor and publish results. If taste-makers can be told that so many more sales, so many more calls, so many more postings, so many more anything makes a significant difference, they can mobilize to achieve that. Taste-makers love having the information. If they come close to the goal but fail, they want to know. Armed with that information, a marketer can turn to them repeatedly.

Rewards for Taste-Makers. Taste-makers love to receive anything cool. Just being in the presence of a brand or performer that they think is cool is a reward. Receiving inside information from a company on product design, being awarded cool merchandise, or being recognized as a contributor in any way can count as cool. These are the standard rewards. But taste-makers love making a marketing success. So they love having their advice solicited for each new thing and, in effect, can create their own rewards.

Brand Role. Taste-makers promote the next new and cool thing. Therefore, forms of entertainment, software, fashions, lines of cookware, furniture, and so forth that have regular *new* releases are ideal for taste-makers. A corporate brand that can engage in trendy activity can also benefit from taste-makers. For taste-makers to support any brand over time, it has to be one that is extended year in, year out—even better, season in, season out. Otherwise, the taste-maker cannot be involved. There must be change that the taste-maker can feel responsible for.

To be cool, the brand has to have an appeal that, relative to the sophistication of the taste-maker, is not too personally demanding. An esoteric mutual fund specializing in derivatives would be too demanding for the ordinary financial services taste-maker. Thus, although their delight may appear complex at first, it must turn out to be simple in the end.

Because of the nature of the new and the cool, taste-making is often a matter of crossing communities. To show how marketers can work effectively with taste-makers, we draw on how Brian Cohen and Al Branch of Elektra Records guided Missy Elliott's 2001 summer success single "Get UR Freak On" (on "Miss E . . . So Addictive") from hip-hop's taste-makers to those of the mainstream market. They learned in January 2001 that Missy Elliott would be delivering the tracks of her new album within the month. Missy Elliott is an innovative hip-hop artist who successfully broke new ground with her first album (1997) and subsequently went on to work with many other artists in the hip-hop community. Her second album (1999), as is common in the recording industry, did not succeed commercially.

Traditionally, radio play drives sales, and Cohen and Branch were certain that they could get tracks from the new Missy Elliott played on the traditional Black urban stations. However, the sales that resulted from such limited play would count as another commercial failure. The key to Elliott's success was to get her to move from the mainstream urban to the crossover urban and then to top 40 stations. Achieving the crossover is quite tricky because songs that are too commercial alienate the mix DJs who are the initial influential taste-makers. Yet, if a song is not commercial enough, crossover is never achieved. Having a song that is both noncommercial and commercial is only half the problem. Programmers and DJs at urban and crossover stations do not like to continue playing a song that is moving to top 40 stations. Therefore, marketers have first to get the record played at urban and crossover stations in the 10 prime markets (including Los Angeles, Atlanta, New Orleans, New York, and San Francisco), then keep listener enthusiasm high in these markets as it crosses over to pop markets. Any loss of audience causes a loss in momentum and threatens the crossover.

In preparation, Cohen and Branch developed a list of the 100 most influential (taste-maker) mix DJs who played their own selections on Friday and Saturday nights and who are listened to by other DJs, prime time programmers, and the hip-hop cognoscenti (mavens). They also compiled a secondary list of 500 for the second round of taste-maker network marketing. They set the release date for May 15 to give themselves enough time to get the relevant communities talking before the release and the traditional marketing blitz that would come then. The basic plan included four steps:

1. Secure taste-maker DJs in a core African American hip-hop community by sending them exclusive early versions of the single and following up to get radio and club play.
2. Build buzz by event marketing and quality (commemorative) giveaways at African American elite and middle-class lifestyle events.
3. Use Internet e-cards and tell-a-friend contests to cross over to other taste-makers (especially outside the core hip-hop community).
4. Start standard MTV, broadcast radio advertising, and actual Missy Elliott appearances both before and after the release date to keep interest high and to secure crossover.

When Cohen and Branch heard the album tracks, "Get UR Freak On" and "Lick Shots," they realized that both had single potential but both tracks sounded unedited. There were strong arguments that the tracks should be sent back for editing, but they determined that they could not afford delay. They immediately burned 100 CDs with "Get UR Freak On" that night and sent them to the 100 preselected DJs.

Next, Cohen and Branch had to make "Get UR Freak On" part of people's lives in the communities where the song was played. They worked the

10 critical urban markets and events that generally appealed to the African American community. They bought Billboard space and sent wrapped vans around the critical urban neighborhoods to establish a presence for Missy Elliott. They also formed street teams of taste-makers to pass out fliers and poster empty walls. At critical African American celebrations like the NBA All-Star Game, they had street teams of taste-makers hand out commemorative Missy Elliott foam basketballs. They also distributed 10,000 "Get UR Freak On" hotel door hangers with condoms and passed out fliers and posters. The goal of the taste-makers involved in the street teams was to get dialogue going. According to Branch, the tools that work best either establish the artist in the community or get people talking about the artist as part of the event. The goal was to motivate taste-makers by enabling them to have a role in creating buzz.

Meanwhile, to keep DJs talking, 12-inch vinyl records of "Get UR Freak On" were shipped to the 600 most influential taste-making DJs. Again, the goal was to increase radio and club play. Branch regularly contacted the DJs to check in on what they thought of the single and how much play they were giving it. Momentum kept building in the African American community.

To begin the crossover, they started an e-mail campaign in which they located 200,000 online Missy Elliott taste-makers and sent them e-cards featuring Missy Elliott's own filming of her video shoot of "Get UR Freak On." (This taste-maker community includes kids who are learning from and promoting what goes on in the African American community.) The one who forwarded the card to the greatest number of friends got the chance to attend Missy Elliott's next video shoot. When sales reached 10,000, Cohen and Branch knew that the single had crossed over to new, non-urban, non-African American taste-makers.

Dissemination Strategies for Maven Communities

Because mavens tend to form highly interactive, thoughtful relationships with relatively small groups of followers, networks of mavens have been slow to emerge. Mavens find space in solidarity, appreciator, and taste-making communities. Nevertheless, like offline business, e-businesses have been trying to use mavens; and although robust maven networks have yet to emerge, results to date show the value of encouraging mavens to act as reviewers. A recent study of reviews on Amazon.com, 800.com, and Barnesandnoble.com showed the following value of having mavens—most of the reviewers are mavens—write product reviews:

- Review readers are twice as likely to purchase as nonreaders of reviews.
- Review readers return to the site nine times more frequently than nonreaders of reviews.
- Review readers are twice as unlikely to stop using the site as nonreaders of reviews.

Although review readers account for only one-third of site users, they account for two-thirds of the sales.[23] The importance of on-site mavens is expected to increase as the number of competing market offerings increases and as their quality becomes increasingly complicated and similar.

If you sell erudite goods, the strategy of forming a maven network is essentially to become the *university* of mavens in your category. Once people interested in the product category come to you for learned information, the popularity of the maven information channel will enhance the sales channel.

Organizing Mavens. If you sell products that require sophistication, or that are increasingly valued as you develop increasing discrimination, mavens already know about you, visit your site, read your press, and follow your offerings. Many of them have probably written to ask for additional information. Attracting them often means only giving them better tools for contacting you and for reaching others.

Amazon.com attracts mavens by offering readers the opportunity to write reviews on books and other merchandise that it sells. To enhance the relationship and enable real mavens to stand out, it allows readers of reviews to rate their usefulness. Amazon and Epinion suppose that reviewers whose reviews are highly rated are mavens. Amazon and Epinion thus let readers look up the reviewers, find out what they have reviewed, and see how their reviews have fared. Customers can also find out a little about who the maven is. In this way, an Amazon.com or Epinion customer can feel a sense of familiarity with the maven-reviewer. Even though there is no interactivity, Amazon has assisted mavens in reaching others. Epinion goes further by featuring certain mavens monthly. These features give Epinion users a little more material for building a relationship with a maven.

Communications Approach. A robust communications approach has to enable mavens to build up their own kind of networks, as professors at universities do. The key to this process is enhancing the space and kind of communication that enables customers to identify themselves with the mavens. Mavens gain this identification best when they speak in their own, mostly earnest, voices about who they are and why they care about giving advice. The communications approach should focus on enabling mavens to develop their own niche brands as mini Ann Landers-type advice gurus.

Uplister leads here. This is a site where music mavens explain their lists of favorite songs concerning particular themes. Not only do mavens give general accounts of themselves, but also Uplister encourages them to explain how they understand the theme for which they have collected songs. Mavens on Uplister continually engage in both personalization and education. Potential followers can find ways of identifying themselves with the maven as they learn. Uplister finds that providing the structure in which this identification can occur and where mavens appear admirable to followers can go a long way toward replacing the personal understanding and friendly respect of offline maven relationships.

Both online and offline sites could help mavens with many more additional tools and themes for building their personal advice brands. In the future, for instance, maven communities are likely to become more interactive as mavens begin responding to each other and to one or another of their followers in a public forum, much as occurs for appreciators now.

Reward for Mavens. Mavens live for the opportunity to be acknowledged for their special interests. Any way in which mavens can see that what they say counts is an important reward. For that reason, Amazon's and Epinion's reviews of the reviewers are an important reward for the mavens.

Some maven network builders reward mavens with special conventions for meeting one another. Conventions have had some success with mavens who already use chat rooms and bulletin boards. Mavens also like to have advance and detailed knowledge of product offerings. They are interested in what people in R&D are thinking, and they like special product editions such as the early vinyl releases DJs get in the music industry. Therefore, bringing mavens closer to the inside of the industry remains an important inducement. The more a reward increases knowledge and sophistication that can be passed on, the more appeal it is likely to have.

Brand Role. Maven networks make sense for brands that require a developed understanding. The main problem mavens have is sharing their understanding with others. Consequently, viral strategies in this area are likely to follow the current path of Amazon and the like. This still leaves a range of underexplored techniques. Mavens could issue reviews and recommendations on certain subjects according to the level of the reader, years of experience, and so on. They would love the challenge. Mavens could select the mavens they most like to read or listen to. Contacting highly regarded mavens could then be organized and might even require a membership or subscription. In some cases, certain kinds of mavens could even require that their readers pass an admissions test to receive their reviews and recommendations. Again, look to the university as the model.

Aside from the few pure maven strategies of companies like Uplister and Epinions, mavens are often targeted in conjunction with other networked communities. Hasbro's release of its 2001 game Pox gives a good example of that. That campaign also serves well as an example of the general guidelines for orchestrating viral marketing as part of an overall marketing plan. We turn to this subject next.

INCLUDING VIRAL MARKETING IN A MARKETING PLAN

Orchestrating viral and traditional campaigns involves 10 basic keys deployed in three phases. The keys are listed next:

- *Preparatory.*
  - —Start network marketing generally at least three months before traditional marketing.
  - —Plan to start with several communities so that you can learn from successes. (Include a plan for moving from community to community.)
  - —Develop a clear goal of what you want network leaders to accomplish within the general marketing goals.
  - —Draw on mass promotion to lend credibility to word-of-mouth and then capture a broader market.
- *First set of communities.*
  - —Seed with product or critical information.
  - —Market around lifestyle events or leader appearances.
  - —Use early broadcast marketing to enhance buzz and to establish awareness of events.
- *Climax by adding direct marketing and a traditional media campaign.*
  - —Use early direct marketing to cross-communities and cultivate new network leaders.
  - —Always keep the network leaders ahead with premier information and contests that yield commemorative promotional materials that fit with their lifestyles.

—Begin the traditional media campaign shortly before the product release and enhance it so that it can also serve as the climax of word-of-mouth as well as the beginning of traditional public relations events.

VIRAL MARKETING FOR THE POX GAME

Hasbro's marketing campaign around the release of Pox provides a good summary of how viral marketing works and how it can play a role in an overall marketing plan in terms of the previous points.

Matt Collins, director of marketing at Hasbro Games, was introduced to the brand concept of Pox roughly two years before he took it to a national rollout. Pox is a game played roughly like a Gameboy, except that the device has a radio transmitter and receiver built into it. One Pox player can play against another person directly or play against multiple people. The idea is to train (create) a warrior by giving him certain kinds of armor, weapons, and a basic fighting script. This warrior can play against other warriors and capture their armor if he wins or have his armor captured if he loses. The back story involves these warriors saving earth from a strand of alien DNA that threatens to disable all machinery on the planet.

Collins saw the game as a potential brand for 8- to 12-year-olds. The possibility of collecting different armor types, which could then be used in battles, gave it an appeal similar to Pokemon. The wireless technology took it beyond Pokemon by making it aspirational. Kids, especially 9- and 10-year-olds, aspire to having the technology—cell phones and beepers—of older kids and their parents. It also played into the well-known love among kids of that age for constructing and destroying constructed things.

Pox seemed at first like a toy that could be marketed successfully with a conventional marketing plan. That would involve a strong showing at the February toy show, which all major toy retailers attend. Then, send it out to be manufactured in April, ship to the retailers in August, and start television advertising at the beginning of school to produce "kid nag" and make the necessary sales during the holiday season. (In the toy industry, 60 percent to 70 percent of revenue comes during the December holiday season.)

Collins, however, decided to expand his thinking by working with maven gamers both inside and older than the target range. He found young maven gamers in the New York, Boston, and Chicago areas. The older ones were at Babbages and similar places. The results were unanimous. The game was cool to play alone. The Pokemon-collecting aspect of the game was cool, and that made playing with another kid also fun. However, what made the game awesome was its stealth nature. You could leave the radio on and then attack anyone else within range simply by passing by. Best, you could see kids playing and attack them unseen from afar. The mavens were willing participants in the initial viral marketing phase and, in fact, made a real contribution to the brand concept.

That good result, however, produced a new challenge for Collins. The multiplayer experience drew the greatest "Wow" from players; but for most purchasers, it required a market that already had 15 percent penetration. How could a toy be efficiently launched into markets that required such levels of penetration at the time of launch (not an uncommon problem with so-called networked products)? Launching an advertising campaign that promised a multiplayer experience would lead to insurmountably bad word-of-mouth unless kids could experience it.

Collins decided to start in the Midwest, the region with the greatest Gameboy/Nintendo/Sony use and the best positioning of Hasbro's business customers, and move from there east and then west. He determined to work one Midwestern urban region at a time, starting with the Chicagoland area, which had 400,000 eligible boys. He decided to find the coolest of the cool kids (taste-makers), supply them each with 10 Pox games to give away to their friends, pay them $30, and put them on the Pox mission to spread Pox. Collins started with three cool Pox ambassadors per school in roughly 150 qualified schools. (Schools qualified by meeting criteria involving the size of the population of boys ages 9 and 10; families of middle income; local Target, FAO Schwartz, or Toys"R"Us stores; and sales of hand-held games in the area.) Collins wanted to start the taste-making process in April before school was out, support word-of-mouth with local promotions, and reach the necessary penetration by the end of the summer. Toys"R"Us and Target would track the number of Pox sold to determine if the word-of-mouth strategy lifted penetration to the level where regular mass promotion could effectively begin.

The coolest of the cool kids were selected through surveying. A video was made to excite them about their mission. It showed other kids, like them, playing Pox and finding it cool. The kids knew, of course, that the back story was marketing, yet they loved it. Collins' team delivered Pox to 15 kids at a time in more than 100 orientation sessions and followed up with telephone calls. The most important promise that the kids made was to give the game to 10 other recruits (friends). The second promise was to see to it that the Pox message was not lost. Later, researchers interviewed the kids to keep alive the sense that they were bringing the newest, coolest thing to their communities.

To support these "ambassadors," Pox.com was launched in late April to get the opportunity to reach taste-makers. The efforts of these taste-makers were, in turn, supported by mobile billboards, such as those used in urban neighborhoods for Missy Elliott, deployed in the neighborhoods. Routes were worked out so that kids would see them on their way home from school and while playing with one another after school. Hasbro bought some spot television time for this purpose.

The results from the viral marketing were so strong at the toy stores that Hasbro's main customers, particularly Toys"R"Us and Target, demanded a national launch instead of going from urban area to urban area through the Midwest. Consequently, Hasbro had to prepare a traditional media launch and figure out a way to bring in viral marketing after the start of a mass media blitz. To do this, Collins has had the retailers in new cities agree to biweekly Pox Saturday tournaments during the fall. In these tournaments, kids have the multiplayer experience. Hasbro is targeting key taste-makers to come to these events.

VIRAL MARKETING IN THE MUSIC INDUSTRY

We offer another example of viral marketing as part of an overall marketing plan. This example is drawn from the music industry, long a hotbed of viral marketing innovation.

The recording industry is paradigmatic in its use of networked communities for marketing artists. However, Steve Lerner of Wind-Up Entertainment has outperformed the rest of the industry. His most famous case remains his viral marketing of the rock band Creed around solidarity-networked communities. Lerner was able to do what, at the time, the record industry considered impossible, indeed suicidal. Wind-Up released Creed's album "Human Clay" with radio play in only 20 percent of the United States geographically. Radio play is usually both the most costly and the most critical part of a successful release. But with most regions represented in the online community, Lerner took the chance that the online community would drive an initial burst of widespread sales and that those sales, together with calls to radio stations, would increase radio play. It worked. The album sold virtually everywhere, showing the strength of the community as a driver of sales. Wind-Up had spent no more than $50,000 (an unheard-of small sum) by the time 316,000 copies of "Human Clay" had been sold at the end of the first week. Its sales even exceeded the sales of Garth Brooks's release, which had been promoted with a television special. "Human Clay" has now gone quintuple platinum with the band engaging in the normal kinds of promotion: television appearances, videos, and so forth. In short, Lerner changed the front end of music promotion with the use of a solidarity community. How did he do it?

As part of the decision to sign Creed, Lerner found that Creed had already built up a following among Christian rock fans in the South. So, when he signed the band, he gave them a laptop computer, a digital camera, and spelled out certain online promotional duties. (Lerner also took control of Creed's cyber-rights.) After signing the label, he immediately built an artist site to post news (with a bulletin board and a chat room) and then started driving the artists' listeners to the site. Because it is no longer easy to find fans on the Internet (it used to be a matter of going to the *Rolling Stone* site), Lerner had Creed members prime the pump by posting their journals, engaging in chats, and providing videos and music that could be streamed or downloaded. Also, Lerner promoted the site at all offline Creed appearances.

Lerner even schedules offline events based on what they can do for the site, how they can extend its geographical coverage. Once listeners started posting on the bulletin board and speaking in the chat rooms, he recruited the opinion leaders to maintain and direct the community. Theirs are the authentic voices. Lerner sets the goal of having fans (prompted by leaders) provide 90 percent of the site's content in the form of comments, posted pictures, online diaries, and so forth. Beyond using the community leaders, Wind-Up has to provide some editing and take care of frequently asked questions. After two years of promoting "My Own Prison," the re-release of Creed's earlier self-published album, the Creed site was getting 600,000 views per month.

Most artist promotion begins building interest in a new album four months before its release with concerts, artist appearances, and news releases. Then the label spends the largest amount of its promotional budget on promotion to radio stations to get the all-important play of the single. Getting one radio station to catch on from another to increase radio play is its own science of careful timing and constant persuasion. If the radio promoter's timing is off, a song is quickly categorized as fitting one or another niche and is never heard by a mass audience. Sometimes a video is produced to follow radio play of the single. Finally, retailers are brought into the picture with promotions designed to get real estate in the store.

Lerner used the experience of the Creed site to engage the mass media in a new way. Drawing on retailers' interest in keeping their own Web sites fresh, Wind-Up offered eight major retailers the single "Higher" for download and another exclusive track from the album to stream during the month before release. In exchange, Wind-Up received premium retail display space for the CD, including prominent display of Creed posters and so forth. Best Buy and Musicland were among those who participated. Additionally, members of the online community called retailers.

Wind-Up also offered "Higher" for download at 100 radio stations' own sites. To ensure that the radio stations promoted the song at their site and to enhance the station's interest in playing it, Creed offered a free concert in the listening area of the radio station with the highest number of downloads. Such a concert obviously would promote both the radio station and help build Creed's online community. As with retail, members of the online community called stations asking for more spin.

Lerner then released with only 20 percent geographical coverage in spin. The results astonished the industry. Increasing radio spin and producing a video were key in driving "Human Clay" to its later multiplatinum sales. However, the all-out promotional spending on these elements came much later and was supported by the early success. Indeed, Lerner lengthened the promotional lifetime from four months before release to one year before release. In an industry where only one in ten albums makes back the promotional money spent on it, Lerner's use of the networked community for the initial build-up was a revolutionary addition to the usual marketing practices.

CONCLUSION

Leading companies are currently learning how to use networked communities. We believe that companies that understand the different types of networks and the appropriate strategies for each will succeed. They will take buzz to a new level in terms of ever more innovative viral marketing strategies. Moreover, as viral marketing increases, knowing how to work virally with online communities will be a growing source of competitive advantage.

Beyond this, we think that the viral marketing use of networked communities may well open the door to a new era in marketing—an era in which brand concepts will *emerge* from networked communities of consumers as well as be transmitted to them. We have seen evidence of such *brand emergence* in several of the case examples discussed here. We expect buzz to become not only what marketers try to infect target consumers with, but also something that they try to infect themselves with.

Notes

1. Everett Rogers and F. Floyd Shoemaker, *Communication of Innovations: Across-Cultural Approach* (New York: Free Press).

2. For more on the history of research into opinion leaders, the academic term for influencers or influential lead users, see Emanuel Rosen, *The Anatomy of Buzz* (New York: Doubleday, 2000), pp. 56–57.
3. Ibid., pp. 144–145.
4. "Buzz Marketing," *Business Week* (July 30, 2001), p. 52.
5. Renee Dye, "The Buzz on Buzz," *Harvard Business Review* (November/December, 2000), pp. 139–146.
6. See note 2.
7. Malcolm Gladwell, *The Tipping Point* (Boston: Little Brown, 2000).
8. Ibid., pp. 70–78.
9. Richard Dawkins, *The Selfish Gene* (Oxford: Oxford University Press, 1976).
10. Susan Blackmore, *The Meme Machine* (Oxford: Oxford University Press, 1999).
11. See Robert Aunger, ed., *Darwinizing Culture: The Status of Memetics as a Science* (Oxford: Oxford University Press, 2000).
12. James Surowiecki, "A Basket Case," *The New Yorker* (April 9, 2001), p. 42.
13. Seth Godin, *Unleashing the Ideavirus.*
14. Christopher Locke, *Gonzo Marketing* (Cambridge, MA: Perseus, 2001), pp. 183–202, esp. 195.
15. Gil McWilliam, "Building Stronger Brands through Online Communities," *Sloan Management Review,* vol. 41 (spring 2000), p. 44.
16. These figures are as of December 17, 2001. See Jim Cashell, "Top Ten Trends for Online Communities" (December 17, 2001), http://www.OnlineCommunityReport.com.
17. Jim Cashell, "Interview with Vanchau Nguyen, ezboard," *Online Community Report* (March 15, 2001), http://www.OnlineCommunityReport.com/features/nguyen (Forum One Communications, 2001).
18. See note 7, pp. 70–78.
19. See note 7, pp. 74–87.
20. www.electricartists.com.
21. See note 7, pp. 61–69.
22. See Erin White, "Chatting a Singer Up the Pop Charts: How Music Makers Used the Web to Generate Buzz before the Album Debuted," *Wall Street Journal,* (October 5, 1999). Marc Schiller points out that there is one subtle mistake in this article. Some of the quotations suggest that members of the Electric Artist team impersonated fans. Schiller has a rule that people in his company will only work on products that they like. But he is religious—as are others who successfully engage in marketing to highly-networked communities—about genuineness.
23. Peoplelink.com, "What's the Value of eCommunity?" (2000), based on a study by McKinsey & Co.

CHAPTER 7

Acquiring the Right Customers

LISA A. PETRISON and PAUL WANG

Contrary to conventional marketing wisdom, the ability to acquire new customers is actually of secondary importance in making most companies today succeed in their marketing efforts. Examination of the most profitable companies suggests that they are invariably successful in retaining and cultivating current customers, while in contrast, unprofitable companies spend a disproportionate amount of resources trying to obtain new customers, only to quickly lose their business down the road. To an increasing extent, therefore, savvy marketers are spending fewer resources pursuing their competitors' customers, and instead are focusing more of their attention on increasing the loyalty of their own customers.

Research supporting the relative importance of cultivating existing customers over acquiring new ones has become increasingly convincing over the past years. Studies show that across a wide variety of traditional industries, it is between four and ten times as expensive to acquire a new customer as it is to keep an existing one; and for companies operating on the Internet, the disparities are even greater. Raising retention by as little as 5 percent has often been shown to increase company profitability by as much as 100 percent. Companies that maintain databases with financial information about individual customers (such as direct marketers in the catalog, credit card, magazine, and insurance industries) often find that it can take years to recoup their initial acquisition investments, and many observers believe that this is true in a wide variety of other industries as well.

Thus, in most situations, focusing resources on maintaining and growing business from current customers should be the primary marketing goal, with acquiring new customers, a secondary one. All companies do need to attract some new customers (at least from time to time) if they are to continue to remain in business, if only because even the most loyal customers eventually die or move out of the product category. As a result, the topic of how to efficiently and effectively conduct prospecting activities is one that is well worth examining. Acquisition efforts should still be part of a company's overall marketing initiative, however, and attracting customers who cannot be retained and cultivated over the long run is always a less-than-optimal approach and counterproductive with regard to attaining either short-term or long-term profitability.

COSTS OF ACQUIRING CUSTOMERS

A primary reason that it tends to be more profitable for companies to focus their energies on cultivating current customers rather than constantly prospecting for new ones is that acquisition efforts in today's marketplace are tremendously expensive. The cost of reaching and influencing people through all forms of media has increased dramatically over recent years. The cost of advertising in these media has increased, and, in addition, the media vehicles have become more splintered so that getting people's attention and persuading them of a product's merits have become increasingly difficult.

Twenty or 30 years ago, for example, it was much easier than it is today for marketers to reach large numbers of consumers efficiently. Before the introduction of cable TV, major television networks delivered the majority of the population to advertisers each night, allowing marketers to efficiently bring their products to consumers' attention. Today, however, even the most popular television programs (with a few exceptions such as the Super Bowl or the Academy Awards) do not attract anything more than a small sliver of the population—if people are spending their time in front of the television set at all, they are frequently watching cable channels or movies on their VCRs. Other media vehicles have also become more fragmented—thousands of magazines abound, newspaper readership has declined, and dozens of radio stations operate in every major market. The Internet is the worst of all; although a few service providers and search sites (e.g., America Online, eBay, and Yahoo!) deliver large numbers of consumers, in general, the scope of the Web makes it easy for people to make their way toward specialized sites that are specifically tailored to their interests rather than congregating in places with a broader appeal.

For niche marketers that want to attract only a certain type of customer who can be reached efficiently through particular venues, this focus can be a good thing because it eliminates the waste incurred in reaching people who are not very strong prospects for the product. The problem, however, is that usually the only information available about the kinds of people who are reached by particular media are basic demographic variables such as gender, age, and income. Unfortunately, while demographics have long been used by marketers relying on mass media to communicate their selling messages, they are usually not very predictive of how likely individual people are to buy products in a category or a particular brand. For instance, while drugstore cosmetic brands such as Maybelline may choose to target teenage girls and young women because they are more likely than the rest of the population to purchase those products, older and more affluent women (such as First Lady Laura Bush, who has stated that she often wears drugstore makeup) may also have the potential to be good customers. Or consider that, while Ferrari sports cars are most often purchased by older affluent men, the overwhelming majority of people falling into this demographic category have no potential whatsoever for buying this type of automobile.

Limitations of Demographic Information

The low correlation between demographics and purchasing tendencies can be seen in clustering systems (e.g., Claritas' PRIZM), which attempt to predict how likely people are to buy particular brands of products based on where they live. For the vast majority of products, people living in the neighborhoods where consumption of a particular product is highest are in actuality not that much more likely than the average person to buy and use it. Only in very extreme circumstances (such as purchases of expensive automobiles that the vast majority of the population would be unable to afford) are people in certain neighborhoods more than twice as likely as the average consumer to buy a particular brand of product from a particular category. Even at its best, the "lift" provided by the use of demographic variables is not especially helpful in predicting purchasing behaviors.

The difficulty of zeroing in on prospects who are likely to buy a particular product is one experienced by companies using direct marketing as well as those relying on mass media. Despite the rhetoric of direct marketers claiming they use information about consumers to deliver offers for products that specifically meet their customers' needs, the fact remains that response rates for direct marketing prospecting efforts rarely rise above 2 or 3 percent. Despite the increasing amounts of information available about individual customers, it is obvious that it is still very difficult to predict exactly what type of person is likely to be a good prospect for a specific product even when consumers can be addressed on an individual basis.

There are situations in which advertising vehicles do seem to deliver the desired audience for a particular company's advertisements. Couture clothing lines find it appropriate to advertise in *Vogue*. Upscale cruise lines may choose to run ads in *Travel and Leisure*. Movies aimed at teenagers enamored with pop culture may be promoted on MTV. It makes sense for the arts and crafts furniture company Stickley to advertise prominently in *American Bungalow*. In these instances, the wide variety of media choices available in today's marketplace makes it easier for marketers of specialized products to zero in on the people most likely to buy their products, thus cutting down the costs for ads reaching people who would have no interest in buying the product.

Unfortunately, however, such obvious matches between products and media vehicles are rare. More often, individual media vehicles are targeted mostly at people of particular demographics and are not very good at singling out consumers who are likely to be especially good targets for particular products or services. In addition, even when it is hypothesized that a correlation between a vehicle's audience and a product's target market might exist, it is generally difficult to know for sure whether this is actually the case. For example, *O: The Oprah Magazine* is designed to appeal to women who have the desire for self-actualization. While it is probable that such women also might be attracted to particular products and services related to that goal, it is hard to know for sure which products these might be, at least unless companies do extensive surveys to determine which magazines their best customers read and/or use direct marketing to gauge response rates. More often, the selection of the right vehicle is determined by the best guess of the media planner—a time-consuming, as well as an inexact, process.

Thus, given the fact that in today's environment there exist an increasing number of media vehicles, all of which target smaller and more specific groups of people than they did in the past, this targeting is of real help to only a small sub-segment of marketers. For most companies, this trend has merely increased the overall average costs of reaching people through mass media or direct mail, which is how most companies (except for those using personal selling appeals) actively prospect for new customers. For one thing, the activities of evaluating, selecting, buying, and coordinating advertisements in a large number of different venues—which is necessary for companies that hope to get any substantial reach in today's marketplace—are time-consuming and, therefore, costly for companies and their advertising agencies. (This expense is such that many advertisers refuse to even consider vehicles that do not have a minimum audience size, but even piecing together a media buy that includes only the most prominent choices can be very labor intensive.) Moreover, while advertising in a particular vehicle with a small circulation is obviously cheaper than advertising in a larger one, the average CPM (cost of reaching a thousand audience members) is almost always much higher. Unless a brand's target is closely correlated to that of a particular media vehicle, the cost to reach (much less acquire) relevant prospects is likely to be much higher than it would be if more vehicles with larger audiences were available. (The few vehicles that do command large audiences—again, the Super Bowl and a few very highly rated network television shows—tend to attract much advertiser interest. Even though they are expensive on a total-cost basis, their CPMs still tend to be relatively low.)

Customers' Divided and Saturated Attention

A bigger problem is that even when people are reached by a particular media vehicle, they may not pay very much attention to the advertising supporting it. Consumers today have been inundated with millions of advertising messages during their lives and, as a result, have become very good at screening out the ads that reach them so that they are not overwhelmed with stimuli. People watching television, for example, may avoid being exposed to advertisements in a number of ways: by flipping channels during commercial breaks, by recording television shows and then fast-forwarding through the ads when later watching the shows, or by switching to another activity (e.g., paying bills, reading, talking, leaving the room) when commercials come on the screen. Similarly, most people have become practiced at avoiding looking at ads when reading magazines or newspapers (although in some cases, when advertising is perceived to be part of the "content" of the publication as in some fashion magazines, attention may be higher). Automobile radios are specifically designed to let drivers easily flip from station to station when commercials are played. Studies show that consumers spend about the same amount of time (about two minutes per day) going through their mail regardless of how much they receive; well-defined sorting strategies allow those people who receive 20 or 30 pieces of mail per day to efficiently dispose of those items that are unlikely to interest them with little more than a glance.

The Internet is perhaps the worst of all media when it comes to getting the attention of potential customers. Searching for information on the Web can be a time-consuming process, and many people do not want to spend more than a limited amount of time sitting in front of their computer screens. As a result, impatience with Internet advertising runs high. Click-through rates on banner advertisements have fallen far below 1 percent, and consumers encountering company home pages that are littered with advertisements for various products are frequently inclined to move quickly past them into the site if they know what they are looking for or abandon the site entirely if they do not.

The increasing propensity of people to screen out advertising information makes the activity of acquiring customers far more expensive than it was in the past. For instance, a traditional rule of thumb was that marketers should expose each consumer about three times to a particular ad to give people enough opportunity to sufficiently absorb its message. If people pay attention to only a fraction of the advertisements to which they are exposed, however, the number of times that companies need to run their messages so that they can reach an optimum level of effectiveness can increase dramatically; for example, to an average of nine times rather than only three times if people notice ads only one-third of the time. Given that mass media (including direct mail) is the only option available for most companies to systematically attract new customers, inefficiency contributes to the fact that prospecting is much more costly today than it was in the past.

Extensive Customer Knowledge and Experience

Another problem is that even when people today do absorb an advertising message, they are often unlikely to be affected by it very much. The majority of consumers in many categories have already tried most or all of the available options and are much more likely to trust their own experiences than the claims made in a particular advertisement. Frequent business travelers, for instance, have usually flown on a variety of airlines and thus have a great deal of knowledge about what to expect from carriers—a fact that United Airlines acknowledged when, after decades, it pulled its "Fly the Friendly Skies" ads because consumers stated that they were lacking in believability.

In other cases, people may not have previously purchased a particular brand but have already made the decision that they are not interested in it. In the direct marketing industry, for instance, many companies have found that when they send out increased numbers of solicitations, their response rates begin to drop—mostly, research suggests, because they are reaching people who have already tacitly rejected the offer repeatedly.

Even when people have not previously tried a particular brand and have some potential to buy it, they may be much more inclined to trust the recommendations of people whom they know personally than anything that might be stated in an advertisement or in other promotional materials. Consumers today have been exposed to so much advertising that they often are skeptical about what marketers tell them, and, therefore, they rely much more on the advice that they receive from fellow purchasers. Heavy cellular phone users, for instance, may spend time talking with other similar people about issues such as customer service and connection clarity in different cities and base their purchase choices much more on these conversations than on what is stated in advertising or recommended by store personnel.

Overall, then, advertising in the early twenty-first century is usually relatively ineffective at influencing people's behaviors even when it manages to catch their attention. As a result, marketers generally need to run a huge amount of advertising or to invest heavily in other types of marketing activities to attract new customers. Doing so means that to recoup their upfront acquisition costs, companies need to retain these customers' business over time. If not (e.g., if new customers are dissatisfied with product quality or receive a better price from a competitor), the acquisition effort may actually end up being of negative rather than positive value for the company.

Marketplace Commodities

Still another problem in today's marketplace is that products in many categories are very similar to one another. Much of the time, marketers from various companies within an industry focus their attention on the same heavy users in the product category, and thus end up creating products with similar features and benefits. In addition, benchmarking processes often ensure that competing products are similar in terms of overall cost and quality. While this standardization may ensure that no company is "left behind," it tends to result in a situation in which consumers have no particular reason to purchase one company's products over another's because all have the same basic benefits and features.

When product parity exists in the marketplace, as it does in many product categories, marketers have two options with regard to attempting to attract new customers. First, they can advertise heavily to increase brand awareness, knowledge, or liking among the relatively few customers that may have the potential to be influenced by factors other than price. This action is likely to be expensive, however, as described earlier, in many industries, a high percentage of customers are not going to be easily persuaded by advertising messages. Second, marketers can choose to reduce price to attract prospects. However, if there really is no difference between the company's products and its competitors', customers acquired through this strategy may defect very quickly if competitors match low prices or if the company eventually increases its own prices, meaning that profits are not sustained over the long run.

This phenomenon was common in the early days of the Internet, for example, when investors evaluated the potential of start-up companies through their ability to attract new customers. Pets.com, for instance, spent a great deal of money advertising in media such as for a recent Super Bowl, then priced products at only slightly above cost and offered free shipping even on such bulky and heavy items as large bags of dry dog food. In taking this approach, the company's hope was that customers would start to become comfortable with the site and then return in the future. However, once the company began to raise prices, its customers began shopping at other Web sites offering them better deals or went back to buying pet products through local bricks-and-mortar retailers. As a result, the company's losses mounted, its ability to raise more capital disappeared, and, within a few months, it went out of business. As a result of incidents like these, analysts and investors finally began making statements that they had lost faith in the Internet industry because of customer retention problems and that they would henceforth evaluate companies on their ability to keep, as well as to obtain, customers.

Part of the reason that companies in the early days of the Internet had a difficult time retaining customers is that they took a cost-centered approach toward their businesses. Early Internet companies took advantage of factors such as low overhead and virtual inventories to keep prices low, and early customers tended to be technologically savvy people who enjoyed and were comfortable surfing the Internet for deals and who were relatively price sensitive. As a result, sites that were able to offer low prices on standard products tended to do well for a while.

Unfortunately, two factors made this strategy become less profitable as time went on. First, competitors soon copied the cost efficiencies that had allowed early entrants to charge low prices, and price wars ensued. In addition, the next wave of people who began shopping on the Internet wanted to spend less time online, and they were less inclined to use technologically advanced tools to seek the best prices. In addition, many of the newer Internet shoppers were upscale professional people who were relatively price insensitive but were concerned about service quality and whether they could obtain something that was qualitatively different from what they could get by shopping in bricks-and-mortar retailers. As a result, many people visited and made one or two purchases from different Web sites but then decided that there were better ways to purchase products and did not pursue shopping online except in certain circumstances (e.g., from eBay, which provides a wide array of used and specialized products that cannot be easily obtained from traditional retailers). While Internet businesses have gradually begun to focus on how they can create a competitive advantage other than price that convinces people to purchase from their sites repeatedly, retention on most Web sites still tends to be low, making it much more difficult to achieve profitability.

Purposely Seeking out Internet Sites

Another problem with Internet marketing is that people need to make a special effort to seek out sites. People pass physical retailers in shopping malls or on their way home from work and have easy access to finite lists of alternatives through local telephone directories. They usually find relevant stores and the products they stock when they are looking for something specific to purchase. On the other hand, to get people to visit a specific site as a result of a mass media advertisement, Internet companies need to persuade them of the merits of the products or services being offered, get them to memorize or bookmark the site address, and then hope that they actually remember to look for the site the next time they are online. Getting consumers to perform this complex combination of tasks can be very difficult for marketers to accomplish. Moreover, consumers searching for different kinds of products on search engines usually encounter long lists of alternatives; therefore, the likelihood that they will visit any particular site is often relatively low.

In addition, it is still the case that a large percentage of the population (even those who have access to the Web) has no interest in making purchases over the Internet, meaning that advertising through mass media inherently includes a great deal of waste. Moreover, even those people who have some inclination to purchase from the Internet often have considerable reservations about doing so because of fears about privacy and security, worries about out-of-stocks, and difficulties in predicting what the obtained merchandise is actually like. These concerns are likely to be even greater when people have not previously purchased from a particular site.

All of these factors explain why acquiring customers on the Internet is so expensive. Some observers, for example, estimate that in the early days of the Internet, attracting a first-time customer cost firms an average of $250, compared to an average of only $40 for traditional companies. As a result, it is even more important for Internet firms than for traditional companies to ensure that the customers they attract can be cultivated into the future, to recoup the large investment made to find them.

Enhancing Customer Satisfaction

No matter what the type of company, however, attracting customers is an expensive undertaking. Accordingly, marketers need to make sure that they can provide a high degree of customer satisfaction before they begin any acquisition efforts. If customer satisfaction cannot be ensured, firms may switch resources to increase the likelihood that people will continue to be customers after they have made their first purchase. After a large merger, for example, Wells Fargo bank purposely suspended acquisition efforts for a period of six months. This suspension gave the bank the opportunity to resolve internal operating issues and make it less likely that, during the period of inevitable upheaval, consumers would be acquired, become dissatisfied, defect, and be disinclined ever to do business with the bank.

Ensuring that prospects are satisfied with their first experiences with a company has several advantages for marketers. First, it makes it more likely that these people will purchase from the company in the future, even if they have to pay a higher price than they might be able to obtain from a competitor. Moreover, to the extent that customers begin to trust a particular company to satisfy their needs, they may eventually be cross-sold on other products and services offered by that organization. Finally, satisfied customers may tell others about their positive experiences, making it easier and less expensive for the company to acquire more customers in the future.

Therefore, when developing a marketing game plan, managers should first determine what types of things make it more likely that customers will become loyal to the company and then take steps to bring about these conditions. Only after setting this stage should major efforts go into prospecting for new customers.

When an Acquisition Focus Is Appropriate

Despite the fact that most companies generally receive a higher return on their marketing investment when they focus their resources on the cultivation of existing customers rather than on the acquisition of new ones, there are certainly situations in which giving substantial attention to acquisition activities is very important. Adopting an acquisition focus may be especially useful for certain kinds of companies or for companies or brands in particular stages of their life cycles.

Furthermore, nearly all companies need to engage in some customer acquisitions if they are to replace those customers who leave through natural attrition. In some cases, the loyalty engendered by the company's core users passes on to newer buyers, meaning that active acquisition activities on the part of the company are less necessary. In most cases, however, companies need to engage in some systematic acquisition efforts, whether through advertising, public relations, or some other form of communications.

In certain circumstances, however, firms may need to acquire new customers. For example, a company may note that its traditional core customers are moving away from the brand, either because they have outgrown the need for it or because, in some cases, they are aging. For instance, during the early 1990s, Cadillac had by far the highest loyalty of any car sold in the United States (with re-buy rates of almost 80 percent). This statistic suggested that the company had done an exceptional job of cultivating customer loyalty, and, for a long time, the division was indeed a star moneymaker for General Motors. However, the median age of the brand's buyers was approximately 70; many of these loyal customers were going to move out of the market relatively soon as they stopped driving or passed away. A challenge for Cadillac, therefore, has been to maintain its appeal to its core base of older drivers while also attracting a new group of customers to replace them—something that it has attempted to do by introducing models with a "retro" look and running nostalgic advertisements focusing on the glamour that used to be associated with the brand in the 1950s. (General Motors struggled with the same problem with another of its brands, Oldsmobile, throughout the 1980s and 1990s. Eventually, however, the company decided that the car did not have the potential of appealing to a younger market and discontinued it.)

Trends Requiring More Concerted Acquisition Efforts

Even companies that are currently extremely successful with their cultivation efforts may choose to put an emphasis on acquiring new customers if research suggests that the issue of customer die-off will eventually become a problem. For example, Harley-Davidson is a very successful company, so much so that people ordering a motorcycle have to wait up to a year to obtain it from the factory. The problem, however, is that most of the company's customers are people from the Baby Boomer generation or older, who associate motorcycle riding with personalities like James Dean and feelings of rebellion and freedom. Younger people today tend to be much less attracted to motorcycles in general or to Harley-Davidson in particular, often making comments to the effect that they associate the brand with downscale, middle-aged, overweight people. While Harley-Davidson is currently very successful, it may face problems with declining sales in the future as its current core users get to the point in their lives when riding motorcycles (and especially Harley-Davidson's heavy-vibrating and hard-to-maneuver motorcycles) becomes uncomfortable for them. Therefore, while fostering enthusiasm among younger consumers is a challenge, doing so may be necessary if the company is to continue to remain as successful and profitable into the future as it is now.

Acquisition efforts are also especially important when customers move in and out of a particular category on a regular basis. For instance, women getting married generally spend no more than a year or two planning their weddings; after that, they stop being in the market for the many products and services associated with that event. Similarly, new parents need to make decisions concerning the many goods and services related to infant care. Yet, after an initial decision-making period, they are no longer in the market for some products (e.g., car seats) and may have become relatively brand loyal to others (e.g., baby formula). Obviously, the shorter the time period that people remain in the market for products made by a particular company, the more important it is for the company to focus efforts on acquiring new customers to replace the ones who are moving out of the market.

Companies operating in markets characterized by inertia buying (i.e., where customers buy the same product repeatedly because it seems too much trouble to seek alternatives) also may choose to focus more efforts on acquisition efforts at the period in people's lives when they are likely to enter the category. For example, many people open their first checking accounts and obtain their first credit cards when they begin college, and some of these young customers maintain those accounts even after graduation because they do not want to take the time to switch to a different company. Banks may decide to target college freshmen with prospecting efforts, even if they will not generate much profit during their college years, to keep their business after they graduate from school and become more profitable customers.

Another situation in which an acquisition focus may be appropriate occurs when people buy from the product category infrequently. For example, once most people have purchased a Nordic Track cross-country skiing exercise machine, they will not be in the market to purchase another one for a number of years (both because they already have one and, in many cases, because they end up using it less often than they thought they would). Similarly, many people who purchase a Palm Pilot electronic organizer will not feel the need to replace it for some time. For these types of "one shot" or infrequently purchased products, acquisition efforts are extremely important because most sales come from first-time buyers.

However, this category of products is actually smaller than might be initially thought. For example, although most people purchase or lease new automobiles no more than once every four years or so, studies have shown that a new-car salesperson who is able to successfully cultivate a base of only several hundred loyal customers can make a comfortable living, surpassing that of the vast majority of salespeople in the industry who tend to take a more short-term approach. Several factors account for this:

- Most U.S. households own more than one car, and other family members may go to the same salesperson to replace other vehicles if a satisfactory experience is delivered.
- If the salesperson is able to make the car-shopping experience a pleasant one, some customers may come into the showroom occasionally just to see the new models and, as a result, purchase a new car earlier than they had intended.
- Because people tend to be highly involved in their shopping experiences for new cars, and because a high proportion of these experiences are thought to be relatively unpleasant by many people, a salesperson who is able to deliver a good experience is likely to be the beneficiary of strong word-of-mouth recommendations and thus to receive a number of referrals.
- Establishing trust over time may allow a salesperson to credibly recommend features or vehicles that might be more expensive than those that customers had originally intended to purchase.
- The relationship-oriented salesperson wastes less time showing cars to prospects who do not end up actually making a purchase. Thus, the salesperson can spend more time learning about vehicles and paying special attention to needs of loyal buyers, raising the quality of the experience that good customers receive when they come into the dealership and increasing loyalty even further.

In addition, car dealers have the opportunity to cross-sell to new-car buyers a variety of maintenance and repair services, which, in many cases, can provide more profit than the sale of the vehicle itself. To the extent that salespeople give purchasers an experience that makes them more willing to visit the dealership again in the future, they are contributing to its overall profitability. Dealerships that want to increase their overall profits should consider ways to motivate those salespeople who have positive relationships with their customers to encourage them to patronize the service department and return to the dealership for further purchases.

Like car dealers, many companies selling products that might, at first glance, be thought to provide profits on a one-time-only basis actually have the potential for substantial additional sales because of repeat purchases or purchases of related products in the future. For example, while customers who purchase a Nordic Track probably will not want to buy another such machine in the future, it can be assumed that they are at least somewhat interested in physical fitness and, therefore, may be potential targets for certain other products (e.g., upgrades). If the experiences that they had during the Nordic Track buying process and with the product itself were positive ones, these customers may be far more open to purchasing such items from Nordic Track than from other companies that they have not yet grown to trust. This potential to form relationships with customers may provide Nordic Track with the opportunity to sell additional products of its own, or to operate in a joint venture with another company selling products that might be attractive to these people and that would have the potential of increasing positive feelings that customers have about the Nordic Track brand overall. The adoption of this type of framework changes the customer's purchase of the Nordic Track equipment from the sole source of revenue for the company to the first of many opportunities to sell products.

Finally, companies that are just starting up or seeking to expand their businesses need to place a substantial amount of emphasis on acquisition efforts, at least until they have built up a solid customer base. This strategy may be the case both for companies attempting to penetrate established industries and those operating in new or rapidly growing industries. For example, as home users of personal computers moved from telephone lines to faster Internet connections, a variety of companies focused attention on acquiring customers. In this situation, an assumption was made that once customers chose one kind of service provider, they probably would not easily switch to a different provider; therefore, it appeared to be crucial to obtain these customers' business upfront rather than waiting until they had already been acquired by competition. Aggressively pursuing acquisitions in a growing industry is especially appropriate when, as may have been the case here, certain factors (such as customer inertia) make it less likely that people will switch once they have made an initial decision to buy a product that they will use on an ongoing basis.

Nevertheless, even when a company is pursuing rapid growth and needs to actively court prospective customers, a substantial amount of thought should be given to ways to maintain these customers and maximize their profit potential over the long term. The company should consider what types of customers are likely to be most profitable in the future and then focus its attention on acquiring people who fit into this category rather than just attracting as many people as possible. In most cases, this approach means actually acquiring a smaller number of customers than might be obtained if prospects were acquired indiscriminately, given that customers with the potential of being very loyal to a particular company may be more difficult to find and reach. They also may be more likely to carefully consider the choices available to them before making a decision.

Many observers think that failure to identify and attract profitable customers is the main reason for the difficulties of the first Internet start-ups. Start-up companies often measured their success by the number of hits their Web sites received or by the number of initial purchases that were made. The question of whether these people would continue to purchase in the future frequently enough, and at a high enough price for the company to generate a profit, got far less attention. This shortsightedness was particularly problematic because many early sales on the Internet were made at deep discounts to bargain hunters who never would have considered paying full price for the products.

Rather than focusing on offering low prices, companies generally have a much better chance of becoming profitable if they focus their attention on cultivating a particular group of customers who are willing to pay a premium to get what they want. The primary question that marketers attempting to aggressively prospect for new customers must answer is, "What type of people do we most want to attract?" Instead of targeting potential buyers indiscriminately, a company should attempt to determine what types of customers it can serve better than any of its competitors and to what extent those customers are likely to ultimately become profitable for them. After it has these answers, the company can choose acquisition methods to target and attract disproportionate numbers of these people. More importantly, the company can make changes in its products and operations so that these targeted customers have a good experience when they do business with the organization for the first time, and thus are more likely to feel good about and continue to do business with the company into the future.

TRADITIONAL APPROACHES TO CUSTOMER ACQUISITION

Mass Marketing

The most conventional approach to customer acquisition, as well as toward marketing in general, is through the use of mass media. The goal of advertising or other forms of mass communications is to point out the benefits of products both to prospects and to current users, in the hope that these people will be more likely to purchase and use the product in the future. These communications are most often designed to point out how the product is different from its competitors'; that is, what its unique selling proposition is. In some cases, this unique benefit is designed to appeal to only a particular type of customer, but, in general, most companies try to find benefits with a wide appeal so that they have the potential of obtaining as many customers as possible.

For example, the general benefit promised by Pepsi has been that the drink makes the consumer feel younger and more energetic, a theme that has been emphasized over the years by the use of youthful celebrities such as Britney Spears and (previously) Michael Jackson. In contrast, Coca-Cola has generally taken a "classic American" approach, emphasizing how the beverage is a part of the everyday moments that make life more special. Each of these approaches has wide appeal; most consumers are likely to be attracted to both brands. To the extent that segmentation is done for mass-marketed brands, it is often based on the demographics of the people who are the heaviest users in the overall category rather than those of the particular brand in question. For example, all laundry detergents are promoted primarily to women with families because they are the most frequent users of these products.

Even when companies use mass marketing to communicate with customers, it is possible to focus attention on a smaller segment of the market that is underserved by other players. Apple Computer, for instance, owed much of its turnaround success in the late 1990s to the fact that it targeted its computers to different types of person-home buyers who were not technologically savvy and who wanted something fun, typified by Apple's original slogan, "The computer for the rest of us," as opposed to the business and "techie" users that other computer marketers were targeting.

Mass media efforts generally merge acquisition and retention efforts and focus on promoting a single product rather than cultivating customers who might eventually be sold a variety of products, largely because mass media communications cannot differentiate between current and prospective customers. Traditionally, managers have stated that their strategic marketing goal was to win over competitors' customers, an objective that tacitly assumes current customers will stay with the company. Scanner data from companies such as IRI and Nielsen have revealed that this is not the case in many companies because of frequent customer switching, so managers have begun to focus more on the goal of retaining rather than acquiring customers in their marketing planning.

Using mass media as the sole means by which companies communicate with prospects and customers has several drawbacks. First, the approach does not allow companies to learn who their customers are and to establish interactive relationships with them. As a result, the organization will have a difficult time cross-selling its current customers on other products or services that may be especially relevant to them because such appeals must be made through further mass media advertising, which will mostly be received by people who do not have any particular affinity for the brand. In addition, if the organization does not have information about individual customer's needs and wants, it is impossible to customize offers or products to be especially appealing to them. Nor is the company able to direct messages only to current customers; therefore, much of its advertising is wasted on people who are difficult to influence. Finally, because a multitude of factors can influence sales, it is usually very difficult for companies to know whether their marketing communications efforts are having the desired effect.

In many cases, companies have no choice but to rely on mass media to communicate with prospective and current customers. Marketers of packaged goods products, for instance, generally do not interact directly with their end-users and do not make enough money on a per-consumer basis to pay the costs required to build and maintain a database of customer information. Using mass media to communicate the benefits of products to consumers is necessary. However, companies that operate within these constraints may still choose to focus on a particular segment of the market rather than on the market as a whole if they want to acquire customers who will provide them with profits over the long run.

Traditional Direct Marketing Testing

A second type of acquisition approach has been long practiced by traditional direct marketers, although in recent years it has also been adopted by a variety of other types of companies. This approach involves contacting a large number of customers, often through direct mail, although sometimes through mass media, with direct response advertising and then seeing which of the different lists of people or which mass media vehicles produce the highest response rate or profitability. Marketers sometimes refer to this as the *spaghetti approach:* No underlying theory of why certain types of people might be good prospects for the brand needs to exist; rather, just as one might throw a pot of spaghetti at the wall to see which strands stick, marketers test their messages against different target groups to see which ones are most likely to perform the best.

Once such information has been obtained, marketers can direct more marketing resources to the list sources or media vehicles that have been shown to have the highest response rates. In addition, because direct marketers are aware of exactly how much initial revenue they are obtaining from each customer group, they are able to determine whether the money that they need to spend to acquire these people's business will be recovered and an overall profit achieved; if it is not, these lists or media will not be used in the future.

A number of other variables besides customer type may be tested in direct marketing acquisition efforts. Different versions of creative copy—such as what is said about the product or how that message is presented—may be developed and tested against matched groups of consumers to determine which is the most attractive. Pricing, sales promotions, and product variations are also often tested during acquisition efforts to see which ones "pull" the highest. The ability of such testing to allow direct marketers to evaluate the success of their prospecting activities is a major advantage and is in part responsible for the increased propensity of other types of companies to use direct mail or other types of direct response advertising in their marketing communications efforts.

Another factor characteristic of direct marketing is that acquisition efforts and retention efforts are generally separate from one another. These efforts are distinct because "customers" (those people who have purchased in the past) are known to the company, whereas "prospects" are totally unknown. Certainly, a direct marketer who runs a direct-response ad in a mass media vehicle does not have the names or any individualized information about the people who are being reached. Because of the way in which the direct marketing list industry works, the same thing is usually true when direct marketers use lists of people to receive direct mail solicitations.

Several different types of lists are available to direct marketers. The most commonly used consist of people who are the customers of particular companies or organizations, such as L.L.Bean or Williams-Sonoma. Also frequently used are compiled lists, which consist of names of people who meet certain criteria (such as unmarried women ages 25 to 34). This information is obtained from public sources by companies specializing in such data collection (called *list bureaus*). Other types of lists also exist, such as data on interests (e.g., gardening, photography) that are collected through customer surveys by specialty companies. Regardless of what type of list is used, marketers almost never obtain permanent access to information about the people being prospected for storage in their own databases; rather, they "rent" the names for one-time solicitations. Only if a response is obtained does the prospect become a "customer" and an interactive relationship have the potential to be developed.

This distinction between current customers and prospects is in many respects a good thing. Current customer names are free while prospect names must be purchased. The cost difference encourages managers to put more emphasis on cultivating current customers. However, in practice, direct marketers may be more short-term oriented with regard to their prospecting activities than might be desired. Marketers tend to judge whether their prospecting efforts have been successful based on the number of customers responding or the amount of money that those people spend on their first purchase. The extent to which these people continue to purchase profitable products from the company into the future, on the other hand, is much less often considered when managers decide which sources of names or which promotions to continue to use in the future. Thus, short-term profits may be optimized with this type of approach, while long-term profits may be less so.

A second limitation of traditional direct marketing testing is that while the approach is very good at providing a definite answer as to which of two or more different approaches performs the best (over the short-term), it does not explain why or give any information about what types of other approaches may be even better than the ones being tested. Therefore, although the "scientific" component of direct marketing is helpful in allowing marketers to determine whether specific marketing activities perform well, the overall strategic direction and development of various ideas for appropriate tactics must still result from the creativity and understanding of the marketplace possessed by the marketer.

Long-Term Focused Direct Marketing Testing

As we have just described, one of the drawbacks of the way traditional direct marketers have evaluated the performance of their prospecting activities is that success has usually been measured based on response rates or immediate profits obtained. A list with a 2.5 percent response rate would be preferable to one with a 2 percent response rate. Similarly, a promotion that delivered an average initial profit of $2 per customer obtained would be preferable to one that delivered an average profit of only $1.

However, this type of approach says nothing about the amount of money that the company earns on customers acquired through different methods over the long term. For instance, consider the true example of a company that sells through direct mail a variety of books related to natural health.

Over time, the company has tested a variety of different creative approaches for promoting its books through mailings, some making exorbitant claims (e.g., "Lose up to 15 pounds in one month without dieting or exercising!") and others, more reasonable ones. In addition, the company has tested various sales promotions, including some that allow the buyer to purchase a $30 volume in "three easy payments" over a three-month period. Because the company consistently found that the more hyperbolic copy and the easy payment promotions had better response rates, it gradually moved toward using them in all of its direct marketing activities.

These tactics ensured that the company maximized its sales and profits with regard to prospecting for customers in the short term. However, the question is whether it was optimal for the long term. For instance, it might be hypothesized that people who purchased a book that overstated the benefits of the products in question would be less than satisfied and thus unlikely to purchase more books from the company in the future. Similarly, it is conceivable that a person who was unable to pay for a $30 book in one payment might have limited resources to purchase more books later on. Therefore, even though short-term sales are high, it is possible that cross-selling opportunities over the long run might be less so. Indeed, the company's experience was that most people purchased only one or two books, and most sales came from first-time buyers. While it is possible to make money by selling products only to one-time buyers, companies that are able to create a strong base of customers to whom they sell a variety of products over time almost always find it much easier to make money over the long term.

Questions concerning the extent to which various marketing tactics result in long-term profits are testable by companies that maintain information about their customers over the long run through a technique called *Lifetime Value Analysis*. This technique requires adding up all the revenues associated with a particular type of customer (adjusted to net present value) and subtracting the expenses attributable to that type of person. Calculating this value over an extended period (generally five years or less) allows marketers to determine how much segments of customers are worth to them, not just in immediate sales, but also in the future.

This technique can be used to allow companies to determine the effectiveness of various means of attracting new customers in creating long-term profits for the organization. If a particular promotion draws people who are especially likely to purchase profitable products numerous times in the future, then those customers' average lifetime value may be high even if response rates are only average or even below average. Companies that are concerned about making money over the long term may decide to run more such promotions to add strength to the organization in the future.

Despite the apparent attractiveness of making acquisition decisions based on long-term as well as short-term profit considerations, relatively few direct marketers have attempted to take this approach. Some exceptions do exist; for example, direct-mail insurance companies always make long-term profitability projections to calculate risk and set prices for different types of customers, using their actuarial data to decide what types of consumers to prospect with offers.

Several reasons for the low propensity of other companies to use this methodology exist. First, like most companies in today's environment, direct marketers tend to be under pressure from the investment community to produce short-term profits. Therefore, marketing managers may be encouraged to look primarily at how immediately profitable their activities are likely to be even if long-term profit is not fully optimized.

Even companies that are very oriented toward the long term may have good reasons for looking only at short-run rather than long-run profitability when evaluating the effectiveness of acquisition efforts. For one thing, determining which activities attract customers who will be especially profitable over an extended period takes an equally long time (even years). Thus, this type of testing cannot be used to judge the appropriateness of alternatives such as specific lists or copy phrasing. Rather, it is useful only when a company is evaluating alternative approaches that are substantially different from one another.

For example, in the case of the publisher of the books on natural health, vastly different audiences (downscale versus upscale) and copy approaches (factual versus exaggerated claims) might have been tested in terms of their long-term profitability. The results could be used to drive the overall philosophy and strategic direction of the company with regard to its marketing efforts in the future, even though copywriters and marketers would still have to use their judgment when considering how to describe each individual book and what specific lists to rent for prospecting efforts.

Another problem is that even at relatively sophisticated direct-marketing companies, databases may not be organized in a way that allows information about acquisition and retention efforts to be easily merged. Because acquisition and customer cultivation have generally been viewed as distinct activities at most companies, relevant data—such as how specific customers have been obtained, marketing and other costs that have been associated with them, and the revenues that they have generated over time—may be stored in different places and in different formats in the company's computer systems. Organizing this information in a way that allows long-term profitability calculations may require a considerable amount of effort. As a result, this sort of initiative may not come to fruition unless upper management has a very strong interest in determining the answer to particular questions concerning the profitability of different types of acquisition efforts.

Finally, this type of long-term profitability analysis is valuable only to the extent that the future is likely to be the same as the past. Industries characterized by rapid change will find it to be much less helpful because as different competitors or types of customers enter the market, what worked in the past may not work in the future. For example, many Internet companies set up their operations based on how early adopters (mostly computer-savvy individuals) acted and what they said they wanted; unfortunately, customers of Internet sites who entered the market later were quite different in their shopping behaviors. Therefore, managers need to look at the marketplace and consider how much it has changed or is likely to change over time. The more that change is taking place, the more appropriate it will be for marketers to use their best judgment of what is likely to work in the current environment rather than to look to what has happened in the past.

In summary, the use of direct marketing testing that takes into consideration long-term profitability implications has a specific role in helping marketers to be more successful. It should be used primarily to allow marketers to evaluate different alternatives for broad strategic directions in industries that are changing relatively slowly. When used in this manner, it may provide reassurance that the company will continue to be profitable not only over the short run but also into the future.

Current Customer Profiling

A somewhat more complex and sophisticated approach to acquisition efforts is to profile a company's current best customers and then attempt to find more of this type of customer through the purchase of external data. Such analysis is done by statisticians who use regression and related analytical approaches to determine those variables that are the most predictive about what kinds of prospects will purchase from the company and be profitable over the long term.

Customer profiling differs from traditional direct marketing testing because a variety of information may be included in the model. These variables may include such things as geographics (e.g., region of the country, ZIP code), demographics, psychographics (e.g., hobbies), and previous purchases from other companies.

For instance, during the early 1990s when the Lexus line of automobiles was introduced, marketing modelers determined that the most important variables that predicted whether an individual would purchase a new Lexus were income level (wealthier people were more likely to purchase), current car ownership (regardless of their incomes, people driving Mercedes were especially likely prospects), model year of their current cars (people driving cars that were three to four years old were especially good targets), and geographic area (people living within a certain radius of a dealership were more likely to be interested). The company decided to send this profile of potential customers a direct mailing that offered a gift of an auto safety kit or picnic basket just for test-driving the car. Although these items were expensive, the company found that the offer was necessary to get these busy people to visit the dealerships. The company also found that conversion rates after they did take a test-drive were high. The model, therefore, achieved its goal of allowing the company to efficiently target a valuable offer to those people who might be inclined to buy, while at the same time preventing the company from wasting money giving costly items away to people who were not likely to make a purchase.

One major advantage of such modeling is that it allows companies to focus on attracting customers who are likely to be profitable over the long term rather than only those who are likely to immediately respond. For instance, credit card companies have long used statistical modeling to solicit only those people who are likely to be valuable over the long run (mostly using variables from credit reports such as payment histories and outstanding debt). This technique has been especially useful for companies in this industry for two reasons:

1. Credit card companies do not want to extend credit to those people who are unlikely to pay their bills in the future, so it is important that they try to predict risk as well as response rates.
2. Even for customers who are likely to be responsible in paying bills, response rates for credit card solicitations tend to be so low that most companies do not make a profit for up to a year or more after people sign up for the card.

Therefore, looking at long-term profitability allows companies to direct solicitations to those customers who are likely to stay with the company in the future and to be willing to pay high interest rates on the larger sums of money that they have borrowed.

In some cases, statistical modeling may be used to direct different sorts of solicitations toward different kinds of customers. For instance, one cable company selling multiple services used a variety of data to promote cable modems to some potential customers and expanded cable TV packages to others. People with certain characteristics (e.g., under age 30, sports enthusiasts) received specific creative communications suited to their expected needs as well.

While some companies have had success in acquiring customers with this type of statistical modeling approach, others have found its applicability to be more limited. If the model is used to predict long-term profitability, data on individual customer's profitability over an extended period need to be available. As described earlier, many companies do not have this information organized appropriately and need to spend a substantial amount of time and effort to make it available.

In addition, commissioning a statistical model and then purchasing the necessary data about prospective customers to include is an expensive undertaking. Unless such activities substantially increase the ability of the company to efficiently target only those customers who will be especially profitable, the investment may not pay off. Unfortunately, because demographic data (the most prevalent type of information available for purchase from outside sources) is not generally very predictive of buying behaviors, models are not always as useful as might be hoped. Because it is difficult to know in advance how much efficiency will be obtained through such an endeavor, marketers commissioning analysts to develop such statistical models should be prepared for the possibility that the return on the investment may not pan out.

Also problematic is the assumption that a company's current best customers are its ideal customers. In many cases, this equation may be true, but in others, a change in strategic focus might allow the company to bring in people who look different from existing customers but who might prove to be very profitable over the long run if the organization made appropriate changes to serve their needs. This potential is especially likely when a company currently offers an undifferentiated product to a broad segment of the marketplace. In that case, the company's best customers look exactly like its competitors' best customers, and these people are solicited frequently by a variety of companies in the industry while other people are relatively ignored. For example, historically, in the credit card industry, people with good credit histories and large monthly balances have been bombarded with solicitations, whereas people who pay off their bills regularly are much more rarely targeted.

When companies want to solicit new customers who look similar to their current ones, the development of analytical models can sometimes increase the efficiency of a company's marketing efforts. This efficiency may occur because the model may allow a company to reduce marketing costs and improve response rates by targeting only those people who are likely to respond, at the moment in time when they are most likely to do so. Considering how expensive it is to solicit new customers, when it works right, this method can be very helpful. Nevertheless, companies that rely too heavily on the use of models to run their marketing efforts can easily lose sight of the fact that it may be more beneficial over the long run to try to find a core group of people who prefer the company's products or services to its competitors' and, therefore, are more likely to respond to its solicitations and to pay a premium price for its offerings.

In other words, analytical models should not replace strategic marketing thinking. Marketers working for companies where models are frequently and successfully used should still make an ongoing effort to consider whether their company is strategically positioned to offer something that is of unique value to a particular segment of the marketplace. If not, managers should consider how the organization might be able to accomplish that objective. Then they should implement necessary changes to appeal to desired customers even if what is done is not necessarily attractive to the current customers of the organization. If possible, this goal should be accomplished through the development of products and services that are customized for particular groups of customers, so that both existing and new customers are served optimally.

For example, a credit card company that has traditionally targeted business customers who are over their heads in debt but eventually do pay their bills (in the process incurring high amounts of interest and late fees) may develop specialized cards that target start-up businesses, established companies that are continuing to grow slowly and responsibly, or frequent travelers—all groups that have been previously ignored by such companies. If this is not possible, the organization may gradually make incremental changes that will make its products and services increasingly appealing to its desired customer base, even if it means that its offerings become somewhat less appealing to current customers. In many cases, the achievement of this goal may mean adding or refining benefits while raising prices. For example, Banana Republic gradually changed its apparel from basic casual clothing to more sophisticated items designed for fashion-conscious young business people. While some previously loyal customers were annoyed and stopped shopping at the stores, the large number of newer and more profitable customers made the change worthwhile.

After such new or revised products have been successfully introduced and new customers courted, analytical models may be developed to profile the most profitable members of this new customer segment, so that similar people can be recruited. This recruitment should not be done, however, until the organization has already made changes that are necessary to satisfy these new customers because otherwise the people who would ultimately have been the most valuable are less likely to stay with the organization. Even when such internal changes have been made, it always takes some time for people to learn about and believe in the ability of the company to serve their needs. This fact usually leads to a transition period in which analytical models suggest that traditional customers are more profitable than the new segment being targeted. It is, therefore, important that marketers in this situation not be discouraged and that they give their new strategies and customers sufficient time to become profitable rather than let an analytical model dictate their marketing strategy.

DEVELOPING AN ACQUISITION STRATEGY

Marketers wanting to make an active attempt to acquire customers for their companies need to attend to several different factors if they are to be successful. They need to determine the overall marketing strategy; that is, to figure out what type of customers they want to serve and what they can offer to those customers that the customers cannot obtain elsewhere. Otherwise, the company will inevitably be engaged in a battle for those customers with competitors, resulting in high acquisition costs and low retention rates. When this happens, long-term profitability becomes a difficult endeavor. Increasing the efficiency of prospecting efforts is of some help to companies offering undifferentiated products. However, to be truly successful over the long term, marketers will be better off if they can determine exactly what kind of competitive advantage they can offer rather than focus all of their attention on tactics that are designed merely to save money.

In addition, managers need to consider whether their organization is capable of serving the customers that it wants to reach. If the company's products or services are not going to be delivered appropriately, it is pointless or counterproductive to engage in active acquisition efforts because people who purchase for the first time and are dissatisfied are less likely to give the organization a second chance. Therefore, it is important for managers to get to know the people that they are targeting and to understand their needs and wants, and then to go about making any changes necessary to satisfy them. While improvements in products or services should certainly be an ongoing process, companies should ideally develop at least a minimum level of attractiveness (i.e., beyond what competitors can offer) to the particular customers that they are targeting before engaging in active prospecting efforts. Otherwise, customers will be unlikely to remain with the company and to pay a premium price for its products or services, and, therefore, the high costs associated with any acquisition effort are less likely to be recouped.

After the company's strategy is set and it is in a position to serve customers appropriately, managers should attempt to attract the right customers in as efficient and effective a manner as possible. As we have described, each of the available ways in which companies can prospect for customers has positives and negatives associated with it, and none is appropriate for all circumstances.

For example, companies that would find it practically or economically infeasible to create customer databases obviously need to use one-way mass media communications to communicate with prospects as well as customers. (Note that they can, nevertheless, focus their acquisition and retention efforts on a select group of customers with particular needs and wants that are not being met well by other companies rather than on the market as a whole.) Other companies that plan to engage in interactive customer relationships through the use of database marketing, but that find it difficult to predict who would be a good target through the benefits that their products or services offer, may need to "fish" for prospects through mass media, persuading people who are good targets to identify themselves so that a two-way relationship can begin being built. Finally, when appropriate external data is available, it may prove efficient to use direct mail or other forms of direct solicitation (including, cautiously, the Internet) to target those individuals who have been determined (through testing or through analysis of information about current customers) to be likely to make the most money for the company (immediately or over the long term).

CONCLUSION

It is up to the marketing manager to determine which of these approaches is likely to be the most successful in a particular situation. Most important, the marketer must ensure that the prospects being sought are more attracted to the company than to its competitors. When those people have been acquired, they must be satisfied enough with their experience to buy from the company in the future, to consider other products and services sold by the company, and to recommend the firm's offerings to other people. Only by focusing on this goal will companies manage to achieve success and profitability, both immediately and into the future.

CHAPTER 8

DATABASE SUB-SEGMENTATION

EDWARD C. MALTHOUSE

Great things can be reduced to small things, and small things can be reduced to nothing.

(Chinese proverb)

WHY SUB-SEGMENT A DATABASE?

This chapter discusses a critical component of any customer relationship management (CRM) strategy: sub-segmentation. Imagine that a company has successfully launched some product, which is usually targeted at a single market segment, and that it has compiled a database of information about its customers. A sub-segmentation partitions the database into smaller groups of customers, whose members are similar to each other.

At one extreme, it is possible to have groups of size one, which is the idea of one-to-one marketing.[1] This extremely fine segmentation is problematic in that it can be impractical to manage sub-segments of size one, particularly when the database is large. At the other extreme is one group, in which case every customer in the marketplace or database is treated in exactly the same way. Marketers have long recognized the problem with this view—that not all customers have the same wants, needs, and expectations of the product or service, even if the customers are all members of the same market segment. A sub-segmentation is a compromise between these two extremes, providing a practical way to tailor interactions with a customer.

The author thanks Bobby Calder, Robert Blattberg, Jock Bickert, and Scott Schroeder for helpful discussions on this topic.

Many companies want to offer customized versions of their products. The term *customization* has been used broadly to cover all aspects of interactions between customers and the company, including:[2]

- *Selection of benefits or features that are emphasized in communications:* Consider the Whole Foods supermarket chain, which targets both natural foods and gourmet shoppers with perishable and organic products. Even within these market segments, there are distinct groups with different motivations. Some customers shop there because of the gourmet products—to them, Whole Foods is the best place to find the freshest, high-quality, often difficult-to-find products to prepare gourmet meals. Another group of customers is loyal because of the selection of health foods—Whole Foods offers all-natural, organic products grown without pesticides. Still another group may shop there because of their political views on the environment. Whole Foods would want to emphasize different benefits to these different groups. For a second example, consider a telecommunications company that is sending offers for Internet services to existing residential telephone customers. The company would describe the service to a technophile in a different way than to a low-tech family wanting to provide Internet access for its children.
- *Configuration of the product or service:* Following the telecommunications example, the company may want to offer a different bundle of services to a technophile than to the family. Alternatively, a catalog company selling clothing, such as Lands' End, may want to create a special tabloid for a sub-segment of customers having an interest in outdoor activities.
- *Information communicated to the customer:* A financial service company may want to send a more detailed statement to its sophisticated investors and a minimal statement to customers who have only basic investments.

Companies often charge customers different prices for the same product or service. Credit card companies offer low interest rates for balance transfers and increase these rates after a period of time. The cost to renew a magazine subscription is sometimes higher than the cost of subscribing to the magazine through another offer.

Sometimes customization means "surprises and delights." An organization may want to show its appreciation to its best customers. American

Airlines sends fresh-baked cookies to its best customers. Hotels may surprise guests with chocolate before bed.

A particular supermarket chain may offer incentives, such as encouraging less profitable customers to shop during off-peak times to reduce their traffic in the store during peak times for their most valuable customers. Incentives are used to change the behavior of a group of customers.

HOW TO CUSTOMIZE?

A very difficult task is deciding exactly how to customize interactions between the organization and the customer. How should an organization decide among the numerous ways to configure the features of the product, the positioning, and so on? Answering this question is a central focus of this chapter. The solution begins with understanding the customers. When an organization understands why a sub-segment of customers chooses to use its goods or services, the way they use them, the way the products fit into their lifestyles, and their expectations, it becomes easier to customize interactions.

Many marketers have emphasized the importance of building long-term relationships through customer loyalty programs.[3] Sub-segmentation is a key component of a loyalty program. Once a company has acquired the "right customers," it wants to maximize its relevance with this customer base. A natural way to do this is to use the sub-segmentation methods described in this chapter.

One of the easiest and least costly ways to customize a product or service is to tailor its description to different segments. For example, an online catalog company used the Cohorts[4] system to sub-segment its database. When a customer visits the catalog's Web site, the company customizes the descriptions of its products. Consider the way it describes a particular sweater:

- When an "Alec and Elyse" (affluent empty-nesters with dual incomes who use their high discretionary income to enjoy all aspects of the good life) visit the site, they see: "Soft, natural fibers in honey-comb weave add a touch of style to your casual outings. Our 100 percent cotton sweater is perfect for an early morning stroll on the beach or a fireside aprés-ski with friends. Available in cranberry, heather, charcoal, loden, honey, jet, or ecru."
- The same sweater is described to an "Elwood and Willamae" (retired couples with modest incomes who dote on their grandchildren and,

> when not touring the United States, engage primarily in domestic pursuits) as follows: "From spring planting to fall harvesting, our cable-knit cotton sweater keeps you toasty warm. Sturdy weave resists snags and invites compliments. Available in red, light gray, dark gray, olive, yellow, black, or tan."

Customizations such as these have been shown to increase click-through and buy rates substantially.

Segmentation and sub-segmentation are tools to facilitate customization. The word *segmentation,* unfortunately, has many different meanings. To direct marketers, segmentation means a "scoring" model (a model that predicts the likelihood of customer response to an offer). To a brand manager, "Segmentation involves dividing the market of potential customers into homogeneous subgroups."[5] After segmenting the market of potential customers, the brand manager targets a brand at a single segment.

The approach described in this chapter—sub-segmentation—takes place after targeting a brand at a market segment and acquiring a database of customers. It divides a market segment into further subgroups. The marketing manager must have marketing plans for each sub-segment, because all sub-segments are customers. Other direct marketers use the term *customer segmentation* or *market segmentation* to describe this activity, but the term *sub-segmentation* is less ambiguous (even the term *customer* can mean different things to different marketers). Although the focus of this chapter is on sub-segmentation, many of the techniques described herein could also be used for market segmentation in data-rich environments.

TYPES OF DATABASE SUB-SEGMENTATIONS

Sub-segmentations can be categorized as off-the-shelf or customized. A sub-segmentation system that can be purchased from a company and applied to a database is called *off-the-shelf.* Off-the-shelf systems can be based on geodemographics (such as PRIZM[6]), which are defined using aggregate-level data such as census blocks and zip codes so that people living in the same neighborhood will belong to the same sub-segment. The underlying idea behind these systems is that "birds of a feather flock together." For example, neighborhoods with a PRIZM code of "Blue Blood Estates" have residents that tend to belong to a country club, watch golf on television, and read business magazines. Those living in "Shotguns and Pickups" tend to smoke pipe tobacco, drink Canadian whiskey, and read hunting, car, and truck magazines. Those in "Hispanic Mix" tend to buy dance music, use postal money orders, and read tabloids and fashion magazines.

Off-the-shelf approaches can also be based on household data (Cohorts[7]), which are defined using demographic and lifestyle data at the household level. Cohort groups are named using first names that commonly appear in them. For example, the "Stuart" group is composed of affluent, health- and fitness-minded men with investments and upscale interests. "Elmer" is composed of sedentary older men with fixed incomes and few interests beyond their grandchildren and gardens. "Kenny" is composed of younger men who spend their free time in the garage or outdoors. "Randy" is composed of single fathers who enjoy outdoor activities, home workshops, and electronic entertainment with their kids.

A second sub-segmentation system can be *customized;* that is, it is developed for a particular company. There are two types of customized sub-segmentations, depending on the data-mining methodology used to find the sub-segments. First, there are "unsupervised learning methods" (obvious splits, clustering, latent class analysis). This approach yields segments of people who are similar to each other on some customer attributes. For example, if age and income are used as the customer attributes, the resulting segments are "homogeneous within" and "heterogeneous across" with respect to age and income.

The second type of customized sub-segmentation is based on *supervised learning methods* like Chi-Squared Automatic Interaction Detector (CHAID) and bump hunting.[8] These approaches yield segments using a set of "predictor" variables that have similar values of some dependent variable, such as long-term value (LTV), attrition, and so forth.

If the objective of the analysis is to "explain" some criterion variable such as LTV or attrition, a supervised learning method is appropriate. If the objective is to find homogeneous groups with respect to the customer attributes, an unsupervised learning method is appropriate. Examples of both approaches are described later.

While there are many situations where it is appropriate to explain some dependent variable, we should note one limitation. Dependent variables are usually a function of what was done to customers in the past that influence whether a customer remains loyal. Estimates of customers' LTV are usually based on how similar groups of customers behaved in the past. These analyses raise some important questions: Is a sub-segment of unprofitable customers intrinsically unprofitable, or is it unprofitable only because of the way its members were marketed to in the past? If the product were reconfigured, would these customers become profitable? In using a dependent variable from the past, you are "marketing in the rear-view mirror." We shall see how unsupervised learning methods can escape the past by focusing on customer needs, wants, and motivations.

Examples Using Supervised Learning

One marketing question that was recently answered using these techniques is, "Who owns pets in the San Francisco Bay Area?" A bump-hunting analysis[9] of a large marketing research survey identified two sub-segments:

1. Age under 45; 14 or fewer years of education; lived in Bay Area four years or more; lives in a house or mobile home; ethnic background was White, East Indian, Native American, or unknown.
2. Number of children greater than 0; owns home; and ethnic background White, East Indian, Native American, or unknown.

The dependent variable is whether someone has a pet. The "customer attributes" (predictor variables) are demographic variables.

Another marketing question addressed through these methods is, "Who is likely to cancel their membership?" A company sells different types of memberships for its services, which cost different amounts and offer different levels of service. New members make an initial down payment and, if they do not pay the entire cost of the membership up front, a monthly payment. They can select among monthly payment methods: checking electronic fund transfer (EFT), credit card EFT, or check. With the EFT methods, the monthly payment is paid automatically from a credit card or checking account.

The company sought to identify types of people who are likely to cancel their memberships within the first three months of membership. It wanted to define the sub-segments based on what is known about the members one month after joining. This information includes age and gender, total cost of membership, type of membership, down payment amount, monthly payment amount, method of payment, number of times that the member used the service during the first month, and enrollment date.

Figure 8.1 shows a Classification and Regression Trees (CART) model applied to this scenario. CART functions by splitting the database on the customer attributes. In this example, the first split is on the amount of the down payment. Those customers with a down payment over $73 have a 3.98 percent default rate. The CART technique performs no additional splits on this group, hence it is a sub-segment. Those customers with a down payment of $73 or less have a default rate of 23.69 percent. This

Figure 8.1
CART Sub-Segments for Attrition Example

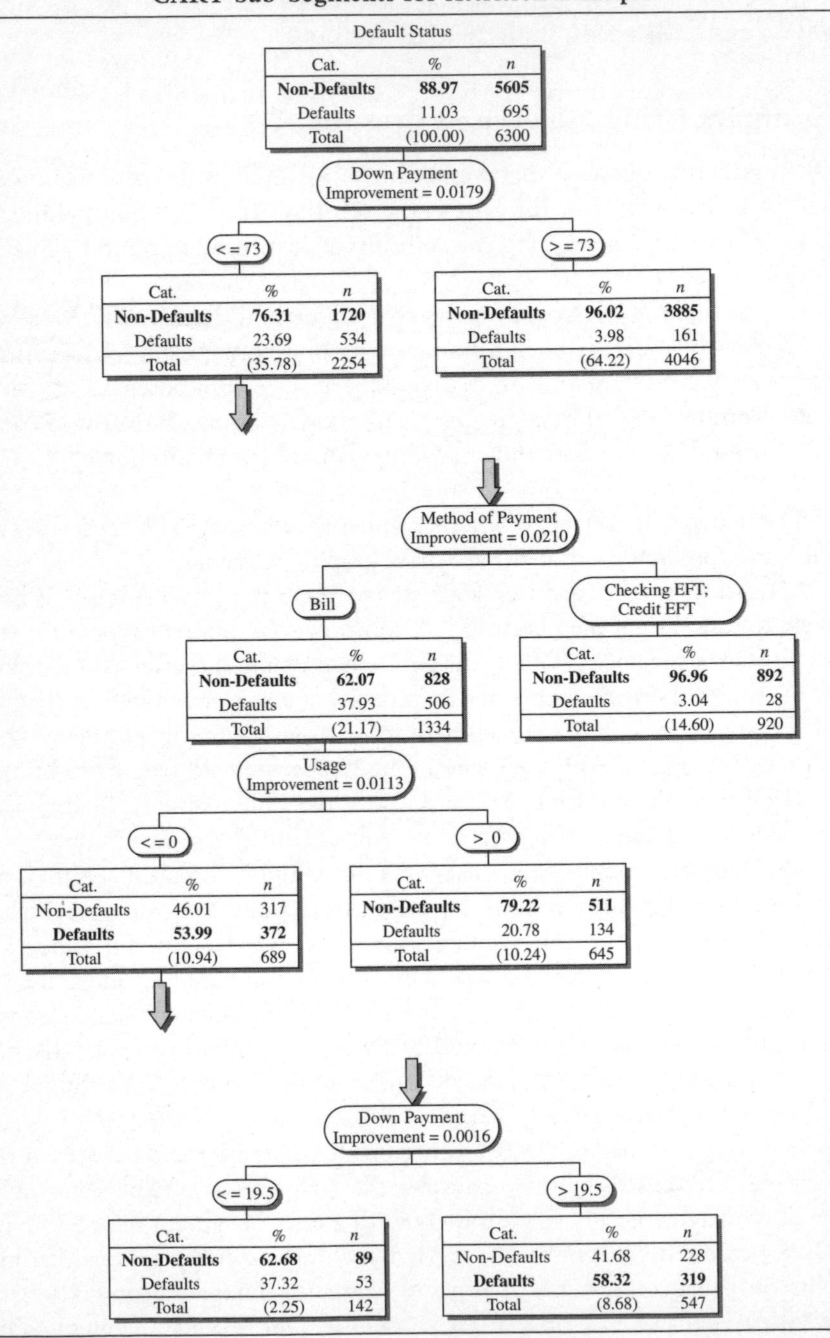

group is split further on their payment method. Those customers with a down payment of $73 or less *and* some form of EFT payment have a 3.04 percent default rate. This group is not split into finer distinctions, hence it is the second sub-segment. Those customers who pay bills have a 37.93 percent default rate. This group can be split further by usage. Those who use the service have a 20.78 percent default rate, while those who do not use the service have a 53.99 percent response rate. The latter group is split once more on down payment size.

The boxes without any further splits are called *terminal nodes* and are the sub-segments. The CART model has identified five sub-segments with different default rates. A useful story emerges from these results for the marketing manager: Those with large down payments or EFT payment methods are not likely to cancel. A small down payment and the billing method is a bad combination, especially if the customers are not using the service. The company should consider discontinuing the billing method, or it could provide incentives for people to use the EFT methods. It should also consider offering incentives to get new members to make large down payments and encourage inactive new members to use the service.

The sub-segments offer interesting findings, but leave many questions unanswered. Why do some people join but never use the service? Why do those who use the services at least once cancel? Are they dissatisfied with the experience? Why did they join in the first place? While some of these questions could be answered with qualitative marketing research, it is possible that the reasons are unrelated to segment membership. An alternative approach is to define segments entirely using these types of attributes. The process of doing so is described in the next section.

Example Using Unsupervised Learning

Different analytical methods were used to address another firm's marketing question. Specifically, a cellular phone company[10] wanted to identify sub-segments among its current customers. The company had available data on each customer's cell phone usage and demographics. The following segments were identified using latent class analysis:

- *Communicating families:* Families with multiservice accounts, above-average revenue, higher than average roaming usage, and a tendency to make calls of short duration.
- *New customers:* Those with less than three months of data and slightly below-average revenue.

- *Convenience users:* Single-service customers with "convenience" price plans. They tend to use more than their allowed minutes and have a high proportion of weekend calling.
- *Safety users:* Based on usage patterns, these customers seem to have their phones for security reasons. This is the largest segment, and members tend to have long-term relationships, but they contribute a small proportion of total revenue.
- *Super users:* Customers have multiple services, heavy usage, digital price plans, and the highest revenue per account. They tend to exceed time allowances. There is a high representation of business customers.

After classifying customers into one of these five segments, the company can customize its marketing activities. The Super users have the highest usage and generate a disproportionately high amount of revenue. A top priority should be to keep this segment loyal. The company should do some further research to understand the needs of this segment better. This research should also identify sub-segments and design special loyalty programs.

The Communicating Families group also generates a disproportionately high amount of revenue, and the company should invest in keeping them loyal and extending its relationship with these customers. This segment has a low percentage of users with digital phones, yet digital price plans are more convenient for the user and easier for the company to service. Therefore, the company should offer incentives to these customers to switch from analog to digital services.

The Convenience users are a large segment, although they do not contribute exceptional amounts of revenue. The company has an overriding goal of retaining customers. Given that these customers regularly exceed their allowed minutes, it might make sense to offer them price plans with more allowed minutes and a higher minimum monthly charge. Finally, the Safety users generate little revenue, and their profitability could be evaluated further.

The key point of this example is to show how a company can use sub-segmentation to help it create configurations of its product or service.

THE UNSUPERVISED SUB-SEGMENTATION PROCESS

The basic steps in conducting an unsupervised sub-segmentation are as follows:

1. Perform the initial splits.
2. Select bases for sub-segmentation; that is, attributes to define the sub-segments or provide hypothetical, likely sub-segments.
3. Identify the variables in the database that relate to the attributes, or collect same via survey.
4. Develop the segments (using judgment, cluster analysis, or latent class analysis).
5. Profile the segments.
6. Develop and implement more relevant marketing and communications programs.

Initial Splits

If groups of customers are obviously in different segments, the database marketer should first form groups and then sub-segment within each group. Do not make your data-mining technique do the obvious. For example, a bank may have customers that are large businesses, small businesses, wealthy consumers, and other consumers.[11] Because there is probably no reason that large businesses and individual consumers would ever be in the same segment, it makes sense to treat them as separate groups. The bank then finds sub-segments within the large businesses, small businesses, and so on.

Credit card companies often do an initial split based on whether the cardholder carries a revolving balance. Those who carry a revolving balance are called *revolvers,* and those who pay their bills off in full each month are called *transactors.* Credit card companies also do an initial split on active and inactive cardholders. An inactive cardholder is one who has a credit card but never uses it nor carries a revolving balance.

Another common initial split is based on profitability. An organization may have a group of customers that have not been, and probably will not become, profitable to serve. It might make sense to drop these customers from further sub-segmentation efforts.

Catalog companies do initial splits based on whether a customer is "new," meaning that the customer has made a purchase for the first time within a certain recent duration. One reason for this split is that the nature of data available on new customers is quite different from data on others. By definition, the previous purchase history is skimpy for a new customer. Often the contact history, the record of previous solicitations sent to the customer, is also short. The company may have only the source of the name and one order.

Publishers form an initial split on "bad debt," indicating that a customer has subscribed to a magazine but did not pay for it. Those people may be eliminated from future mailings.

Dell's Web site illustrates an initial split. Visitors are asked to select between consumer, business (small, medium, and large), and public (state versus local, federal, education, health care).[12] A large business would want to buy a very different type of computer from the type that the typical consumer would want. Why distract customers by showing them products they would never buy?

Select Basis for the Sub-Segmentation

Perhaps the most difficult and important step in developing sub-segments is selecting the attributes that will be used to define them. Seemingly unlimited attributes can be measured on customers—so which should be used?

The way people are grouped depends on the attributes used to define the sub-segments. People are grouped one way if height is used to define sub-segments and a completely different way if political views are used. Selecting the attributes is a subjective task, one that is presumably informed with experience and knowledge of the industry, category, and brand.

Selecting the attributes requires striking a balance between many, often conflicting, objectives. The choice depends on:

- The objectives of the customizations to be done.
- The data available for developing the sub-segments.
- The data available for implementing the customized marketing programs.

Two (Conflicting?) Objectives. One seemingly straightforward objective is that the marketing manager should be able to take action as a result of the sub-segments that are identified. At the same time, we often want to identify the sub-segment membership of everyone in the database with reasonable accuracy. Objectives may be incompatible, and selecting attributes requires striking a balance between them. Sometimes we can think of groups that would be great to have, because we can envision "perfect" marketing programs for each; however, it may not be possible to classify these members of the database accurately. Conversely, using the information available for everyone in a database may yield rather bland segments that do not lend themselves to the creation of relevant marketing programs.

The marketing manager should participate in the selection of attributes. The data-miner cannot do this step alone; the result is often a sub-segmentation system that is not actionable and that is never used. The manager usually has important knowledge about what can be done from a marketing perspective and, at least intuitively, about what types of customers exist. The brand manager and data-miner should always have a discussion about what can be done differently from a marketing perspective. What are the marketing objectives? What tactics can be considered? For example, is it possible to change only the way the product is described in the offer? Or, is it also possible to create versions of the product by creating different configurations of features?

The first criterion may seem obvious, but it is difficult to do well. Some thought exercises may be useful before jumping into the data. First ask, "If I formed sub-segments based on a certain set of attributes, what types of groups are likely to result?" Anticipate the results from the cluster analysis; hypothesize the resulting sub-segments. Second, "What sorts of marketing programs could be offered to each of the groups?" If the answer to the second question is that there is little that could be done differently to the groups, the attributes selected are probably not good.

Types of Data. Before discussing the second criterion (assigning everyone to a segment with reasonable accuracy), we must summarize the types of data available to companies. The data available to database marketing can be classified into three general types:

1. Data are available for everyone, including purchase and contact histories; other behavioral data such as in-bound telephone calls; payment information (VISA, MasterCard, house credit card, American Express; does the customer pay on time?); information that is gathered at the time of enrollment; and, in the United States, city block-level demographics from the census. The amount of this type of information available often depends on the length of the relationship with the customer. A credit card or catalog company knows far more about the consumption habits of a long-term customer than a new customer.
2. Data are available for a somewhat representative sample from the database, such as marketing research survey data. Syndicated sources of marketing research data such as Simmons, Scarborough, and Mediamark Research Institute also may fit into this category, as well as some demographic or lifestyle data.

3. Data are available for a convenience sample (not representative) from the database. For example, the database may contain indicators of hobbies and interests. Some interest variables are populated by mail-order purchases. An individual has an interest in gardening if he or she has purchased gardening supplies from mail-order catalogs in the past. Another gardening interest indicator variable might take the value "yes" if an individual has subscribed to any gardening publication in the past. Yet, these gardening indicators are flawed—a person could be keen on gardening without making mail-order purchases or subscribing to gardening magazines. Conversely, someone without an interest in gardening could purchase gardening magazines or supplies through the mail as gifts.

There are some important points to consider regarding different types of data. For example, it is best to use data available for everyone whenever possible, because it can be difficult to classify those not part of a sample into a sub-segment. For example, if a sub-segmentation is defined by a customer's education, but education is available only for a sample, how should someone whose education is unknown be classified? In addition, note that marketing research surveys can gather information about virtually any topic of interest to the marketer, but they are usually substantially more expensive than using variables already available from syndicated sources.

When a sub-segmentation is developed with data from a representative sample, variables from a convenience sample can be useful in classifying people not in the representative sample. For example, suppose a marketing research survey of 2,000 people was used to develop sub-segments, including a gardening variable. A gardening interest indicator from an overlaying data source can be useful in assigning to sub-segments people who were not in the focal marketing research survey.

There has been little success in using variables from a convenience sample to develop the sub-segments themselves (as variables in a cluster analysis). If the only available data come from a convenience sample, it is important to understand how the data were collected, the biases inherent in the collection process, and how the biases will affect the conclusions.

Sub-Segmentations Based On Survey Data and Survey Projection. Sub-segmentations based only on data that are available for everyone can be bland, in that the marketing programs created from them do not really connect with a customer. In these cases, the company wants to develop the sub-segmentation using survey data and then *project* the sub-segments onto the entire database. Another application of projection occurs when segments are developed using information that is available only for customers who have been active for, say, six months. The task of classifying a new customer to one of these segments requires projection.

Projection[13] means developing a classification model, such as CART, generalized logistic regression, feed-forward neural networks, or discriminant analysis, to classify people.[14] Information that is available for everyone is used to make the classifications. The problem with this approach is that the classifications are sometimes not sufficiently accurate. When this is the case, the company misses an opportunity to be relevant and may even do more harm than good with the sub-segmentation. For example, suppose that a customer is really a "Stuart," borrowing sub-segment names from the Cohorts system. Stuart is an affluent, health- and fitness-minded man with good investing habits and upscale interests. The classification model, however, is not so accurate and misclassifies the customer as an Elmer, who is a sedentary older man on a fixed income who has few interests beyond his garden and grandchildren. The company sends offers to the Stuart that are intended for an Elmer, and the result will surely be reduced response rates.

When survey data have been used to develop the sub-segmentation and classification models make insufficiently accurate classifications, the company can improve classification rates by asking supplementary questions. This additional data collection is particularly practical with Web sites. For example, the Lands' End Web site offers the Personal Shopper option. The first time shoppers use this option, they are first shown about six pairs of outfits and asked which they prefer. Next, they are asked whether there are certain types of clothing that they would never wear, such as wool, suede, polyester blends, plaids, stripes, and various colors. The rest of the Web session is customized based on the responses to these and other questions.

Other companies ask supplementary questions in billing statements. For example, after subscribing to a magazine, customers may receive a short questionnaire about their interests, which are used to craft more targeted cross-selling offers, and perhaps also more sophisticated sub-segmentation schemes.

The decision to gather additional information should be based on several factors. These include: (1) the cost of acquiring the information, (2) the degree to which the additional information improves classifications, (3) the degree to which improved classifications allow for more relevant marketing and profitability, and (4) response rates.

Ideally, the decision can be quantified. For example, suppose a catalog company is interested in maximizing its customers' average order size. The firm has developed a sub-segmentation system using survey data, but it cannot classify people with perfect accuracy using only information available for everyone. Asking additional questions improves the accuracy of classifications. The catalog company should then measure average order size if it uses a one-size-fits-all approach, customized marketing without asking additional questions (resulting in higher misclassification rates), and customized marketing with additional questions (resulting in lower misclassification rates). The catalog company should also quantify the additional cost of creating customized marketing programs and the additional cost of gathering additional information. In doing so, it can make a final judgment about the optimal approach.

Customer-Insight versus Reach, Frequency, and Monetary (RFM) or Demographic Sub-Segmentations. The purpose of a database sub-segmentation is to make more relevant connections with customers. Certain databases facilitate these connections more than others. For example, consider sub-segmenting a database on monetary value: How profitable has a customer been over the past two years? A more sophisticated version of this is long-term value: What is the (discounted) amount that the company expects to make from a customer over the next three years? Suppose, as is usually the case, there is a sub-segment of 20 percent of the customers that account for 80 percent of profits. Obviously, this group is very important and the company should invest heavily in keeping it loyal; for without it, the company will certainly face financial difficulties. But how does the company achieve more relevant connections with this group if it knows only that they are worth "X" dollars each over the next "Y" years? Monetary value often ignores these important questions:

- Why are these customers buying the company's products?
- How does the product fit into their lifestyles?
- What do the customers value in the products?
- What can be done for this group to grow loyalty?
- How can the company better serve them?
- What rewards or incentives do they value?

Different customers in this prized 20 percent might have different answers to these questions.

Another problem with monetary value is that it is heavily influenced by the way the product was marketed in the past. There could be customers who are not currently highly profitable, but could become highly profitable if the product were configured differently. As a simple example, suppose that a company has targeted high-end power users in the past. The firm learns that there is a sizable sub-segment of low-tech families who want to provide basic Internet access to their children, and that this sub-segment is being underserved in the company's market. The packages it currently offers are not well received by this sub-segment. If the company created different packages designed to meet the needs of this sub-segment, it could become a valuable sub-segment.

Adding *recency/frequency* (RFM) or demographics to the mix often does not help. For example, suppose there is a group of customers that is highly profitable, whose ages are between 50 and 65 years old, and whose household incomes exceed $100,000. We still cannot answer the previous questions. Sub-segmentations based entirely on RFM and demographic variables are nondiagnostic in that they do not help a company achieve a lasting connection with customers. These variables should not be ignored. Rather, they should be used in conjunction with variables that get at customers' motivations for using the product.

Identify Variables in the Database that Relate to the Expected Segments, or Use Survey Data

After selecting the general attributes that will be used to sub-segment a database, the next step is to operationalize ideas about the expected segments. Customers must next be classified in the database into one (or possibly two or three)[15] of the types. To do so, we must find the variables in the database that are indicative of the hypothesized sub-segments.

It often helps to conceptualize sub-segmentations at a higher level than the individual variables that are available. For example, a publisher may want to identify people who are interested in keeping physically fit. Their discussions about the hypothesized sub-segments should be about people who keep fit versus those who do not. To operationalize the notion of keeping fit, an analyst must identify variables in the database that are indicative, such as lifestyle variables indicating an interest in running, sailing, tennis, sports in general, and so forth. The individual indicators are combined using data-mining methods to form a composite measure of interest in keeping fit.

As a second example, a supermarket chain with a frequent-buyer program may be interested in sub-segmenting based on whether a person has a healthy diet. The conceptualization of the segments takes place at the level of people who eat a healthy diet and people who do not. To operationalize this notion, the supermarket might look at what these customers have purchased in the past. They would classify certain items as being healthy, such as fresh fruits and vegetables, and others as being unhealthy. They would form a composite measure based on previous buying patterns indicating how healthy a person's diet is.

The higher-level concepts are sometimes called *latent variables*. They are concepts that cannot be directly measured and about which we can make inferences only. Latent variables are common in marketing research. For further discussion, see a good textbook on marketing research.[16]
An important advantage of thinking in terms of latent variables is that they provide great simplification. The task of forming strategies by considering the tens of thousands of Stock Keeping Units (SKUs) offered by the typical supermarket is overwhelming. There would be far too much detail, and the details would likely only cloud your reasoning.

Develop Segments

Sub-segments are usually formed with one of the following methods.

Judgment/Obvious Splits. When only a few variables are to be used in defining the segments, the *obvious split* approach is reasonable. This approach uses judgment to select certain values to form splits of the variables. For example, a catalog company might want to form segments using only the average size of previous orders—large, medium, and small. A reasonable approach would be to select cut points such as $25 and $50; orders less than $25 are "small," between $25 and $50 are "medium," and greater than $50 are "large." Alternatively, the catalog company could examine the distribution of their customers' average order size before selecting the cut points and then choose those three roughly equally sized groups, or identify the top 20 percent of the customers, the vast middle, and the bottom 20 percent.

When there are two variables, it is common to form obvious splits on both and then look at combinations of groups in a grid. For example, a catalog company may want to form segments based on recency and frequency. In the grid shown in Table 8.1, there are two variables rather than one, but the principle is the same in terms of looking for trends in the data.

Cluster Analysis. A problem with obvious splits arises when there are many variables. The number of combinations of variables grows quickly with the number of sub-segments and can become overwhelming. Cluster analysis[17] provides a way of finding natural groupings of customers, especially when multiple variables are to be used in defining the groups.

Table 8.1
Example of Split Sub-Segmentation using Recency and Frequency

	Recency		
Frequency	*< 1 year*	*1–2 years*	*2+ years*
1 time			
2 times			
3+ times			

Latent Class Analysis (LCA). LCA[18] performs a task similar to cluster analysis in that it finds natural groups of customers based on multiple variables. One advantage that LCA has over some forms of cluster analysis (such as the popular *k-means*) is that LCA is specifically designed to handle categorical variables. Once the attributes have been selected and a data set compiled, it is easy to find segments using either cluster analysis or LCA. The choice of a solution should be based on how actionable it is.

Selecting the Number of Segments. Judgment, cluster analysis, and LCA all require the analyst to decide how many sub-segments should be extracted. This decision should first be governed by marginal cost/revenue considerations. Marginal cost/revenue can be used to identify a ballpark number of sub-segments; for example, 5, 10, 20, 50, 100, 200.

Adding sub-segments usually increases costs. A company may have to hire additional people to create the additional customizations. It may encounter programming or other costs to implement customization. Costs depend in part on how much the process of creating customizations can be automated with technology.

At the same time, additional segments should allow the company to become more relevant to its customers. The company should enjoy higher retention and response rates, larger order sizes or donations, more card usage, and higher long-term customer values. The ballpark number of segments should be where the additional (marginal) cost of managing segments equals the marginal benefit of adding more. Marginal cost and revenue are often difficult to estimate at the time a sub-segmentation system is being developed. The revenue generated through customization is partly a function of intangibles such as the marketing manager's creativity.

Once a ballpark number has been determined, the data-miner and marketing manager must agree on a specific number and solution. At this point, the data-miner should find candidate solutions using data. For example, perhaps the ballpark number is 10. The data-miner might find various 8 to 12 sub-segment solutions. The solution ultimately selected must make good business sense. Some software packages offer statistics that evaluate, for example, how well a particular cluster solution "fits the data,"[19] but there is no magical way of determining the "correct" number of sub-segments for a specific marketing application.

Profile Segments

After sub-segments have been selected, the next step is to learn more about each one. This investigation is conducted by comparing the segments on variables that were not used to define them. A company may want to do further qualitative marketing research on segments, for example, by conducting in-depth personal interviews. Additional quantitative marketing research may be necessary if the sub-segments are defined using, for example, only previous purchase history.

The Case of Country[20]

We present a case of a publisher to illustrate steps 1 through 5. In addition, after these steps have been demonstrated, we show how these analyses lend themselves to step 6, which is "to develop and implement more relevant marketing and communications programs."*Country Homes* and *Country Living* have accumulated large databases of loyal readers who subscribe to the magazines, which they currently receive every month or so. The publisher wondered whether it was possible to expand the relationship with these people. Is it possible to connect with these people beyond their reading the magazines?

In talking with readers of these magazines, we learned that for many of them, a country lifestyle is far more than reading country magazines. *Country* often symbolizes a quiet escape from all the pressures and noise of daily life. It represents a way to relax and return to simpler values. Many of the readers also actively participate in "country activities," which are as diverse as the contents of these magazines and include gardening, home decorating, cooking, quilting, sewing, antiques, and travel to country inns.

Are there ways for these magazines to provide additional country moments? We believe so. Our qualitative research suggests that not everyone is interested in the same types of country moments. We also sense that any publisher attempting to expand its relationships with readers had better be relevant. Not everyone is interested in bed-and-breakfast travel.

Standardized, one-size-fits-all offers seem to lack the intimacy expected by readers. To develop and sell additional country moments, we need to answer several questions.

Are there sub-segments (types) of readers? How large are these sub-segments? It is certainly not practical to develop customized country moments for everyone in a database, but it should be practical to develop several distinct types of country moments. How can the publisher identify these types? The answer is to start by identifying sizeable groups in the database with distinct country interests.

After finding sub-segments, we need a way to classify readers. To which sub-segment does everyone in the database belong? How likely is it for each individual to be a member of each of the sub-segments? With this information, a publisher can send offers that are more relevant.

Finally, what else do we know about each sub-segment? What else do the members of a particular sub-segment do in their free time? Could we describe their lifestyles? What are their demographics? This information also helps in developing relevant country moments.

If those are the marketing questions, the marketing research questions are these: How should these marketing questions be addressed? What sort of research design is required? A quantitative design is probably necessary. We would need information from a large, representative sample from the database, or perhaps even the entire database. A qualitative design would not allow us to estimate the size of the sub-segments, develop a classification methodology, or do some of the profiling, although some additional qualitative research could be very useful in further understanding lifestyles and motivations.

Data Sources. There are two possible sources of data. The company could use either a survey or other data it has about customers (such as other subscriptions they own). The advantages of one method tend to be the disadvantages of the other. An advantage of using existing (secondary) data is low cost; these data are much cheaper than surveys. Large publishers likely have a large amount of such information already in the database. Another advantage is that it is possible to know the values of "hobbies and interests" variables for a large number of people in the database, which makes classifying people into sub-segments much easier; if we use a survey of 3,000 people to develop the segments, how do we accurately classify the remainder of the database?

A major disadvantage of syndicated data is data quality. The information is not available for everyone in the database, and the sample of names for whom data are available may not be representative of the entire database. Not all characteristics of interest to us will be available from data providers, and whatever is available will not be exactly what we want. For example, many data providers offer a variable that indicates an "interest in travel." But what does "travel" mean? If it means visiting bed-and-breakfasts in the country, then travel is a country activity. If travel means flying to New York City for the weekend and staying at a four-star hotel in Manhattan, then it is not country. One data provider uses the wording, "Someone in my home participates in the following activities" and then lists many activities including "Travel-U.S." Travel could thus mean either of these forms of travel. With a survey, we could ask specifically about bed-and-breakfasts and country inns. Also, it would be nice to be able to distinguish between infrequent and frequent travelers; the indicator variable mentioned previously would not allow this.

We have a random sample from the database of a country magazine with extensive overlay variables, and we use these data in this example. The publisher who provided us with this data has supplemented it with additional information from multiple sources, so that the values of these variables are known for a large fraction of households in their database. Sources of additional information include information about other magazine subscriptions and self-reported data from short questionnaires included in billing statements. Because of the care this company has taken to assemble a reliable set of variables, it is reasonable to start with this information. If the sub-segments that result are nonsensical or not actionable, the publisher can always take the survey route later.

Selecting a Basis. We want to be able to offer customized country moments that fit into subscribers' lifestyles. To create these country moments, we need to know what types of country activities are of interest to individual readers. Therefore, the attributes should include indicators of how people spend their free time engaging in country activities. Note that we are not using demographic information or previous purchase information. We feel that the most effective way to connect with these people is to focus on something important to them, namely, how they choose to spend their free time.

Selecting Variables. We now select the variables to be used in the cluster analysis to define the sub-segments. Table 8.2 gives a list of variables that are commonly available from overlay variable providers. A critical question is: Which should be used to define the sub-segments? The key point of this section is that selecting variables requires a deep understanding of the brand

Table 8.2
Common "Hobbies and Interests" Variables to Overlay and Supplement Demographics

Upscale merchandise	Decorating	Quilting
Gardening	Do it yourself (DIY)	Cooking
Crafts	Sports	Collectibles
Needlework/cross stitch	Golf	Music/video
Sewing	Travel	Fashion
Woodworking	Books	

itself and of the types of marketing programs that will be created for sub-segments.

For example, if we include golf, the data-mining methods will find some segments that like to golf and others that do not like to golf. But is this characteristic useful in creating country moments? The answer would be yes if we were planning to create some country moments that center around golf. However, if golf has nothing to do with the types of marketing programs that are created, it should not be used. Based on the types of programs we envision creating and our understanding of the country brand, we decided to omit golf. Golf does not seem to be much of a distinguishing country activity.

We also dropped travel, for reasons mentioned earlier–"travel" is too broad. Gardening, cooking, decorating, collectibles, and crafts have similar problems. Not all types of gardening are country. Nevertheless, we feel that these activities are closer to the country concept and should be included. Sewing, quilting, and needlework are probably all less ambiguously country and were also included.

Sub-Segmentation Methodology. The first step in developing a customized sub-segmentation is to choose whether to proceed with a methodology that involves a dependent variable or one that does not. Should we use CHAID/bump-hunting or some clustering method? For this particular problem, there is no obvious dependent variable. We might be tempted to use something like number of previous subscriptions or total dollars from previous subscriptions, but these would not suit our present purpose. We are not trying to sell these people more subscriptions, nor do we want to identify groups of people based on their free time activities who have a large or small number of subscriptions, and so forth. Without a dependent variable, we cannot use CHIAD or bump-hunting; thus, some sort of clustering is appropriate.

The choice between cluster analysis and latent class analysis partly depends on the type of data we intend to use. If we intend to use many categorical variables, we would certainly want to consider latent class analysis. Otherwise, *k*-means clustering often produces satisfactory results.

We decided to use *k*-means clustering. We ran several different solutions and selected the one that seemed the most actionable to us. The key question was whether we could think of distinct things to do for each sub-segment. The cluster means are shown in Figure 8.2 in a multipanel dot-plot. A cluster's average interest in an activity is indicated with a dot; the dotted line indicates the average interest in an activity. Dots to the right

Figure 8.2
Five-Cluster Solution for "Country" Case

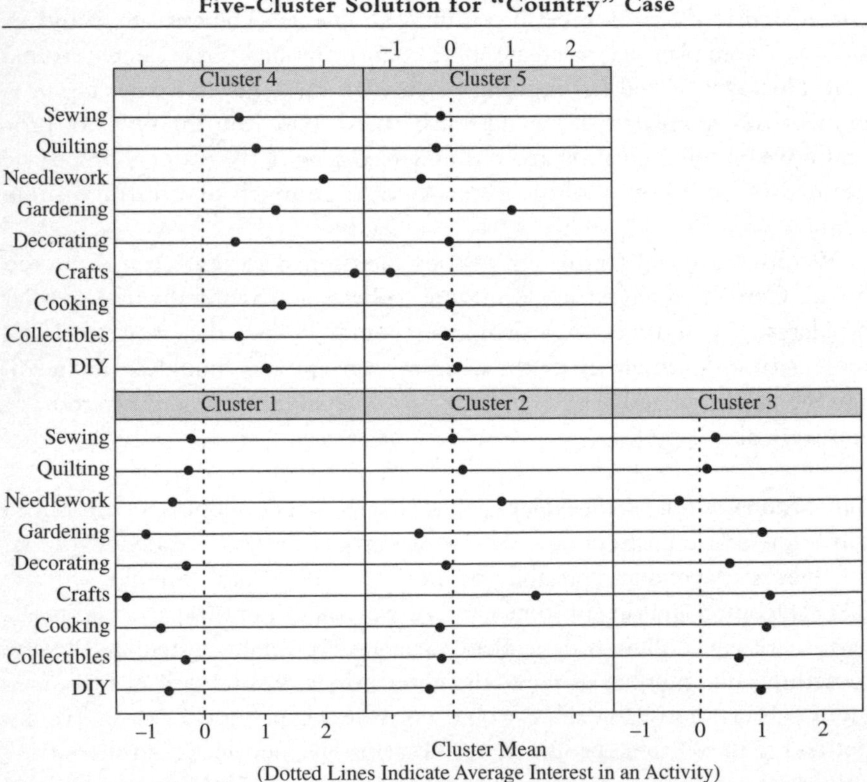

of the line indicate above-average interest in an activity; dots to the left indicate below-average interest. Our interpretations of the clusters follow:

Cluster 1, *Dreamers,* has below-average interest in all activities. We profiled the clusters on demographic variables and found this group to be younger and more likely to be employed than the others. We, therefore, hypothesize that this group is composed of armchair country people. They do not currently engage in country activities, perhaps because they do not have time.[21] When they receive an issue of the magazine, they go to their favorite armchair and escape from their busy lives. When members of this group retire, perhaps many of them will become more active participants in country activities. This character sketch could be confirmed with further marketing research.

Cluster 2, *Crafters,* has above-average interest in crafts and needlework, and roughly average interests in the other activities. They are a bit below average on gardening.

Cluster 3, *Active, No Needles,* has above-average interest in anything that does not involve needles. That is, they are not interested in sewing, quilting, or needlework.

Cluster 4, *Do Alls,* has above-average interest in everything. They are also the oldest group and the most likely to be retired or homemakers. They are particularly interested in crafts and needlework.

Cluster 5, *Gardeners,* is particularly interested in gardening. They have roughly average interest in the other activities, with the exception of crafts.

The relative sizes of the clusters are 40 percent, 16 percent, 17 percent, 11 percent, and 17 percent, respectively. Usually, the main thing to look for in cluster size is that a group is not tiny. A tiny group may not have enough people to justify creating customized marketing programs. (When tiny groups result from a cluster analysis, the cause is often statistical outliers.)

Marketing Programs. We have identified sub-segments with different lifestyles. Now it is the marketing manager's job to create customized country moments for them. First, consider the Gardeners. One way to expand a relationship with this sub-segment is to create additional publications for them. For example, the specialized magazine *Country Gardens* would appeal to this group. There are also books designed for this sub-segment including *Kitchen Garden Planner* and *Garden Aviary*. But the publisher should not stop with additional books and magazines. It owns a great brand and has a database of names that connect with the brand and have an interest in gardening. It should consider forming partnerships with other companies that sell gardening accessories, such as seeds, gloves, furniture for the garden, and so forth.

The obvious way to sell, for instance, genuine country heirloom tomato seeds, is through direct mail via catalogs. If, however, there are concentrations of country gardeners in certain geographic areas, it might make sense to investigate distribution through retail centers. You could visualize a "Country Corner" at local gardening supply stores and use the database and direct mail to promote it.

It is important to note that these cross-selling efforts must be consistent with the country brand. The country brand represents quiet, simple, old-fashioned values. Partnering with a company whose reputation is incongruent with the values is not recommended.

A different tack would be required for the Dreamers, because this group does not seem to be actively engaging in any country activities. If this is indeed the case, the way to expand a relationship with this group is to make it easy to sample country experiences. Perhaps this group would be interested in adding more country to their life by taking a "Country Getaway," staying at a specially selected bed-and-breakfast in their area, visiting suggested antique stores, touring country gardens, and enjoying country-style meals. Alternatively, perhaps they would be interested in house tours, where they can get decorating ideas from other people who share their values. We could also hypothesize that this group would like to engage in country activities, but does not currently. If this were true, then perhaps they would be interested in, for example, furniture refinishing classes.

The marketing possibilities are limitless. The key points of this example are as follows:

- The sub-segmentation is used to select among all the possible ways of expanding a relationship with these customers.
- The attributes used to sub-segment the database go beyond demographics and recency and frequency. By using leisure activities, we are able to connect with subscribers in a way that is important to them—how they choose to spend their free time.
- All subsequent marketing programs are consistent with the brand.

CONCLUSION

This country case illustrates, in some detail, the points presented in this chapter. The techniques and analytical choices in identifying sub-segments are important, but the goal is most important of all. Namely, the understanding of sub-segments can prove to be an extremely useful marketing tool.

Notes

1. Don Peppers and Martha Rogers, *Enterprise One to One: Tools for Competing in the Interactive Age* (New York: Currency Doubleday, 1999).
2. David Shepard, *The New Direct Marketing: How to Implement a Profit-Driven Database Marketing Strategy,* 3rd ed. (New York: McGraw-Hill, 1999), Chapter 35.
3. See Tom Collinger's chapter in this volume, and Frederick Reichheld, *The Loyalty Effect* (Boston: Harvard Business School Press, 1996).
4. See www.cohorts.com.
5. Brian Sternthal and Alice M. Tybout, "Segmentation and Targeting," in *Kellogg on Marketing,* ed. Dawn Iacobucci (New York: Wiley, 2001), p. 3.
6. See www.claritas.com.
7. Jock Bickert, "Cohorts: A New Approach to Market Segmentation," *Journal of Consumer Marketing,* vol. 14, no. 5 (1997), pp. 362–377.
8. Trevor Hastie, Robert Tibshirani, and Jerome H. Friedman, *The Elements of Statistical Learning: Data Mining, Inference and Prediction* (New York: Springer-Verlag, 2001).
9. See Jerome H. Friedman and Nicholas I. Fisher, "Bump Hunting in High-Dimensional Data," *Statistics and Computing,* vol. 9, no. 2, section 15 (1999), pp. 123–143.
10. This example was originally described in "Driving Customer Insights through Segmentation: A Case Study in Wireless Telecommunications," in *In the Works,* ed. Berham Hansotia, Infoworks, vol. 3, no. 2 (2001), pp. 3–5. Also see www.infoworks-chicago.com.
11. See www.infoworks-chicago.com/newsletter/2.1/planning.htm, and Hansotia, "Customer Segmentations."
12. One could argue that these are market segments.
13. See note 2. Chapter 30 also discusses survey projection.
14. See note 8 or Brian D. Ripley, *Pattern Recognition and Neural Networks* (Cambridge: Cambridge University Press, 1996) for further discussion of these methods.
15. People are not always clearly a member of one particular segment. A customer may have some characteristics that indicate one type and other characteristics that indicate another. Latent class analysis gives the probability that a person belongs to a particular segment. For a person who is not clearly a member of a particular segment,

latent class analysis might indicate that the person has probability .5 of being a type A customer, .4 of being a type B, and .1 for other segments. Such a person may be receptive to marketing treatments designed for either segment A or B (or perhaps neither, as the customer is not clearly a member of either segment).

16. See Gilbert Churchill and Dawn Iacobucci, "Psychological Measurement" in *Marketing Research,* 8th ed. (Fort Worth: Harcourt, 2002), section 9A, and "Factor Analysis," pp. 796–819. The concepts of reliability and validity are particularly important.
17. See Brian S. Everitt, Sabine Landau, and Morven Leese, *Cluster Analysis,* 4th ed. (London: Edward Arnold, 2001).
18. See http://ourworld.compuserve.com/homepages/jsuebersax for a latent class Web site with a bibliography and listing of software.
19. See note 17 and David Bartholomew and Martin Knott, *Cluster Analysis* and *Latent Variable Models and Factor Analysis,* 2nd ed. (London: Edward Arnold, 1999).
20. This case was developed with Bobby Calder, who did all of the qualitative research on readers of *country* publications. We acknowledge all of the students in our courses that have assisted in developing this case. We also thank Hearst and Meredith for their assistance.
21. Another possible explanation is that we do not know if these people engage in *country* activities. Some data sources cannot distinguish between a "no" and an "unknown." Perhaps many of these people are really "unknowns."

CHAPTER 9

CUSTOMER PROFITABILITY AND DIAGNOSING A CUSTOMER PORTFOLIO

FRANCIS J. MULHERN

We can assess the degree to which a company is market-oriented by considering the measures it uses to evaluate business performance. In most businesses, the most widely used performance measures pertain to products, brands, business units, employees, marketing tactics, and a host of other organizational units and activities. As a simple example, consider sales promotions. Sales promotions typically are evaluated in terms of incremental sales, return on investment, response rates, promotional awareness, and a variety of other measures that help managers develop more productive promotions.

Improvements in performance measures and technology have brought about dramatic gains in the efficiency of production, distribution, procurement, and other internal business facets. What about marketing? Despite the fact that organizations exist for the primary purpose of, in Peter Drucker's words, "getting and keeping a customer," businesses in general have done a poor job of measuring customers in financial terms.[1] Today, however, marketing is in the midst of a data revolution made possible by automated data collection systems such as point-of-purchase systems. These systems now provide data at the finest level of resolution—individual customer purchase transactions.[2] Such data is revolutionizing marketing decision-making, which, until now, has been based on aggregate data describing product and brand sales in retail chains, geographic markets, or sales territories.

One of the first steps in the progression of companies from product-oriented channel managers to consumer-oriented entities is an understanding of the profitability of individual customers. In fact, in the widely acclaimed "new" approach to marketing, whether it is called *database marketing, one-to-one marketing, customer relationship management,* or *integrated marketing communications,* a fundamental first step is the evaluation of customer profitability. In this marketing approach, emphasis shifts away from acquisition-dominant marketing toward retention marketing.[3]

This chapter presents an overview of the analysis of customer profitability. It emphasizes the evaluation of profit distribution across customers and the factors that determine or correlate with customer profitability. We'll look at how such analyses make possible more integrated approaches to marketing that truly are customer-driven.

CUSTOMER PROFITABILITY ANALYSIS

Customer profitability analysis can be partitioned into three areas of analysis: (1) profitability measurement, (2) evaluation of profit distribution, and (3) the factors that determine or correlate with profitability. Several measurement issues are addressed in detail elsewhere[4] and are not discussed in detail here. Suffice it to say that profit measurement can be a complex matter that requires many decisions about measurement specifications. Measurement specifications include the length of time over which to measure, the choice of which customers to include in the analysis, and the handling of the time value of money. The one measurement topic addressed in some detail in this chapter is cost allocations, because it is such an important and thorny issue. Following a brief discussion of cost allocation, I provide a detailed overview of the distribution of profitability and the analysis of the factors that relate to profitability.

COST ALLOCATION

The need to assign marketing costs to customers has increased over the years as marketing and related costs have grown. As a percent of corporate budgets, marketing costs grew from 20 percent to 50 percent between 1947 and 1997. Cost allocations can be very difficult in many consumer marketing situations because costs are not tracked on a per-customer basis. Customer costing is usually more feasible in business-to-business marketing where customers are more likely to be identified and their behavior tracked. Accounting systems are also more likely to assign costs to business units, profit centers, production facilities, and product categories. While recent advances in automated customer relationship management systems are facilitating customer cost tracking,[5] customer-level costing remains a difficult and uncertain area of analysis. Cooper and Kaplan note that operational cost systems that provide detailed information on process efficiencies and business unit performance do not generally provide information in the form necessary for activity-based costing—a requirement for customer cost allocation.[6]

Many organizations treat marketing costs as fixed costs. Expenditures on personal selling, advertising, promotion, and other marketing efforts are budgeted and evaluated as lump sums. This practice is no better illustrated than by traditional top-down budgeting approaches that allocate monies to functional areas, products, and marketing tactics. The obvious shortcoming of such approaches is that when costs are not allocated to customers, customers can be evaluated only on a revenue basis. If the ratio of marketing and service costs is constant across customers, revenue-based analyses are sufficient. However, in the more likely instance that costs are unevenly distributed across customers, proper evaluation of customers can be made only after costs have been allocated to customers.

What Costs Should Be Assigned to Customers?

To conduct a complete customer profitability analysis, marketing analysts should allocate to customers all marketing, customer service, and related costs. Activity-based cost systems diminish the relevance of the traditional distinction between fixed and variable costs. Kaplan and Cooper note that nearly all costs of doing business are variable costs and should be allocated to customers.[7] These costs include the costs of personal selling, advertising, promotion, direct communications, training and installation, delivery, call centers, and the like. The traditional definition of *fixed costs* is a cost that remains unchanged no matter what the level of production or sales. Kaplan and Cooper add the more stringent criterion that the only costs that are truly fixed are those that pertain to entities of which only one exists in a company, like a CEO's salary. To allocate costs, an organization must do the following two things:

1. Capture costs at the customer level. This measurement issue is becoming less of an obstacle as automated data collection pervades more aspects of business. Examples of capturing customer cost data include the assignment of customer calls to call centers or charges for late payments on accounts receivables.
2. Match costs to customer revenue streams. In many organizations, customer revenue analysis and cost accounting are separate entities. Revenues are traced to customers, business units, and sales territories, while costs are linked to production-related aspects of the business.

Often, revenue and cost accounting systems exist on different software platforms. A complete customer profitability analysis requires a single database that contains both revenue and cost data.

An important facet of customer costing is the tracking and allocation of supply chain costs. Marketing researchers[8] are extending fundamental profitability models[9] to incorporate supply chain costs. They show that profitability analysis is improved when accommodations are made for supply chain costs including distribution, financing, shipping order processing, and accounts receivable. Supply chain costs are most important for businesses in which dramatic differences exist in the cost of acquiring and servicing customers through different channels. For example, many companies find it less expensive to serve customers through Web sites or other direct communication channels than through a sales force or network of retail stores.

Problems with Time

Profitability analysis can be plagued by asynchronous occurrences of revenues and costs. Consider a sales representative who makes two visits to a company in the first quarter of the year and none in the second quarter. The cost per sales call is $500. The customer makes no purchases in the first quarter but, in the second quarter, makes a $10,000 purchase, which has a gross margin of 30 percent. When the first two quarters are analyzed jointly, the profitability of this customer is $(.30 \times 10,000) - (2 \times 500) = \$2,000$. However, when profitability is computed on a per quarter basis, the customer represents a loss of $1,000 in the first quarter and a profit of $3,000 in the second quarter. While this is a simple problem, it can be a serious sticking point because accounting systems are based on rigid time periods, while analysis from a marketing perspective should be more oriented toward customer purchase cycles that may or may not match with calendar periods.

Customer profitability analyses are frequently conducted on an annual basis to serve as inputs into annual budgetary and planning processes. From a behavioral perspective, one year often represents a reasonable time frame for analysis for the obvious reason that each of the seasons is represented. However, in some instances, different time windows are more appropriate. Time spans of greater than one year are likely to be appropriate for products that are not purchased frequently, such as appliances and computer equipment. Marketing analysis should participate in the design of cost tracking and assignment methods so that revenue and costs are matched in a way that facilitates profitability analysis.

Time periods should not be too short. The inherently stochastic nature of purchase behavior can lead to dramatically different levels of profitability and profit distribution for periods of varying lengths. For example, computation of customer profit on a per quarter basis can lead to erratic levels of profit per customer and misguided marketing practices.

DISTRIBUTION OF CUSTOMER PROFITABILITY

Almost without exception, businesses that measure customer profitability find that a small portion of customers account for a large portion of profits. The so-called 80/20 rule, also known as the Pareto principle, describes this phenomenon. (Note that when profit concentration is described this way, there is no need for the two percentages to sum to 100 because they are each a percent of something different.) One source of high levels of profit concentration is the interaction of the frequency with which people purchase and the quantity of units purchased. A "natural" purchase concentration exists because the customers who buy most often tend to buy the most volume. Hence, we should evaluate the distribution of purchase frequency across customers, because it is a primary source of the skewed distribution of profits.

MEASURES OF PROFIT DISPERSION

We can easily assess the distribution of customer profitability by visually inspecting profit curves. Consider an example of profit distribution for a customer database that consists of all purchases from customers buying from the supplier during the entire calendar year of 1999. The database includes customer identification numbers, all items purchased, the corresponding prices, and a set of descriptor variables including geographic location, industry type, and company size. The firm measured customer profitability by aggregating purchases into company-designated product categories and applying average profit margins for the category. It then summarized profits across all categories for each customer. The profit distribution for the 630,000 customers, compressed into 100 percentiles, is shown in Figure 9.1.

This example demonstrates a case of extreme profit concentration among a very small set of customers. About $9.4 million dollars, representing 17 percent of profits in gross margin, come from only 1 percent of the customers. A few large businesses purchase a large amount of equipment from this supplier. A second characteristic of this profit distribution is the presence of a

Figure 9.1
Distribution of Customer Profitability

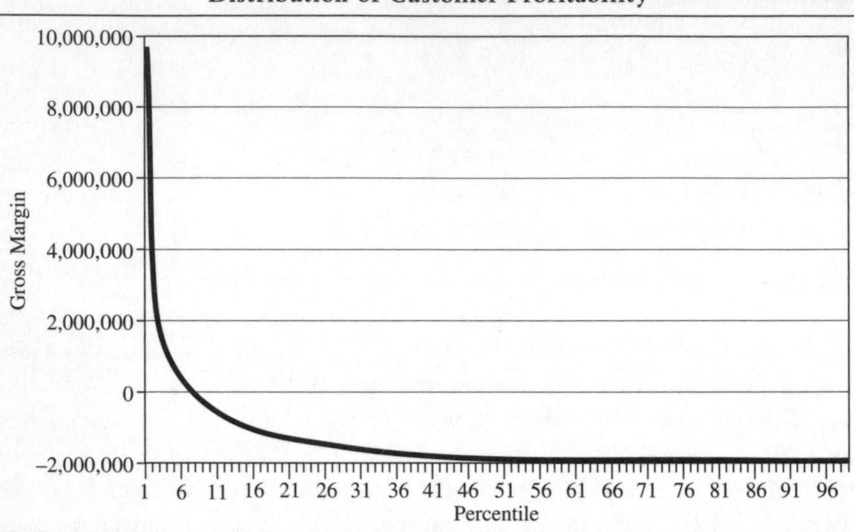

set of customers, the bottom percentile, which has a total negative gross margin of $244,000.

In addition to such graphical representations, it is useful to have summary measures of the distribution of profit that managers can quickly compute and evaluate. Next, several such measures and an assessment of their appropriateness for customer profitability analysis are described.

Relative Mean Deviation

One way to evaluate the distribution of profits across customers is to aggregate the deviations of each customer's profit from the mean profit level. This mathematical operation uses the relative mean deviation, which is defined as:

$$RMD = \sum_{i=1}^{n} | \overline{x} - x_i \mid n\overline{x}$$

where

x_i = Profit level of the ith customer,
$\overline{x}$ = Mean profit level across all customers, and
n = Number of customer.

The relative mean deviation has the advantage of providing an overall representation of profit distribution ranging from zero, in the case of all customers being equally profitable, to $2(n - 1)/n$, in the case of all profit coming from a single customer. The shortcoming of this index is that it is not sensitive to changes in profit distribution among customers who are on the same side of the mean. For example, if there were a shift in profit from a customer at the 5th percentile to one at the 20th percentile, the relative mean deviation would remain unchanged. Customer portfolios with dramatically different distributions of customer profit could have quite similar measures of profit concentration with this measure.

Variance

One way to overcome the problem with the relative mean deviation is to square each of the deviations from the mean before summing them. This can be achieved by simply using the variance:

$$V = \sum_{i=1}^{n} \frac{\left(\bar{x} - x_i\right)^2}{n}$$

A variance puts a greater emphasis on observations that are further from the mean. One quality of this measure is that any transfer of profit from a lower profit customer to a higher profit customer always increases the variance. Thus, more uneven distributions of profitability (between high- and low-profit customers) have greater variance than more uniform distributions. The shortcoming of the variance as a measure of profit concentration is that it is highly dependent on the mean profit level. A distribution with a greater relative variation than another could have a lower variance if the mean profit level is lower. To overcome that deficiency, we could compute the coefficient of variation by taking the square root of the variance and dividing it by the mean. The benefit of this measure is that it places equal weights on changes in profit at different levels of profit.

Still, the relative mean deviation, the variance, and the coefficient of variation are all based on the mean level of profit. The argument can be made that the mean is not an appropriate foundation for evaluating profit distributions because of the high degree of skew in the distributions, which renders the mean distant from other measures of central tendency. To circumvent this dependency on the mean, we can use alternative measures that rely on differences in profits among all pairs of observations, rather than comparisons of each customer's profit with the overall mean. Such measures follow.

Standard Deviation of Logarithms

A common practice for handling skewed distributions is taking logarithms. Doing so has the effect of giving greater relative importance to observations with lower values. Taking logarithms also has the desirable property of eliminating the impact of unit levels when pairwise differences are taken. Dispersion of profit can be represented by the standard deviation of the logarithms:

$$SDLOG = \sqrt{\sum_{i=1}^{n} \frac{\left(\log \bar{x} - \log x_i\right)^2}{n}}$$

However, the customers at the lowest end of the distribution are the ones in whom managers have the least interest. Most customer databases contain an enormous number of very low dollar customers. Because taking logarithms accentuates the importance of the lowest-dollar-volume customers, measures such as the standard deviation of the logarithm are less desirable.

Statistical Distribution Parameters

An alternative approach to representing profit concentration is to fit a probability distribution to the ordered histogram of customer profit, as exemplified in Figure 9.1. Several distributions such as the negative binomial and the gamma distribution can be fit to the customer profitability curves. The inverse of the *r* parameter in the gamma distribution serves as a useful measure of profit concentration.[10] However, statistical parameters are not as easily communicated to managers as some of the previous mathematical methods, or the geometric measures described in the following section.

Gini Coefficient

The *Gini coefficient* is a widely used measure of income inequality in welfare economics. It is most easily explained geometrically in the context of a Lorenz curve. The *Lorenz curve* is a two-dimensional plot depicting the relationships between the cumulative percent of customers and the cumulative percent of profits, as shown in Figure 9.2. The straight line on the diagonal represents the condition in which all customers are equally profitable. The Gini coefficient equals the ratio of the geometric area between the diagonal line and the Lorenz curve to the triangular area between the diagonal line and the two axes.

Figure 9.2
Lorenz Curve

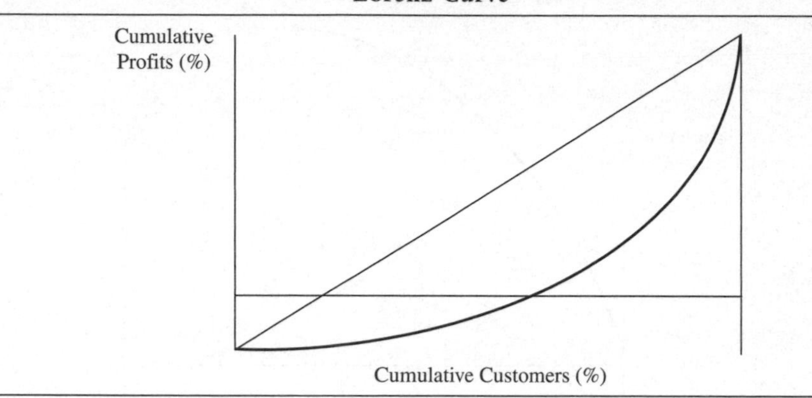

The mathematical specification of the Gini coefficient is:

$$GINI = \frac{1}{2}n^2\overline{x}\sum_{i=1}^{n}\sum_{j=1}^{n}|x_i - x_j|$$

The Gini coefficient also has a mathematically attractive interpretation. If we computed the pairwise differences in the profitability of all customers, aggregated the absolute values of these differences, and took an average, the resulting number would be the Gini coefficient. We can think of the Gini coefficient as a weighted sum of different customer profit levels in which the weights are a function of the position of each customer in the profit ordering.

A Lorenz curve for customer profitability is best shown[11] in an inverted format such that cumulative percent of profits is on the vertical axis and is free to stretch above the 100 percent mark in cases where a portion of the customers represent more than 100 percent of profits, as shown in Figure 9.3. If a standard Lorenz curve were used in those situations, the curve would drop below the horizontal axis, resulting in the awkward representation of a negative percent.

Another prevalent measure drawn from income economics is the *Schultz coefficient,* defined as the greatest vertical distance between the 45-degree line and the Lorenz curve. With a standard Lorenz curve, the Schultz coefficient ranges from zero (all customers have the same profitability) to one (all profits come from one customer and all other customers net zero profits). With a modified Lorenz curve, Schultz coefficient values exceeding one are possible.

Figure 9.3
Modified Lorenz Curve

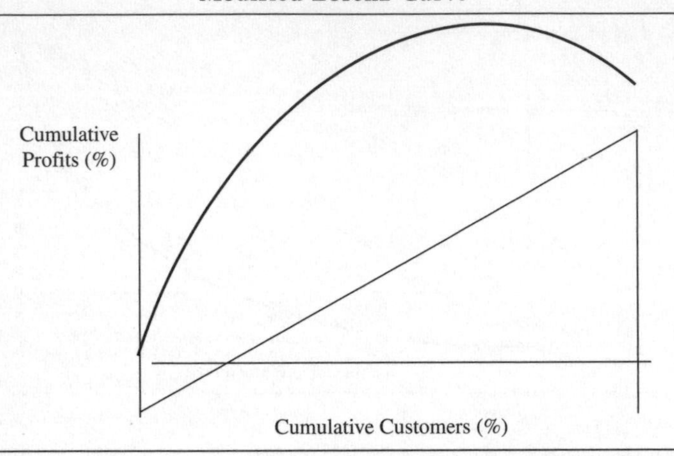

We refrain from suggesting any one measure of profit distribution is necessarily the best. The Gini coefficient has a wide level of acceptance, is easily computed, and has many desirable properties. It represents an attractive measure. However, the other measures described can also be useful for profitability analysis. Last, we note that all these measures are invariant with respect to overall magnitude of profits. They address strictly distribution, not level. While distribution of profit across customers is critical, its importance should not overshadow the absolute dollar amount of profits contributed by customers.

EMPIRICAL ANALYSES

To demonstrate customer profitability analysis and subsequent evaluations, we provide an extensive empirical example using a large-scale customer database of individual customer purchases of ready-to-eat (RTE) cereals at a major supermarket chain. The data spans six months, ending in March 2001. Data were collected at the supermarket checkout as part of a frequent shopper program. The club card is used for two-thirds of the transactions, representing 80 percent of the dollar sales in the chain. Figure 9.4 shows the distribution of profitability across customers. To facilitate presentation, we group customers into demideciles—twenty groups of customers each representing 5 percent of the customer base. We partition customer profit dollars into full price purchases, represented by the shaded area, and promotion purchases, represented by the white area.

Figure 9.4
Customer Profit Distribution for Ready-to-Eat Cereal Category

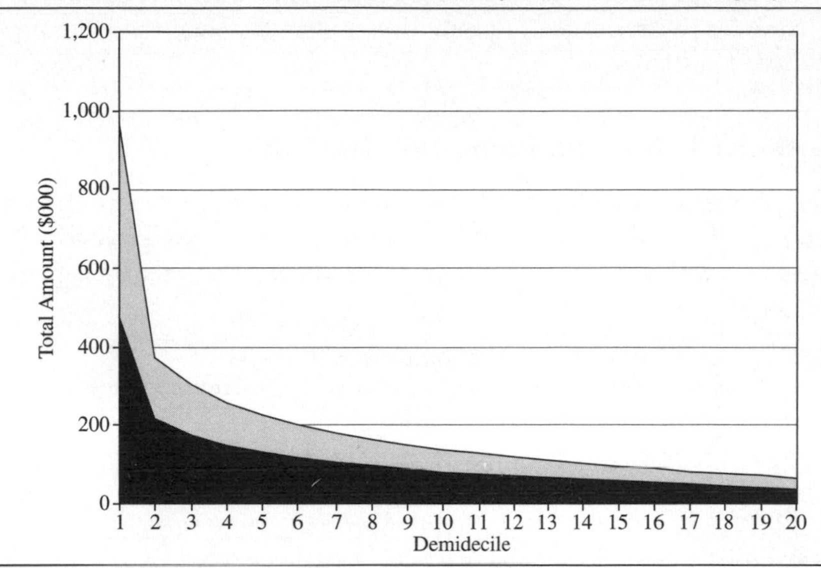

As in the business-to-business example described previously, we see the familiar curve representing a high level of profit concentration among a small set of customers. The detailed information in a customer database allows for further description of purchase behavior. Here we investigate the profitability of shoppers to breakfast cereal manufacturers in the context of managing a portfolio of customers.

DIAGNOSING A PORTFOLIO OF CUSTOMERS

Once we have a profitability analysis, we can diagnose a portfolio of customers and determine what factors either cause or correlate with profitability. In an extensive treatment in the literature of the determinants of profitability, several hypotheses about the determinants of customer profitability for a catalog merchant are empirically tested.[12] The research finds that customer profitability is not positively related to the length of a customer relationship, a result that contradicts the finding espoused in a service marketing setting.[13] The research also indicates that the cost of serving customers does not diminish as the length of a relationship increases, and that long-term customers do not necessarily pay higher prices. Results suggest that simple generalizations about the factors that relate to customer profitability cannot be made. For the empirical setting we evaluate here, we consider the relevance of promotion and brand buying to the profitability of customers.

Customer Profit and Promotion Buying

Sales promotions are used widely by manufacturers and retailers and have been extensively researched in academics and industry. Most promotion research deals with aggregate sales levels for brands, as represented by aggregate

Figure 9.5
Promotion Buying and the Distribution of Customer Profit

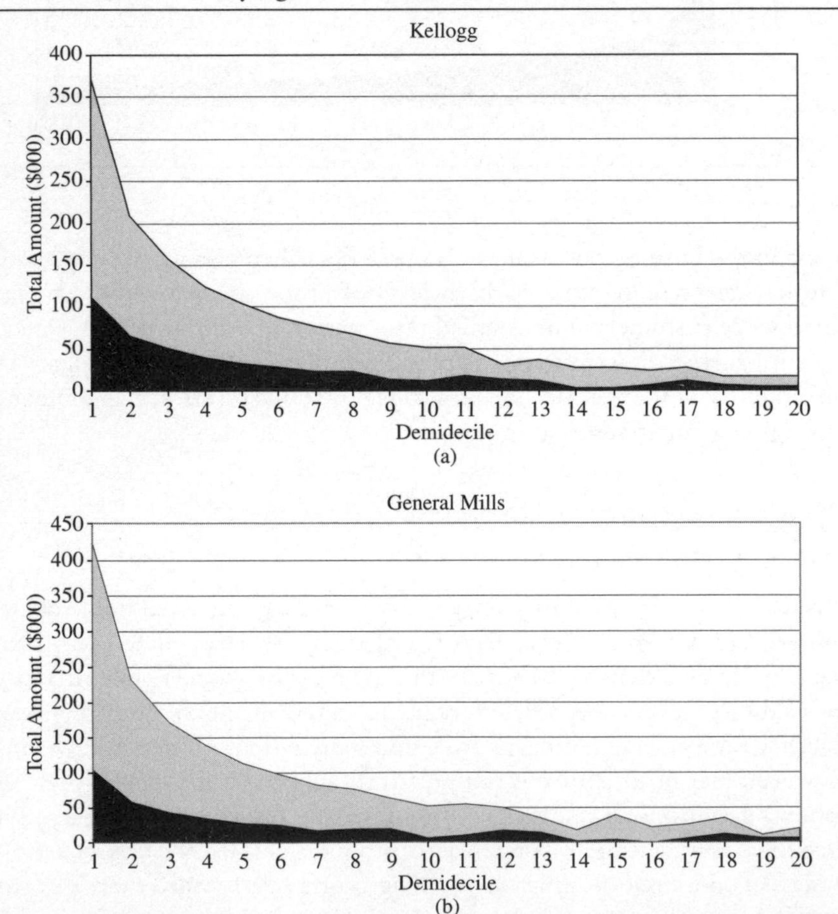

scanner data, or customer-level choice among brands, as revealed by studies using scanner panel data. Little research has looked at how promotion buying relates to the profitability of customers. Promotions are often criticized for serving the less profitable, brand-switching segment of the market. However, this claim has little empirical support. Here we explore how promotion buying by individual customers relates to their profitability. Figures 9.5a through 9.5d show total customer profits and customer profits from promotion purchases for each of the four major manufacturers in the RTE breakfast cereal category. The shaded area represents full-price purchases, while the white area represents promotion purchases made under

Figure 9.5 ***(Continued)***

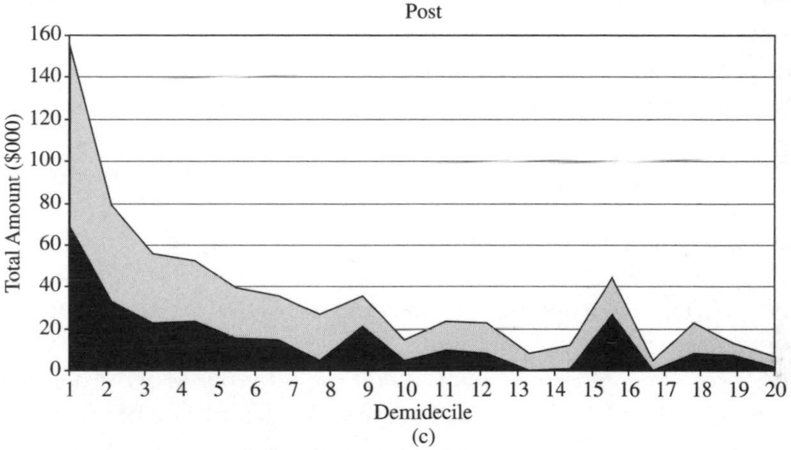

Post

(c)

Quaker

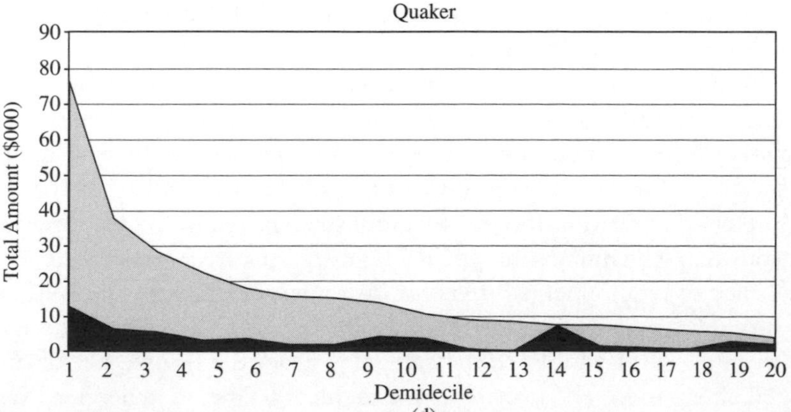

(d)

temporary price discounts. Information about coupon purchases was unavailable for this analysis.

Comparison of the four figures reveals that the distribution of profit across customers is fairly similar for each of the four major brand manufacturers.[14] However, notable differences exist in the portion of profit that comes from promotion purchases for customers at different profit levels for each of the brands. One obvious cause of these differences is the different frequency of promotion at the four brands. For example, Post gets a larger portion of its profit from promotion purchases than does Quaker. It appears that for Quaker, promotion response is higher among the less profitable customers. This result is unfavorable for that manufacturer, because it indicates that its promotions are serving a less attractive set of customers than the promotions of the other manufacturers. The value of this type of analysis of customer profitability is that it reveals which customers, in terms of profitability, are served by promotional activities. With such knowledge, companies can better manage promotions as profit-generating activities, as opposed to revenue-generating activities.

Share of Requirements

One shortcoming of many customer profitability analyses is that they typically are limited to the purchases a customer makes from one company while ignoring purchases made from competitors. When data on purchases from competitors is available, profitability analysis can include the computation of share of requirements. *Share of requirements* is essentially a customer-level market share. The benefit of knowing share of requirements is that firms can identify unmet potential and adjust target marketing strategies accordingly. Share of requirements is included as a measured component in some profitability models.[15]

Continuing the empirical analysis, we compute share of requirements for each percentile of customers for each of the four major brands in the category. What is important in target marketing is how share of requirements differs for customers at different levels of profitability to the firm. To explore that relationship, we measure share of requirements for each of the four major manufacturers of RTE breakfast cereal. Figure 9.6 shows how share of requirements differs for customers at different levels of profitability. Each line depicts the relationship between share of requirements and customer profitability in the category. From the figure, we can make several observations about share of requirements. First, in general, a brand's share of requirements decreases as customers become less profitable. Stated differently, companies have the highest share of requirements among the

Figure 9.6
Share of Requirements for Customer Percentiles

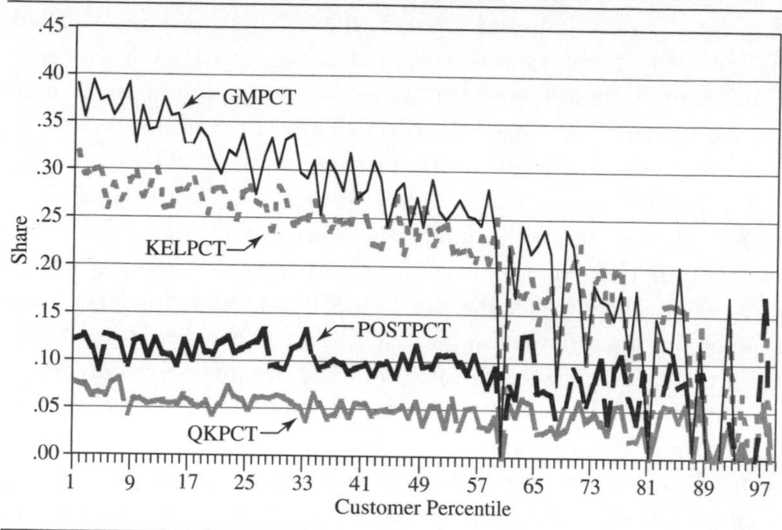

most profitable customers. This finding reflects several underlying aspects about purchase behavior. First, we can conclude that more profitable customers are more likely to concentrate purchases within a single brand. Second, among the less profitable customers (toward the right of the figure), share of requirements is erratic. This outcome stems from the frequency of zero market shares among some of the low-volume customers for some of the brands.

Next, consider the differences in the patterns for different brands. The brand share plots appear to be linear, so we fit simple linear regression lines to each. The dependent variable is the market share for each percentile (comparable to customer level share of requirements), and the independent variable is the customer percentile. Table 9.1 shows regression coefficients

Table 9.1
Regression Coefficients for Brand Share Plots

Brand	*Kellogg*	*General Mills*	*Post*	*Quaker*
Kellogg	1.0			
General Mills	−0.12	1.0		
Post	−0.08	−0.10	1.0	
Quaker	−0.07	−0.07	−0.04	1.0

for the lines fitted to each of the brands. The fitted lines for Kellogg and General Mills, the two leading brands in the category, have much higher slopes than the lines for Post and Quaker, the small-share brands. These results indicate that Kellogg and General Mills have relatively higher portions of sales going to customers with high shares of requirements. In contrast, Post and Quaker have generally lower shares of requirements that do not vary dramatically across customers at different profit levels.

Also note that while all brands get most of their sales from a small portion of customers, as shown in the brand-level distribution curves, the small-share brands are not as dependent on the heavy category users as are the large-share brands. That is, small-share brands draw sales from the entire distribution of customers in the category, while large-share brands draw primarily from the heavy users in the category. The upshot of this outcome is that large-share brands are more at risk and, therefore, must do more in terms of engendering repeat purchases or offering promotion incentives to maintain their market positions. Small-share brands, on the other hand, are less at risk because their sales come evenly from category purchasers at all levels.

We next explore how the shares of requirements for two brands are related. Table 9.2 shows the Pearson correlation coefficients for each pair of share of requirements on a per-customer basis. Each pair of share of requirements has a low negative correlation. The correlation figures are low because of the prevalence of zero share of requirements, especially among low-volume buyers. Nevertheless, the low correlations indicate that customers are not loyal to multiple brands. Despite the heavy presence of promotion in the category, customers who patronize one brand at a high level tend to do so at the exclusion of other brands.

One final note with respect to share of requirements concerns the importance of achieving a high share of requirements as a marketing objective. In general, achieving a high share of requirements is perceived as a good thing, because it represents a brand's acquiring more of the potential dollars from a customer. However, share of requirement objectives cannot be

Table 9.2
Pearson Correlations between Shares among Different Brands

Brand	*Slope*	t *value*	R^2
Kellogg	−0.27	19.6	0.94
General Mills	−0.37	26.6	0.90
Post	−0.10	12.1	0.78
Quaker	−0.05	6.5	0.56

divorced from the fundamental volume of purchases from a customer. It is often more profitable to have a low share of requirements from large-dollar customers than to have a high share of requirements from low-dollar customers. This realization brings to mind the sometimes-overstated assumption that a high-market share is a necessary prerequisite for profitability. There is a relationship between share of requirements and customer profitability, much as there is a relationship between market share and corporate profits. However, this relationship should not be oversimplified and should not be asserted without consideration of the actual dollars in profit each customer represents.

Finally, we consider how customer profitability and promotion buying relates to brand purchase behavior. We operationalize brand loyalty as percent of purchase dollars a customer spends on the brand with that customer's highest share of requirements. In Figure 9.7, brand loyalty appears as the horizontal axis, and promotion sensitivity, defined as the percent of purchases made on deal, is on the vertical axis. The circles in the figure represent segments of consumers at various levels of brand loyalty and promotion sensitivity. The magnitude (diameter) of each circle represents the total dollar volume in profitability for that segment. The plot reveals that the largest consumer segments have moderate levels of promotion expenditures with medium-to-high levels of brand loyalty. The results of this analysis at the individual customer level show the importance of not making simple generalizations about purchase behavior for all consumers. The combination of behavioral characteristics with financial information about customer profitability shows distinct groups of customers. Both manufacturers and retailers can use such information to target customers more selectively.

Figure 9.7
Promotion Buying, Brand Loyalty, and Customer Profitability

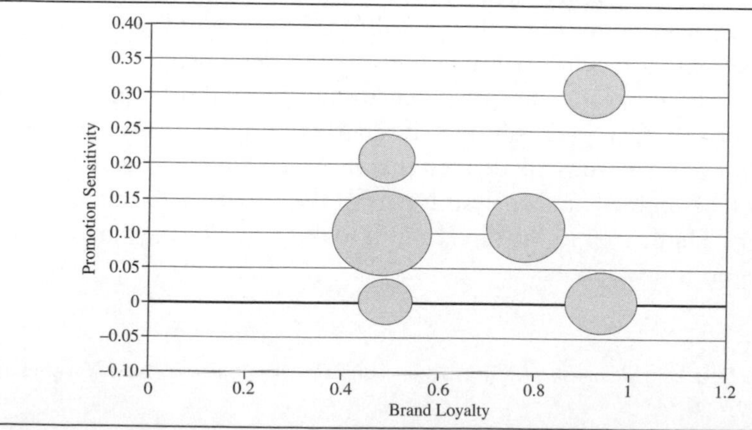

Profitability and Customer Trajectory

So far, we have discussed customer profitability strictly in a historical perspective. Future profits can be represented in models that incorporate future cash flows—called *lifetime value models.*[16] A useful diagnostic is to relate historical profit levels to the growth rates of customer revenue. Doing so allows a business to determinc whether its growth is coming from high–, intermediate-, or low-profit customers. Cases in which the most growth comes from low-profit customers, or the most profit comes from the lowest-growth customers, are causes for concern.[17]

CONCLUSIONS

Customer profitability plays a central role in marketing planning when it is measured and incorporated into day-to-day operations. As companies adopt stronger orientations toward customers and the external marketplace, the idea of managing customers supersedes the management of product and brands that dominates most businesses today. Marketing is becoming a practice that manages customer portfolios and treats segments of customers with an array of market offerings and marketing communications at the appropriate level—be it mass marketing, segment-oriented target marketing, or direct marketing.[18]

Many of the issues raised in this chapter—profitability measurement, evaluation of profit distribution, and the relationship between customer profits and promotion and brand buying—lay the foundation for customer-based marketing planning. Technological developments in the form of customer databases and customer relationship management systems will continue to contribute to the inclusion of customer-based financial measures in marketing practice as opposed to more product- and business-unit-based financial measures that prevail. In today's world of increasing financial orientation, with palpable pressures to demonstrate the financial outcomes of marketing practices, customer profitability plays a more prominent role than ever. Ultimately, marketing must answer to the demands on corporations to deliver shareholder value.[19] Customer profitability measurement and analysis is part of the answer to that demand and represents a large step in the direction of making marketing a more financially rigorous discipline.

Notes

1. Peter Drucker, *Management: Tasks Responsibilities and Practices* (New York: Harper & Row, 1974).

2. Robert C. Blattberg and John Deighton, "Interactive Marketing: Exploiting the Age of Addressability," *Sloan Management Review* (1991), pp. 5–14.
3. Jacquelyn S. Thomas, "A Methodology for Linking Customer Acquisition and Retention," *Journal of Marketing Research,* vol. 38 (May 2001), pp. 262–268.
4. Francis J. Mulhern, "Customer Profitability Analysis: Measurement, Concentration and Research Directions," *Journal of Interactive Marketing,* vol. 13 (winter 1999), pp. 25–40.
5. Ronald S. Swift, *Accelerating Customer Relationships* (Upper Saddle River, NJ: Prentice Hall, 2001).
6. Robin Cooper and Robert S. Kaplan, "The Promise and Peril of Integrated Cost Systems," *Harvard Business Review* (July/August 1998), pp. 109–119.
7. S. Kaplan and Robin Cooper, *Cost & Effect: Using Integrated Cost Systems to Drive Profitability and Performance* (Boston: Harvard Business School Press, 1998).
8. Rakesh Niraj, Mahendra Gupta, and Chakravarthi Narasimhan, "Customer Profitability in the Supply Chain," *Journal of Marketing,* vol. 65 (July 2001), pp. 1–16.
9. Paul D. Berger and Nada I. Nasr, "Customer Lifetime Value: Marketing Models and Applications," *Journal of Interactive Marketing,* vol.12, no. 1 (1998), pp. 17–30; also see note 4.
10. David C. Schmittlein, Lee G. Cooper, and Donald G. Morrison, "Truth and Consequences in the Land of 80/20 Laws," *Marketing Science,* vol. 12, no. 2 (spring 1993), pp. 167–183.
11. See note 4 and K. Storbacka, "Segmentation Based on Customer Profitability—A Retrospective Analysis of Retail Bank Customer Databases," *Journal of Marketing Management,* vol. 13 (1997), pp. 479–492.
12. Werner J. Reinartz and V. Kumar, "On the Profitability of Long-Life Customers in a Noncontractural Setting: An Empirical Investigation and Implications for Marketing," *Journal of Marketing,* vol. 64 (October 2000), 17–35.
13. Frederick F. Reichheld and Thomas Teal, *The Loyalty Effect* (Boston: Harvard Business School Press, 1996).
14. Note that the erratic distribution of profit among some of the lower-profit customers reflects ties in the number of customers per group and the fewness of customers buying some of the smaller share brands.
15. Don E. Schultz and Philip J. Kitchen, *Communicating Globally: An Integrated Marketing Approach* (Lincolnwood, IL: NTC, 2000).
16. See note 9.
17. See note 8.
18. Robert E. Wayland and Paul M. Cole, *Customer Connections: New Strategies for Growth* (Boston: Harvard Business School, 1997).
19. Rajendra K. Srivastava, Tasadduq A. Shervani, and Liam Fahey, "Marketing, Business Processes and Shareholder Value: An Organizationally Embedded View of Marketing Activities and the Discipline of Marketing," *Journal of Marketing,* vol. 63 (1999), pp. 168–179.

CHAPTER 10

Decision-Guidance Systems

NIGEL HOPKINS, ADAM DUHACHEK, and DAWN IACOBUCCI

Today's Decision-Making Environment

Whether it's a new product launch, a new advertising campaign, a regional promotion, or the allocation of resources across various functions in a customer service organization, managers are constantly faced with a multitude of decisions. Sometimes, the choice is between yes and no; other times, the number of choices seems infinite. The route to the decision differs from decision to decision, manager to manager, organization to organization, and time period to time period, with some approaches being highly calculated and others appearing close to random. In a situation in which shareholders' assets are at stake, a random approach to decision making would hardly be favored, and rationally, managers seek to eliminate as much uncertainty as possible from the probable outcome of their decisions.

Decision Calculus: The Early Vision

John D. C. Little's early (1970)[1] "decision calculus" philosophy proposed an approach to methodically reduce the uncertainty associated with managerial decision making by structuring and supporting the decision process with data, models, and simulation and optimization analytics. Central to the decision-calculus philosophy is the creation of mathematical models that explicitly represent phenomena in the manager's business environment, such as models of customers' responses to price, advertising, and promotion activities; models of the perceptual positioning of competing products; models of customer brand preference; and so on. These models are created and updated using timely and relevant data from the business environment.

They are then subjected to rigorous simulation and optimization questions that allow the manager to evaluate a number of explicit alternatives and pick an optimal solution from a range of possibilities.

ALAS, ADOPTION HAS BEEN SCANT

As appealing as Little's approach was, today's practices rarely resemble that vision. Data are often collected and assembled in great swaths with little, if any, distillation; and managers are left to wade through the enormous, intricate, and usually unimportant detail of its raw form, often throwing their hands up in frustration and resorting to a heuristic, "gut-feel" approach to decision making (in many cases, these intuitions differ only nominally from a random choice). Business managers clearly appreciate that data should be used in the guidance of decision making. However, the best way to do it eludes many—even those charged with delivering technologies, products, and services aimed at serving this need. Before we look at what has made the adoption of a seemingly logical and elegant approach to guiding decision making so slow and difficult, we revisit the needs of the decision maker.

NEEDS OF THE CONTEMPORARY DECISION MAKER: NOT MUCH HAS CHANGED

While the last two or three decades have seen incredible change in the speed at which business operates and change occurs, the basic needs of the decision maker remain essentially unaltered. If anything, those needs have been amplified by a world that is now more informed, more competitive, and moving much faster. These are some of the basic needs of the decision maker expressed in terms of the properties decision-guidance information must embody:

1. *Timely.* Decision-guidance must be timely, happening interactively, in real time. Typical lead times on traditional market research projects, for example, can run anywhere from four weeks to six months. Rarely in today's environment does a manager have the luxury of prolonging decision making until "all the data arrive." This fast pace calls for speeding up the cycle time through, for example, Web-based data collection and continuous real-time data analysis.

2. *Specific.* Unless the data and subsequent analyses address specific, tangible aspects of the business, the results are unlikely to be actionable. Consider the difference between these two statements from the standpoint of actionability: "Product quality must be improved to retain customers" versus "The reliability of the system software must be improved by two points to reach our goal of 80 percent customer retention in six months." In operationalizing issues for measurement, or simply storing secondary data, managers should always be aware of exactly how the information will be used. Stating the goal before collecting and analyzing the data increases the chance that the goal will be achieved.

3. *Prescriptive.* Decision-guidance must be prescriptive. That is, instead of focusing on a description of the state of the business, decision-guidance should focus on what a manager might or should do next and the likely outcomes. Decision-guidance should be a "state of mind," necessitating the employment of different, often more complex, approaches in the analysis of data. Before any prescription for decision can be delivered, there must be an orientation to the future, an ability to predict, and an ability to evaluate alternative actions. That, in turn, would imply the presence of a predictive model and a mechanism or framework capable of presenting alternative scenarios to such a model for evaluation.

4. *Parsimonious.* Decision-guidance must be easy to understand and communicate. Today's manager has a complex multidimensional environment to contend with and cannot become expert as a statistician or management scientist. Traditionally, an understanding of technical concepts such as external validity, confidence, and variance has been a prerequisite to developing an understanding of information presented for decision-guidance. Task specialization, as well as organizational hierarchical structures, can impede information transfer. These barriers to adoption are unnecessary and can easily be replaced with more natural and user-friendly approaches to presenting information.

5. *Valid and reliable.* To be useful, decision-guidance also has to be valid and reliable. If a manager is advised that a 10 percent (±2 percent) increase in customer satisfaction will arise from a $200,000 investment in a new service and support telephone system, a 10 percent (±2 percent) increase in customer satisfaction should result when $200,000 is spent on a new telephone system. Many factors contribute to achievement of this result: reliable data, valid models, timeliness of the underlying data, effective integration of these pieces, and so on. Valid and reliable guidance is a function of the quality of each of the components creating the solution and the quality of overall governance joining them.

6. *Financially anchored.* Decision-guidance must be delivered in a financial framework. For example, in conjunction with return-on-investment analyses, it is generally not enough to say "product concept X is more attractive to the target audience than product concept Y," especially when product Y would be cheaper to manufacture. The explicit inclusion of financial considerations in the creation of prescriptive guidance is imperative if it is to have meaning and usefulness in an organization with a bottom-line, financial focus.

7. *Scalable.* To be really useful, decision-guidance solutions should be scalable, which usually means leveraging technology in deployment. For example, in a large organization where thousands of new products are tested every year, a solution for pretest market sales forecasting should not be dependent on the talents of a single analyst and his or her capabilities with a statistical analysis program. It should be codified into processes and systems so that it may be used consistently organization-wide at a reasonable cost and in a fashion that allows for direct comparison of competing opportunities.

It would be difficult not to agree that these seven properties, if delivered, would dramatically change the nature of business decision making forever. The question is: Why don't today's systems already embody them?

Most organizations and managers implicitly know the potential of the data they possess, but various factors make it difficult to extract that value. In the next section, we discuss some of the factors that have impacted the satisfaction of these needs.

BARRIERS TO THE ADOPTION OF EFFECTIVE DECISION-GUIDANCE

A number of factors have hindered the adoption of systems that provide effective decision-guidance. Perhaps one of the most visible of these is the explosion in the amount of data available to managers in recent years, which has left little time to focus on anything but storing and organizing what is coming through the door (see the next section, The Distraction of the Data Sirens). Sometimes the data sources need better integration (see the Let's Get It Together section). Another factor in many organizations is the tradition of rote behavior, or process inertia. That is, certain kinds of data are collected and certain methods of analysis are conducted because "This is the way we've always done it" (see section titled The Tail Wagging the Dog). Another barrier to adopting more effective decision-guidance systems is the misperception that they are costly and complex (a problem we discuss in the Deer in the Headlights section). Decision-guidance systems are sometimes not adopted merely because marketing managers may be ignorant of their value—they do not know the kinds of questions these systems can address. We discuss this issue in the section titled Head in the Sand.

Distraction of the Data Sirens

Following the instinct that a business run by "databased decision making" has a competitive advantage, many firms have fallen into the trap of focusing strictly on the first part of that strategy. That is, "databased." In doing so, they have mounted and promoted many substantial and expensive initiatives around the collection, storage, and dissemination of data in the firm in the hope that it somehow translates into better decision making. Unfortunately, the entire value of databased decision making lies in the very detail of that translation—a fact brushed over by most. Owning or having domain over "data" does not make you a better decision maker. Yet, it is ever so tempting to continue to add to your databases and management information systems when data are "available." And "available" it will be: Recent headlines[2] read, "More original data will be created in the next two years than in all of human history." For anyone with a data problem (read: habit), this does not bode well.

At one time or another, all firms have been lured by the *data sirens.* And indeed, many companies in several industries, including consumer banking, retailing, and financial services point to successes they derive through the effective leverage of a portion of the vast repositories they have amassed:[3]

- Ritz-Carlton hotels have long recorded and stored guest preferences to drive the delivery of services tailored to individual customer needs.[4]
- Hyundai supplements its own data with census information to locate growing towns that share the same demographic profile as its current customer base. The identified towns become prime candidates for new dealerships.[5]

Surprisingly, while there are many stories like these, they are the exception rather than the rule: The potential of available data goes largely untapped. The landscape is littered with data-oriented technologies, systems, and solutions that have delivered less guidance for decision makers than was originally expected. For example, we can all think of public instances in which customer relationship management (CRM) and enterprise resource planning (ERP) systems, loyalty programs, customer satisfaction and feedback programs, syndicated and industry information sources, survey data, and so on have fallen flat in terms of the guidance they provide to decision makers.

So, what's the solution? Firms need to realize that the volume and number of data sources they have access to is unlikely to correlate with their success as decision makers. It's how that data (and they won't require all of it) is translated into decision-guidance for decision makers that is most important. Therefore, instead of focusing and obsessing on the "databased" portion of "databased decision making," it is appropriate for the firm to turn its attention to the "decision making" component. That is, what decisions require databased guidance? What analytical methods are appropriate for producing that guidance and transforming the raw data? Subsequently, what data is required to support these methods? In essence, the firm needs to shift its focus from "data" to one of "decision" and work backwards. Whether it's determining how to segment a market or determining how to allocate resources, unless the correct data has been collected and assembled, decision-guidance will be suboptimal. We referred to this previously as *specificity*. The firm must become specific around the decisions it is interested in guiding before it can resist the lure of the *data sirens*.

Let's Get It Together

Another factor impacting the delivery of effective decision-guidance is the fact that supporting data derive from multiple sources that tend to coexist in distinct, discrete locations, rather than as an integrated unit. We now examine the need to integrate data sources across internal storage units, channels and countries, and even competitors.

Marketers are savvy enough to advocate holistic views of customers—analyzing customer demographics, attitudes, historical behaviors, perceptions about competitors, and their estimated economic value, such as lifetime customer value assessments.[6] Yet, again, reality falls short of advocacy. How could the ideal integration be achieved? The integration of data is a means to an end—that is, there is no point in integrating or bringing together the data sources unless it is clearly understood what is and is not important to building a "commercially useful" model of the customer—so that the model can be applied by the marketing manager user. The kinds of necessary integrations follow:

1. The data sources need to be accessible on one common platform so that they can be used simultaneously in modeling efforts.[7] Analytical software and data transfer protocols have become versatile enough that they allow simultaneous access to data stored on different machines in different locations.[8] Historical purchase data might exist in a spreadsheet on a desktop in the sales department, while customer demographics and credit information may exist on a Unix server in the finance department. Front-line service transaction information might exist on multiple, small-capacity machines at the points of service. Integrating these sources allows for a full profiling of customers.

2. Data need to be coordinated *across channels* and *internationally*. Businesses are multichannel today, having retail presences as well as customer access online.[9] Customers value complementary channels; for example, at Victoria's Secret, customers can order apparel online because they know their sizes, but they may visit the retailer to try out a more experiential good, such as the scent of a new perfume offering.[10] Other customers conduct research online but buy at stores. Still others buy online but pick up at local stores to avoid shipping and handling costs and to obtain the merchandise more quickly. As data capture and integration technologies become more prevalent and accessible, a company could capture and capitalize on these patterns by integrating multiple sources of data, that is, syndicated data, perceptual surveys, qualitative interview responses, behavioral choices (obtained via interactive retail kiosks), and e-commerce data collected through online tracking.[11] Data coordination across channels allows the marketing manager to take advantage of synergies and cross-pollination, so a holistic picture of the customers can be formed and a more complete model of customer behavior developed. Rarely is our consumption limited to one venue; thus, data extracted from only one channel present the marketer with a biased, incomplete view of the customer.

3. Data need to be *integrated across competitors*. There is an "organization-centric" bias in many industries, whereby managers seek to obtain answers from analyzing "our data only." This proposal may appear controversial, and surely there would be some limits as to which databases would be shared industrywide, but consider the advantages gained from integrated data sources provided by AC Nielsen and IRI for manufacturers and distributors of consumer packaged goods, or the benefits accrued to automobile manufacturers and dealerships from data provided by J. D. Powers. Industry-level promotional campaigns could be shared (e.g., Got Milk; Eat Beef). If managers could share some standard data across the industry, the impacts of marketing efforts could be measured better and market share estimates refined. Financial and marketing strategic planning would be more reality-based than wishful thinking. Furthermore, environmental and competitive indicators are obtained only in this data-share manner—they cannot be inferred from single provider information. The model of customers in the marketplace could not possibly be complete if competition were left out or assumed away. If we were to call for companies to "share your data with one another," we might be labeled naïve, but it could happen in one of several ways: through multiclient programs or syndicated research from which it is too expensive to be "left out," or through a firm whose purpose is to collect explicit data about competition.

Process Inertia or "The Tail Wagging the Dog" Problem

Organizations and marketplaces are dynamic entities in a constant state of flux. A system designed to guide decision making at one time may be rendered irrelevant and useless at a later time because of a changing organizational structure, changing market dynamics, a changing customer population, and so on. Combine this phenomenon with various other human traits such as risk averseness, inertia, a tendency to stick with what is known, and a need to conform, and it is hardly surprising that we often see obsolete systems continuing to "chug along." In effect, these systems are still being implemented because "this is the way it has always been done." When the relevance of the system to the decisions it is supposed to guide has dissipated, the system is no longer serving the decision maker. In fact, it is often the case that the only thing being served in this situation is the system. That is, while the system fails to provide meaningful guidance, the firm is still burdened by its ongoing operation. The tail now wags the dog, so to speak. This situation represents a significant opportunity cost for the firm: A sizable portion of the effort required to provide relevant decision-guidance is being expended on a system that doesn't deliver.

In particular, data collection and analysis are expensive undertakings; therefore, a business-as-usual approach and a lack of understanding around the applicability of results seem wasteful. The exercises of data collection and analysis should pay for themselves in benefits if they are better planned so as to address relevant, real, and timely marketing issues and imminent decision-making tasks.[12]

In reality, this situation is very common. Most companies would have little difficulty in identifying a system or process originally designed to guide decision making that categorically fails to provide meaningful decision-guidance. However, more often than not and even with a visibly "marginal" deliverable, these systems continue unchallenged in the organization. Organizations mostly lack the mechanisms to adequately evaluate and deal with underperforming systems to be used in guiding decision making.

A firm wishing to avoid being wagged by this tail of obsolescence needs to maintain a vigilant watch. This can be achieved by frequently exposing all existing systems, whether "tried and proven" or "new," to rigorous critical evaluation. This includes evaluations of systems, solutions, and processes in relation to the decisions they are supposed to be supporting: Is the system guiding any decision making? Is the system still relevant? How are the decision parameters changing? What are the needs of the decision maker this system is supposed to support and how do the attributes of this solution correspond? How often is the system used and could the decision maker do without it? Without this evaluation on an ongoing basis, a system has no incentive to remain relevant and is unaccountable.

Misperceptions That Decision-Guidance Systems Are Too Complicated or Costly; a.k.a. "The Deer in the Headlights"

Providing quality decision-guidance is a complex task requiring knowledge of data collection methods, database technologies, statistical analysis, simulation technologies, user interface design methods, the decision sciences, and so on. When faced with this reality and the burgeoning supply of data, the firm is often frozen in indecision between inaction and electing to "do what it takes" to create real guidance for decision makers in the organization—usually defaulting to inaction. The expense and complexity of designing and implementing "fully blown" systems for decision-guidance is usually substantial; and combined with the pressures of needing a solution "now," the decision to not do anything "because there's no time" is often the convenient choice. This is unfortunate as more often than not, a well-designed blueprint for decision-guidance can be implemented in a phased fashion, providing value from the very beginning and building to extremely high levels of value over time.

Choosing and implementing new analytical systems can seem intimidating; however, this barrier can be removed in several ways. In particular, ensuring that the system will provide actionable information from the outset by having specific marketing goals that drive development is a useful device.[13] For example, if you have a tactical orientation, it is less useful to know a general index of overall customer satisfaction at McDonald's or Hilton than to know performance on specific attributes such as satisfaction with the temperature of McDonald's fries or the scent of Hilton's linens. If indices are poor in the former case, there is no diagnostic information regarding how to improve features that matter to customers. If indices in the latter case show poor performance, it would be up to McDonald's or Hilton to determine whether an improvement on this dimension would be cost effective in enhancing satisfaction and loyalty. In terms of both the implementation of a decision-guidance system and the content and decision area that the system addresses, specific narrower goals are more readily measured, hence, eventually, more readily achieved.

We have touched several times on the enormous supply of data (e.g., sales call data, customer service center data, actual purchase data), which is obviously a major contributor to the feeling of bewilderment in the planning and implementation of systems for decision-guidance even though it is "supposedly yielding greater insight into customer behavior."[14] The situation would be far less overwhelming if there were some organizing schema, bringing it all together to help the firm pose specific and relevant questions to investigate (provide "specificity"). For example, a metric addressing the "number of calls processed by a call center" is probably less actionable than a metric that addresses the "average time to resolve the customer service call," and so on.

Consider the following list of far-too-general marketing and management goals that have been cited in popular business media as motives for a company's marketing information (e.g., database) efforts. Note that these goals are all relevant and worthwhile, yet the means to their achievement is more often than not hopelessly vague. It is unclear how the firm is supposed to get from its database marketing efforts to "adding customer value," for example. Companies say they are engaging in database marketing to:

- Attract new customers who are profitable.
- Increase customer satisfaction.
- Decrease expenses.
- Achieve mass customization.

- Add customer value.
- Form long-term relationships with their customers.

. . . admirable, but inactionable (it lacks "specificity").

Consider alternatives that may sound less impressive in their ambitions, yet were actually effective in providing specificity to the problem and, subsequently, delivering at least some decision-guidance value:

- Maximize profitability of ongoing promotional campaigns: AFC Enterprises (operator and franchiser of 3,300 Church's, Popeye's Chickens, Seattle Coffee companies, and Cinnabons) used modeling techniques to maximize the profitability of a recent promotional campaign and the sales level of a new menu item.[15]
- Identify new customer prospects: A cell phone company mapped the communication networks of its existing market to identify potential new customers geographically.[16]
- Maximize the effectiveness of Web-banner advertising: An advertising researcher precisely measured and modeled short-term effects of advertising via click-through and conversion rates on banner ads to produce a tool to guide future decision making.[17]

Theses examples are well defined; and while they may sound narrow in comparison to the loftier marketing goals stated previously, they at least pose situations for which decision-guidance can be developed.

The trick to avoiding getting caught in the headlights is to understand upfront that these things take time and these processes are iterative. While the entirety of the system may look overwhelming, it is usually possible to decompose the problem into manageable stand-alone tasks.

What Can We Do with These Data?: "Head in the Sand"

One of the biggest issues working against the design and implementation of effective decision-guidance systems is simply an ignorance of what is possible. The old adage that "you won't know what it's like until you try it" applies here. Without having experienced "quality" decision-guidance, most managers and firms are simply unaware of the possibilities. Similarly, a large proportion of those charged with providing solutions and services to firms to assist in guiding decision makers are also unaware of what is possible. Databases are not goals in themselves; they are the means to achieving marketing goals. Enthusiasm about customer databases has led some proponents to claim that "information about my customers" is my "company's most valuable asset."[18] Not quite. Information about your customers is of little value in itself if the company does not invoke it when formulating strategy.

For example, many firms are unaware of the simple difference between "descriptive" and "prescriptive" information. A manager armed with descriptive information has to make inferences on the fly (and often incorrectly) about what this means to the firm and how it relates to the decision or decisions he or she is about to make. On the other hand, a manager possessing prescriptive information is usually faced with making choices between various courses of action whose likely outcomes have been preevaluated (i.e., the inferences have already been made). To produce prescriptive information, which largely is more useful than descriptive information in guiding decision making, managers need to create predictive models. Models are another concept poorly understood in practice. In many cases, the confusion or ignorance stems from multiple uses of the term in several different lexicons. For example, there are database models, financial models, business models, and so on. Say the term *model* at a meeting composed of the CEO, CFO, and CTO, and you can imagine the corresponding images. A "predictive" model (used in prescription) is usually derived mathematically from a set of data and relates aspects of the business that the manager can control (e.g., sales effort) to aspects of the business the manager would like to influence (e.g., sales). The resulting mathematical form explicitly quantifies the relationships contained in the data. With a limited understanding of these distinctions, a firm has little hope in successfully implementing quality decision-guidance.

Perhaps one of the best ways to counter the head-in-the-sand problem is to lead by example. Until firms and managers have experienced or witnessed the potential of systems designed to provide prescriptive decision-guidance, it is very difficult to get outside the "rear-view mirror" orientation of a majority of today's solutions aimed at guiding decisions. In the following section, we briefly outline a decision-guidance system that might be employed in the quick service food industry to demonstrate the power of leading by example. We highlight some of the principles that have been discussed in the chapter in a system that could be used to provide prescriptive decision-guidance industrywide at all levels of the organization.

A Look at Decision-Guidance Systems as Applied in the Quick Service Food Industry

We could use any industry to illustrate our recommendations around decision-guidance, but we select quick service food (fast food) for its prevalence and familiarity. This industry experiences some 56 million transactions in the United States every day ($100 billion in revenues per annum). Nearly half of the average household's outsourced meals consist of fast food. The market is highly competitive, and each provider is struggling with issues of customer satisfaction and profitability.

In this competitive business, where change occurs quickly and product and service delivery problems can have detrimental and long-lasting effects on the performance of the independently owned store and the franchise or business system as a whole, *timeliness* (the first attribute of an effective decision-guidance system) in issue detection and decision making is imperative. Thus, a useful decision-guidance system for the quick service food industry might involve providing close to real-time guidance around maintaining customer satisfaction to maintain and maximize within-store sales. The data collection opportunities at point-of-sale are staggering. There is a continuous flow of customers and, of course, "potential respondents." In such a system, every *n*th customer could be invited to share his or her experience with the company (across the industry). As depicted in Figure 10.1, the transaction receipt may be the invitation to take the survey.

Respondents would complete the instrument, ideally, onsite or, at least, electronically. This would allow for close to real-time analysis of the responses. Technologies facilitating this kind of collection might involve responses onsite in the store at an interactive kiosk or over the telephone via an interactive voice response system or online via a Web survey (see Figure 10.2).

Ideally, information from all stores in a franchise system and all franchises in the industry would flow into a central data repository managed by a third party. Operating on this data repository would be a decision-guidance information system designed to:

1. Create and update predictive models that relate performance to success measures.
2. Store, track, and report performance data.

Figure 10.1
The Invitation

3. Maintain the integrity of the proprietary, competitive-privacy, and industry-level data pooling aspects of the system.
4. Provide an access point for managers at all levels of these organizations to enter and evaluate ways in which the performance of their respective businesses and business domains can be enhanced.

Figure 10.2
Data Collection: Multi-Mode

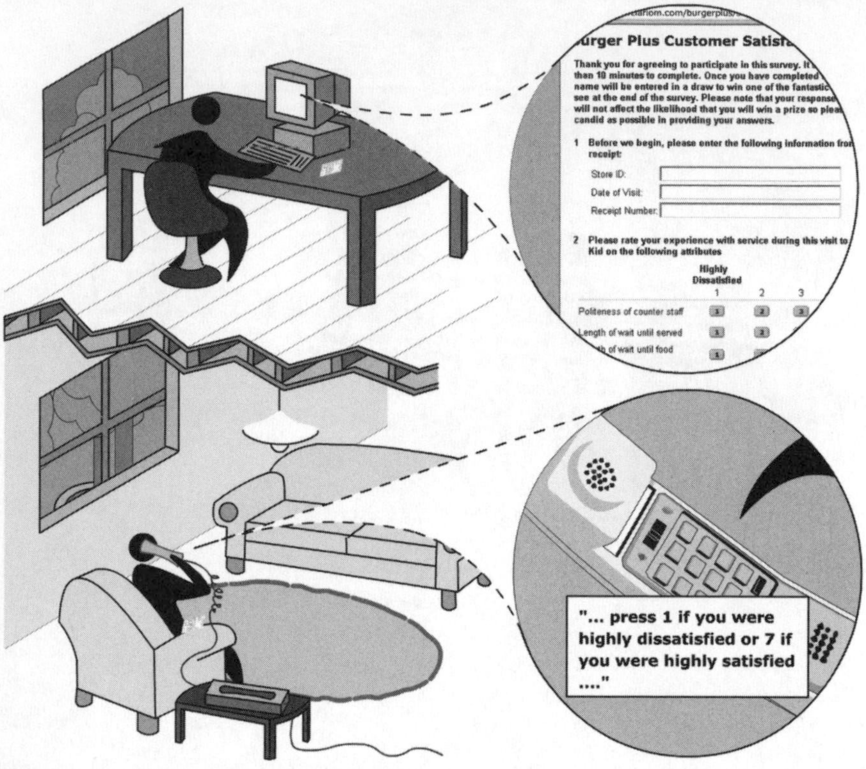

Figure 10.3 offers a view of a portion of a possible user interface for such a system. The example demonstrates options for looking at information in a number of different ways:

1. A focus on your own franchise outlet, the entire franchise chain, or the industry.
2. Examination of indices for customer satisfaction, their drivers, or broader equity scores.
3. Time frames in which any of these indices might have been expected to vary, given marketplace or environmental shifts or company marketing efforts.

Figure 10.3
Decision-Guidance System

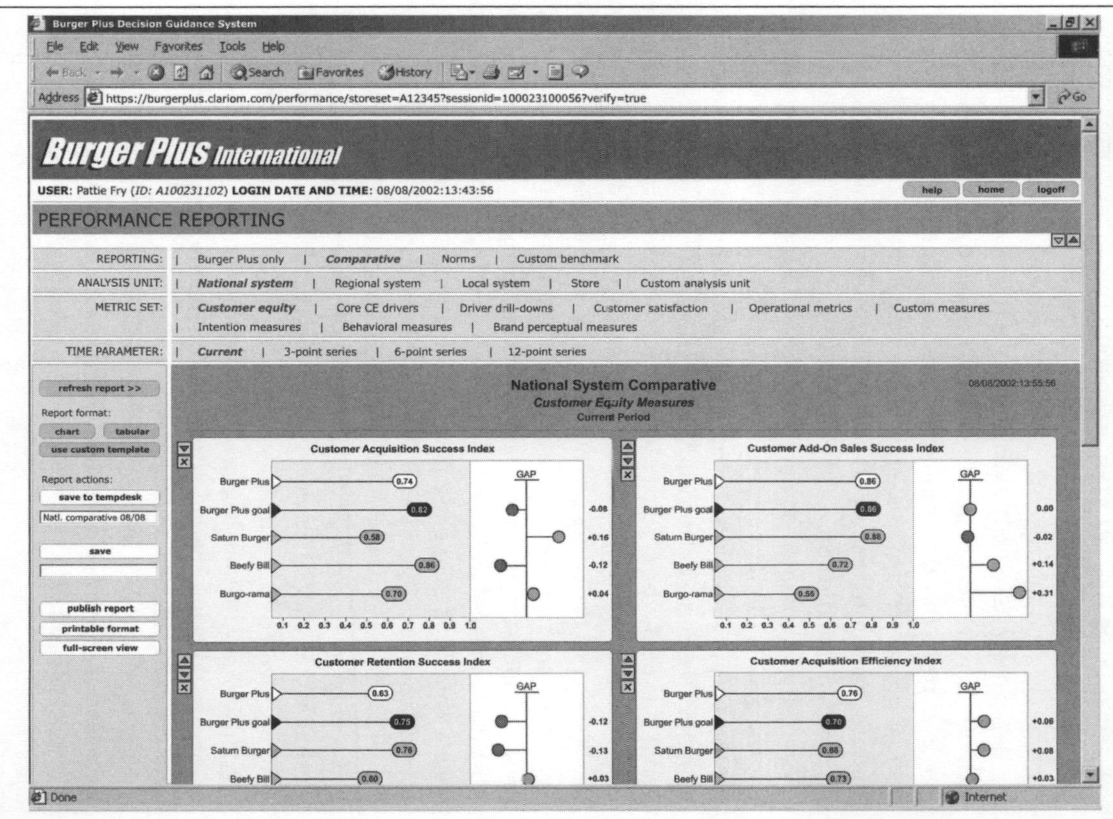

4. Locations defining narrow or broader sampling frames, such as the focal fast food outlet, its metropolitan neighbors, or a broader swatch across the country, and so on.

Depending on the user's role and perspective, these options would allow them to very quickly customize their view to access information that is more *specific* and subsequently actionable (the second criterion of the ideal decision-guidance system). For example, a store owner might be interested in the service delivery issues most heavily impacting retention of their local market share so that they can guide their managers' behaviors individually, whereas corporate decision makers might be interested in the roll-up of this information nationally to perhaps help guide improvements in training programs, and so on.

Attributes three and four of an ideal decision-guidance system were that the results should be *prescriptive* and that the guidance system itself, and the output it produces, should *offer parsimony* (i.e., be simple to understand). In the solution illustrated in Figure 10.3, all modeling that would power the prescriptive aspects of the system would occur behind the scenes, according to agreed-on principles. It does not have to be "black-box" to the corporation, but to a certain extent, it would be to the user. The interface would allow the user to very quickly and simply ask questions such as "What would happen to customer retention if we improved the rating we're getting on food temperature by one point?" "What top three changes could I make at my five stores to maximally increase customer retention?" Without going into detail, the mechanisms delivering these answers to the user would be simulation and optimization technologies, respectively (behind the scenes, of course). The conceptual work and an understanding of the data collection (methods, sampling) would help enhance the *validity and reliability* of the guidance system, and an in-house knowledge of cost structures and profitability factors would help *tie the decisions to financials,* the fifth and sixth of the ideal decision-guidance system's qualities.

Finally, if the system were indeed accessible by all employees in the organization (as implied by the Web-based delivery mechanism depicted in Figure 10.3.), the final ideal of *scalability* would have also been achieved.

In this chapter, we have attempted to outline some of the issues that face companies seeking to effectively leverage data in decision making. There are many barriers and obstacles to overcome. There is no off-the-shelf solution. Systems need to be constructed with a firm view of the decisions they will be guiding, with a view of exactly how that guidance will be derived and, consequently, what kinds of data need to be collected, when, and how.

Notes

1. John D. C. Little, "Models and Managers: The Concept of a Decision Calculus," *Management Science* (1970), vol. 16, B466–B485; John D. C. Little, *Decision Support Systems for Marketing Managers* (New York: American Marketing Association, 1984).
2. *Boston Globe,* February 11, 2001.
3. Michael J. A. Berry and Gordon S. Linoff, *Mastering Data Mining: The Art and Science of Customer Relationship Management* (New York: Wiley, 2000).
4. Christopher W. Hart, "Made to Order: Technology Is Making It Feasible to Reach That Market of One. Make Sure You're the First Mover," *Marketing Management,* (summer 1996), vol. 5, pp. 11–22.
5. Amy Merrick, "The 2000 Count: Counting on the Census—New Data Will Let Starbucks Plan Store Openings, Help Blockbuster Stock Its Videos," *Wall Street Journal* (February 14, 2001), p. B.1.
6. Frank W. Davis and Karl B. Manrodt, *Customer-Responsive Management: The Flexible Advantage* (Oxford: Blackwell, 1996); Gordon A. Wyner, "Taking a Second Look at Customers: Researchers Must Keep Pace with the Changing Marketer-Customer Relationships," *Marketing Research: A Magazine of Management and Applications,* (summer 2001), vol. 13, pp. 4–5.
7. See note 3.
8. Steve Jarvis, "ASPs Bring Complex Tools to Small Firms," *Marketing News* (February 18, 2002), pp. 9–11.
9. See Wyner note 6.
10. Eric Schoeniger, "Successful Retailing: More than Multichannel," *sas.com* (September/October 2001), pp. 14–21.
11. Forrest and Mizerski (1996); Reedy, Schullo, and Zimmerman (2000).
12. Gilbert A. Churchill Jr. and Dawn Iacobucci, *Marketing Research: Methodological Foundations,* 8th ed. (Fort Worth, TX: Dryden, 2002).
13. Darrell K. Rigby, Frederick F. Reichheld, and Phil Schefter, "Avoid the Four Perils of CRM," *Harvard Business Review* (February 2002), pp. 101–109.
14. David P. Hamilton, "E-Commerce (A Special Report): Openers—In Translation: A Guide to the Baffling Jargon of Online Business-to-Business Commerce," *Wall Street Journal* (May 21, 2001), p. R.6.
15. Anonymous, "Mining the Data of Dining," *Nation's Restaurant News,* (May 22, 2000), vol. 34, S22–S24.

16. See note 3.

17. Peter Loftus, "E-Commerce (A Special Report): A Buyer's Market—Pay for Performance: Technology Allows Advertisers to Know Exactly What an Ad Is Worth—To the Dismay of Some Web Sites," *Wall Street Journal* (April 23, 2001), p. R16.

18. Scott McMurray, "Breakaway (A Special Report)—Scott McMurray on Technology: Keeping Tabs on Your Clients Makes All the Difference," *Wall Street Journal* (April 23, 2001), p. 6.

CHAPTER 11

SCORING MODELS

EDWARD C. MALTHOUSE

Prediction is very difficult, especially about the future.

—Neils Bohr

This chapter provides marketing research tools to answer the following questions:

- How can I predict the likelihood of future behavior of customers?
- How likely is a customer to respond if I send him or her a particular offer?
- Which offer should I send to a particular customer?
- How likely is a particular customer to leave during the next six months?

The tool that we use to answer all these questions is the scoring model.

In this chapter, we also address questions about evaluating scoring models. Imagine that you have just received an expensive scoring model from a consulting company—how would you know whether the model was any good? Part of the answer is to use *gains tables* to compare how the new model performs with your current approach. This chapter describes what a gains table is and how to interpret one.

A related question is "How many offers should I make?" Scoring models sort people from "best" to "worst" in terms of their likelihood of responding. Where should you stop "mailing?" At 1 million names? At 1.5 million names? This chapter discusses the strategic issues to consider in making this decision.

The author thanks Pamela Ames, senior vice president emeritus of Kestnbaum & Company, for helpful comments on an earlier version of this chapter.

We also address how a scoring model is built and describe the basic steps that a database consulting company follows in developing a scoring model. This chapter discusses the issues in extracting a data set from a relational database, performing quality checks on the data, selecting a modeling approach (whether linear/logistic regression, CHAID/CART, neural networks), building the model, and implementing the results.

The following example illustrates the importance of scoring models. Suppose a catalog company has a database of 20 million names and plans to mail 2 million copies of its fall fashion catalog. But to which 2 million names? Sending a catalog to someone who will throw it out is not a good practice. How can the company know before mailing the catalog whether a person will respond? Scoring models allow the company to do a better job of picking the 2 million who are most likely to respond.

Suppose further that the average order size is $40. If a scoring model could increase response rates from, for example, 5 percent to 6 percent, there would be an additional 20,000 orders and $80,000 in revenue. The only thing the company does to generate these orders is to do a better job in deciding who should get the 2 million catalogs. When mailing so many offers, even small improvements in response rate can translate into large increases in revenue.

WHAT IS A SCORING MODEL?

A *scoring model* is defined as a data-mining model that predicts the likelihood of some behavior based on other information available for a (prospective) customer. A scoring model assigns every observation in a database a score indicating how likely someone is to engage in a particular behavior. Consider the components of this definition.

Behavior

Many kinds of behaviors might be modeled. Here are some examples:

- *First-time response (acquisition).* If an organization is using direct marketing methods to acquire new customers, a scoring model can help select among prospects by predicting how likely each prospect is to respond to the offer. The customer behavior of interest is "responding to the offer." For example, magazines send mail offers to prospective subscribers. Long-distance companies use telemarketing to acquire new customers. Credit card companies acquire new customers using direct mail and telemarketing.

- *Credit worthiness.* Before a credit card company offers a person credit, it would like to know how likely the person is to default. Credit scoring models provide this estimate.
- *Retention (keep active customers active).* Catalog companies must decide which of its existing customers (those who have purchased within the past three years) should receive a particular catalog. A scoring model predicts the behavior, "making a purchase from the catalog."
- *Reactivation (revive former customers).* Catalog companies must decide which former customers (those who have not made a purchase for three years) should receive a catalog or an offer to reactivate them. A long-distance provider must decide which of those customers who have switched to a competitor to try to win back. Airlines have identified a group of customers who are not buying as many tickets as they have in the past; which of these customers should they try to win back with an offer?
- *Defection (who is vulnerable?).* Companies would like to know which prospects or customers are likely to defect so that they can take steps to prevent the defection. Scoring models can predict the likelihood of attrition within some specified time period.
- *Long-term value.* Sometimes database marketers use scoring models to estimate the total revenue that a customer will generate over a period of time. It is of great interest to a company to know whether a prospect is likely to generate substantial revenue in the future, because it can then allocate marketing resources more efficiently. For example, it can invest more in acquiring customers who are likely to generate substantial future profits. Scoring models can be used to estimate future revenues over a certain duration.
- *Leaving a Web site or number of page views.* E-companies want to understand what causes a customer to quit a Web session before making a purchase. Many also want to know what causes a person to stay at the site longer. These are behaviors that can be modeled with a scoring model.[1]

It is very important that a company model the "right" behavior. For example, companies may make a mistake by targeting customers who will produce a short-term profit but will not be profitable in the long term. Auto insurance companies usually find it very easy to enroll people with poor driving records, but these types of customers are often more likely to have accidents in the future or switch to a competitor for a slightly cheaper rate.

Other Information

Database marketers can use any variables, or fields in the database, that are well populated in the database. Here are some types of *other information:*

- *Contact history.* A contact history is the record of all contacts that have been initiated by an organization in the past, such as mailings, outbound telemarketing calls, and outbound e-mails.
- *Past purchase history.* These histories record all purchases, donations, and so on, that a customer has made in the past. The most common examples include recency, frequency, monetary value, purchase timing (at what times of the year does a customer purchase?), and the product categories purchased.
- *Demographic and lifestyle "overlay" information.* There are companies that gather and sell information about demographic variables such as age, income, sex, wealth indicators, household presence of children, and lifestyle variables, such as having an interest in fitness activities, quilting, gardening, or golf.[2]
- *Geodemographic and census data.* The U.S. Census bureau releases aggregate-level information about a variety of demographic variables, such as the median age, as well as the distribution of age, for every zip code and block in the country.[3] Claritas also sells its related PRIZM and MICROVISION systems.[4]
- *Inbound telephone logs.* A customer calling with a question or a complaint can be an important indicator of future behaviors. For example, a customer calling in to complain about certain types of service breakdowns might be a strong predictor of future defection.
- *Source of name.* People are often referred to Web sites from different sources. It is important to track the route by which the customer came to the Web site, because customers referred by certain sites may be more likely to make a purchase than those from other sources.
- *Mailing lists.* Catalog companies rent lists to acquire new customers. The customers acquired from one list may be more likely to make a purchase or remain a customer longer than those from other lists.
- *National Change of Address (NCOA).* The U.S. Postal Service will tell a company whether a particular customer has moved. Many database marketing companies periodically have this service provided. It

can be valuable information. For example, people who recently moved are often in need of credit. Someone moving into a house for the first time may have a new need to read decorating magazines; therefore, a publisher would want to cross-sell such titles to subscribers of its other magazines.

DATA-MINING MODEL

Data-mining methods include linear and logistic regression, trees (CART, Quest), Bayesian classifiers, and neural networks. These methods are used to estimate the likelihood that a customer will engage in some future behavior. For example, a catalog company might use a linear regression model to predict how likely customers are to purchase from a catalog. They would produce a model such as:

$$\text{Score} = 0.1\ (\text{frequency}) - 0.2\ (\text{recency})$$

In this model, *frequency* is the number of previous purchases made during the past three years, *recency* is the number of months since the most recent purchase, and *score* is an indicator of how likely a particular customer is to make a purchase from the catalog. The larger the score value, the more likely a person is to make a purchase. Those who have made many purchases in the past are more likely to purchase in the future. Similarly, those customers who have purchased recently are more likely to purchase in the future.

Data-Mining Examples

To make the idea of a scoring model more concrete, consider the following examples:

Catalog Example. Suppose a catalog company must decide which of its customers who have made a purchase in the past should receive its 2003 Spring Fashion catalog. The catalog company incurs a cost with every book it sends, so it does not want to send the catalog to everyone. It needs a way to determine, a priori, whether customers will place an order if they are sent a book. Scoring models can help answer this question.

The behavior to predict in this example is whether a customer will place an order if sent a catalog. (Sometimes we may want to take the expected order amount or expected profit into account, so that someone who is likely to place a highly profitable order is given priority. Rather than incorporating this information, we keep the modeling simple and focus only on customers' responses.)

Assume that the catalog company mailed a similar catalog last year and observed who responded (by placing an order) and who did not. Information as of January 1, 2003, can be used to predict response to the Spring 2003 catalog. Other information includes behavioral variables such as how recently a customer has placed an order (*recency*), the number of previous purchases (*frequency*), average size of previous orders (*monetary value*), purchases by product category, purchases from previous spring fashion catalogs (i.e., before 2003), whether the customer holds a house credit card, and contact history.

The next step is to build a data-mining model predicting response to the 2003 catalog from the *other information* category. After the model has been built, the company would apply it to the database as of January 1, 2004, and mail to those customers the model predicts are most likely to respond.

An important problem with scoring models is that they implicitly assume that the future will be like the past. This assumption may not hold. For example, if the catalog company has made a strategic decision to start including more upscale merchandise in the 2003 catalog, customers may not respond the way they did to the 2002 catalog. If the economy has gone into a recession between the mailings, customers may also not respond the same way.[5]

Magazine Subscriptions. Suppose that a magazine wants to acquire new subscribers. A commonly used approach is to rent another company's list of names, and send the people on this list offers for the magazine. Perhaps the magazine company has rented the frequent-flyer list from ABC Airlines. The list of frequent flyers is very large and the publisher does not want to send offers to people who will not respond. Each offer sent may cost, for example, $.50, so the firm must be selective in deciding who gets an offer. A scoring model helps us with this task.

The behavior to predict is whether a customer on this list will respond if sent an offer. Note that if the particular offer does not ask for a payment before the subscription begins, response to the offer is often not the behavior we should be modeling; in this case, the behavior of greater interest is response *and* payment. This is an example of choosing the "right" behavior.

To keep things simple, let us say that the offer requires payment up front, that we want to predict response, and that we have mailed to the customers on the list previously and have observed which customers responded and which did not. Building a scoring model involves the following steps:

1. Select a random sample of names, for example, 100,000 from the airline's data.
2. Compile a database of *other information* about these sampled customers, which would likely include demographic, geo-demographic, and lifestyle information, and perhaps some additional information from the list provider.
3. Build a data-mining model to predict response from the other information. For example, if we built a regression model, we might end up with a model such as:

$$\text{Score} = -0.1\ (\text{Age}) + 0.2\ (\text{Income})$$

   indicating that younger people and those with high income are more likely to respond to the offer.
4. Score the database, sort the database in descending order of scores, and send offers to those with the largest scores.

Scoring the database means applying the data-mining model to every record in the database to predict the likelihood of response. With the example equation above, someone with an age of 20 and an income of 30 (thousand) would have a score of $-0.1(20) + .2\ (30) = 4$, which is a ranking that helps us order people by their likelihood of responding. The question of exactly how many offers we should send is addressed later.

Again, scoring models implicitly assumes that the future is similar to the past. People do not always respond to magazine offers the same way at different times of the year. For example, response rates to gardening magazines might be higher during the spring than in the fall. If the magazine changes the mailing piece itself, it may be necessary to estimate a different scoring model.

HOW TO BUILD A SCORING MODEL

The general steps in building a scoring model are as follows: (1) Create a modeling data set; (2) develop a scoring model; (3) evaluate the scoring model; and (4) score the database and decide how many offers to send. These steps are described in the sections that follow.

Creating a Modeling Database

The first step in developing a modeling database is to identify a *proxy behavior,* which is a behavior observed in the past that is similar to the future behavior you would like to predict, for example, response to a similar catalog mailed last year, response to a subscription offer mailed to a different list in the past, response to a test conducted on this list in the past, and so forth.

The time period when the proxy offer was active is called the *target period.* For the catalog example, the target period was, say, April 1, 2001, through June 30, 2001. The *base period* is a period of time before the target period. Information from the base period will be used to predict the proxy behavior. For the catalog example, the base period could be all information about customers as of January 1, 2001. These periods are illustrated in Figure 11.1. In the nonelectronic world, there is usually a gap between the end of the base period and the beginning of the target period, because the organizations that physically send the offers need some lead time for printing mailing labels and so on.

The data to be used in developing and implementing a scoring model often resides in a relational database. The data-mining methods used for scoring models cannot usually be applied directly to relational databases, however, and the analyst must create a single table (a spreadsheet) with a row for each customer and summary variables as columns. The task of creating summary variables usually means counting, summing, or applying some other descriptive statistic to a field in a relational database.

For example, consider the purchase history of a catalog company. The purchase history is most likely stored in a relational database table with a record for every item that customers have purchased. If someone bought a shirt and a pair of socks on April 17, 2000, there will be two records, one for the shirt and one for the socks. Data in this format cannot be used in a regression analysis, for example, without further processing. Some variables that are commonly created follow:

- *Recency.* Recency is the time (usually in days, weeks, or months) since the customer's last purchase, order, donation, and so forth.

Figure 11.1
Illustration of Target and Base Time Periods

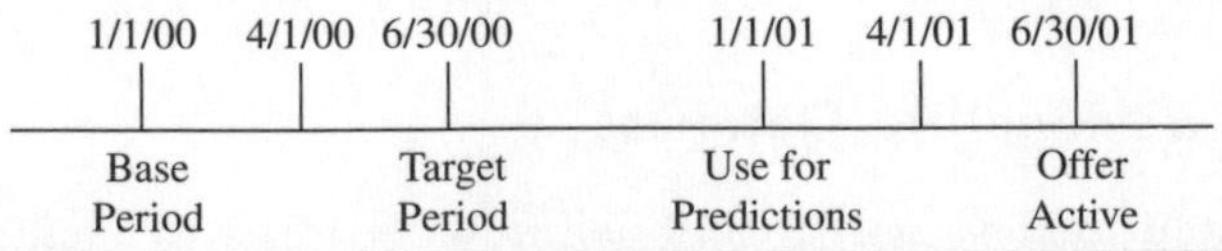

1/1/00	4/1/00	6/30/00	1/1/01	4/1/01	6/30/01
Base Period		Target Period	Use for Predictions		Offer Active

Computing recency requires finding the maximum date by customer in the table.

- *Frequency.* Frequency refers to the number of purchases, orders, or donations during some time period, such as the past two years or the past six months. Setting the length of the time period is somewhat of an empirical process. Are the purchases a customer made from a company 20 years ago still strong predictors of the customer's behavior? Computing frequency means counting the number of unique orders for each customer.
- *Monetary value.* Value indicates how much a customer has spent during some time period. Monetary value is sometimes taken to be the total dollars spent during a period, but this definition is highly correlated with frequency in many industries. Another definition of monetary value is the average order or donation size. Computing monetary value is a matter of summing or averaging dollar amounts in the table.
- *RFM by sub-classification.* Subclasses can make the problem simpler. Recency, frequency, and monetary value (RFM) are often calculated by product categories, responses to specific media, or responses during specific times of the year. For example, RFM values of previous purchases from tall men's catalogs may be better indicators of a customer's proclivity to purchase from an upcoming tall men's catalog than purchases in general. Those customers who place orders during the summer may be very different from those who purchase during the holiday season.
- *Product categories in the first order.* The types of merchandise in the first order can be indicative of future behavior. Someone who buys clothing from a catalog could be a better customer in the future than someone who buys a consumer electronic product, because the purchase of a clothing item indicates that the person is comfortable buying personal items without touching them first. Some consumers feel uncomfortable buying, for example, a sweater without first trying it on for fit, color, and style. These concerns are less of an issue for items such as hand-held video games.
- *Frequency across years.* A customer who has made purchases consistently every year for the past four years is probably a good prospect.
- *Contact and marketing investment.* The contact and marketing investment tracks the number of contacts or marketing dollars spent during some time period. Often, customers who have bought recently and frequently are more likely to purchase in the future. However, there are two possible reasons that they have bought recently and frequently: (1) They are better customers, or (2) they have been given

more opportunities to buy because they have been contacted more often. For example, a customer who has not purchased recently may not have been sent as many offers. Including an indication of previous marketing investment controls for this.

Our focus in these examples has been on retailers, but most other industries face a similar task, and RFM is usually a good place to start. For example, hotel chains maintain relational databases with lists of stays—one record for every visit to a hotel including the customer ID, number of nights, room rate, hotel identifier, and the way in which the room was booked. RFM variables could be created easily from this information. Hospitals maintain a record of visits, including patient ID, type of visit (in-patient, out-patient), amount billed, amount paid, procedures that were performed, and diagnoses that were made. Airlines maintain data on trips, with a customer ID, flight number, ticket price, and class (economy, business, first).

Evaluating a Scoring Model

Recall the question posed at the beginning of this chapter: Suppose you have asked a consulting company to develop a scoring model for you. How do you know if the model is better than what you are currently doing? Alternatively, suppose you have developed two candidate-scoring models, a linear regression and a neural network model. Which one is better?

To answer these questions, we first discuss what *better* means. Then we present the steps for evaluating models.

***What Is* Better?** There are two common criteria for evaluating a scoring model: *fit* and *performance*.

Fit measures how well the model fits the data, as measured by, for example, *R*-squared (proportion of variance in the data explained by the model). Fit tells us how close the predictions from the model are to the values observed in the past. A model that fits well makes predictions that are close to the previously observed values.

Performance measures the number we expect to respond if we send a certain number of people the offer using the scoring model to prioritize the recipients. Performance is usually assessed with a *gains table* (defined shortly).

Most models optimize fit, but performance is of primary interest in many scoring model applications. Consider a company that wants to mail a certain number of offers to customers in the database, whether catalogs, magazine subscription offers, credit cards, or Internet service provider offers. We could argue that fit is unimportant when developing a scoring model for this situation. The most fundamental objective in developing a scoring model here is to partition a list of names into two groups, one that will receive the offer and the other that will not. The partition should be formed to maximize the number of responses (or total profit). Consider the best customer in the database. The accuracy of the prediction—fit—of how likely the best customer is to respond to an offer (or how much that customer is likely to spend) is irrelevant, as long as the best customers get the offer. If one customer has a 90 percent chance of responding and another a 5 percent chance of responding, the estimates of these two probabilities are irrelevant if both are sent the offer.[6]

Gains Tables. The performance of a model is measured with a gains table.[7] An example is given in Table 11.1. (This gains table is derived from a regression that is presented shortly. For now, we simply study the results.) The basic steps in constructing this table are as follows:

1. Compute quantiles of predicted values from scoring model. By convention, database marketers reverse the order of the deciles so that the best decile is numbered one.
2. Compute counts of people, responders, and response rates by quantile.
3. Compute cumulative columns.

Table 11.1
"Gains Table" from the "Standard Regression" Model

Decile	*Number Mailed*	*Number Respond*	*Response Rate (%)*	*Lift*	*Cumulative Mailed*	*Respond*	*Rate (%)*	*Lift*
1	9,541	831	8.71	172	9,541	831	8.71	172
2	9,541	676	7.09	140	19,082	1,507	7.90	156
3	9,541	626	6.56	129	28,623	2,133	7.45	147
4	9,542	565	5.92	117	38,165	2,698	7.07	139
5	9,541	446	4.67	92	47,706	3,144	6.59	130
6	9,541	376	3.94	78	57,247	3,520	6.15	121
7	9,542	383	4.01	79	66,789	3,903	5.84	115
8	9,541	368	3.86	76	76,330	4,271	5.60	110
9	9,541	304	3.19	63	85,871	4,575	5.33	105
10	9,541	268	2.81	55	95,412	4,843	5.08	100

The interpretations of the columns are as follows. The column label *decile* includes the groups of customers most (through least) likely to respond. The 10 percent who are most likely to respond are in decile 1, the next 10 percent in decile 2, and the worst 10 percent in decile 10.

The column labeled *Number Mailed* gives the actual count of people in each decile group. The table was computed with deciles, so there should be 10 percent in each group.[8] Think of this number as the number of people who were sent the offer and given the chance to respond.

The column in the table called *Number Respond* gives the number of people in the decile group who actually responded to the mailing. For example, 9,541 were mailed the offer in the first decile and 831 people responded.

The column labeled *Response Rate* is the percentage of customers in each group who respond. For example, 831 / 9,541 = 8.71 percent of those mailed the offer in decile 1 responded. Note how the response rate decreases in subsequent deciles, which is an indication that the scoring model has been effective in helping to find the customers who are likely to respond.

This column gives the marginal response rate for a particular decile, that is, the response rate for mailing one more decile. To see how this could be useful, suppose that we wanted to mail to the break-even point, which requires, for example, a 5 percent response rate. If we mail to decile 4, we expect a 5.92 percent response rate. Mailing to decile 5 would generate an expected response rate of 4.67 percent, which is below the 5 percent we need; therefore, we would not want to mail to this group. This application is a bit dodgy for the reasons discussed later in this section on deciding the number of names to mail. For example, the economy may have changed or the competitor may be doing something different, systematically affecting the response rates.

Finally, *Lift* is the response rate for a particular decile divided by the overall response rate, which is 5.08 percent (multiplied by 100). For example, decile 1 has a lift of (100 × 8.71 percent)/5.08 percent = 172, indicating that those in decile 1 are 1.72 times more likely to respond than the average person. That is, the response rate is 1.72 times higher if we use the scoring model to pick the best 10 percent rather than selecting 10 percent at random from the database. An advantage of using lift instead of response rate (and cumulative lift over cumulative response rate) is that the indices are less affected by systematic shifts in response rates.[9] For example, instead of using deciles (with ten groups), suppose there are two groups. The top half has a response rate of 10 percent, the bottom half 6 percent, and the overall response rate 8 percent; the lifts are 120 and 75. In the future, suppose that the economy slows down and everyone is half as likely to respond so that the response rates are halved to 5 percent and 3 percent. That is, the lifts do not change because of the economic shift.

The remaining columns in the table are cumulative indices. *Cumulative Mailed* accumulates the Number Mailed column. For example, the number 19,082 in decile 2 is computed as 9,541 + 9,541. *Cumulative Respond* cumulates the Number Respond column. If those in the top two deciles according to this scoring model had been mailed, 831 + 676 = 1,507 would have responded. *Cumulative Rate* gives the cumulative response rate. For example, if we used this scoring model to decide which 20 percent of the file receive the mailing, the overall response rate is 7.90 percent, which is an average of the response rates for the individual deciles (8.71 percent and 7.09 percent). Note that the overall response rate (5.08 percent) is given in the last row of this column. *Cumulative Lift* is the cumulative rate divided by the overall response rate (multiplied by 100). For example, by using this scoring model to select the best 20 percent of the names, we get a response rate 1.56 times higher than if we had selected 20 percent of the names at random.

The cumulative response rate or cumulative lift columns are used to compare models. Suppose that we know that we want to send our mailing to 20 percent of the customers in our file. Using this model, we expect a 7.90 percent response rate. Table 11.2 is the gains table from another regression model (described shortly) that is more sophisticated and, therefore, should do better. Note that the better model does a more efficient job of picking the 20 percent of names to receive the offer, generating an 8.56 percent response rate.

Table 11.2
"Gains Table" from the "More Sophisticated" Linear Regression Model

					Cumulative			
Decile	*Number Mailed*	*Number Respond*	*Response Rate (%)*	*Lift*	*Mailed*	*Respond*	*Rate (%)*	*Lift*
1	9,541	920	9.64	190	9,541	920	9.64	190
2	9,541	714	7.48	147	19,082	1,634	8.56	169
3	9,541	588	6.16	121	28,623	2,222	7.76	153
4	9,542	512	5.37	106	38,165	2,734	7.16	141
5	9,541	447	4.69	92	47,706	3,181	6.67	131
6	9,541	386	4.05	80	57,247	3,567	6.23	123
7	9,542	355	3.72	73	66,789	3,922	5.87	116
8	9,547	359	3.76	74	76,336	4,281	5.61	110
9	9,535	308	3.23	64	85,871	4,589	5.34	105
10	9,541	254	2.66	52	95,412	4,843	5.08	100

The key point is to select the model that gives the largest cumulative response rate (or lift) at the relevant mailing depths. If a model is used only to select the top few deciles, its performance in lower deciles is unimportant.

Scoring the Entire Database and Deciding the Number of Names to Mail

To score the database, we apply the estimated model to all customers. The model's prediction is called a *score.* Scores prioritize who should get the offer; those who are more likely to respond should receive an offer before those less likely to respond. After a database has been scored, the circulation manager must decide the *solicitation depth,* which is the number of names that receive an offer or contact. The term *cutoff point* is also used; names ranked above the cutoff point receive the solicitation and those below do not.

Ideally, the solicitation depth should be the break-even point, where the marginal cost of the solicitation equals the expected revenue generated from the contact. The problem is that true marginal costs and revenues are not easily quantified. For example, narrow definitions of marginal cost and expected revenue take marginal cost to be the cost of the specific contact and marginal revenue to be probability of response multiplied by the unit contribution (expected order amount less cost of goods). These narrow definitions lead us to maximize the short-term profit generated from the mailing, but they can produce suboptimal circulation plans when other factors are considered. Broader definitions are needed. Unfortunately, many of the factors that determine costs and revenues are difficult to estimate reliably, but we must take them into consideration during the decision-making process.

Long-Term Strategic Goals. Corporations often have long-term strategic goals that supersede maximizing profits from a single mailing. For example, a catalog company may have a long-term goal to increase in size. Perhaps it has already invested in infrastructure such as Internet servers, call centers, fulfillment centers, and warehouses, and it needs to increase the number of active customers to justify these investments. The definitions of cost and revenue are complicated. In the short term, such a company might need to mail below the point where the unit contribution equals the cost of the mailing.

Or, a credit card company may have a long-term strategic goal to increase its market share by acquiring new cardholders. It is difficult to estimate revenues because they depend on many other factors. How much will new cardholders use their card, if at all? Will they carry revolving balances, or will they pay the full amount of their balances each month? If the new membership was generated by offering a low interest rate on a balance transfer, will the new member leave or move the balance to another card when the interest rate is raised?

Long-Term Customer Value. The long-term value of a customer is often greater than the unit contribution (price paid less cost of goods), and we should consider it when making circulation decisions. A classic example of this is a record or CD club. A record company enrolls people into the club by offering them, for example, six CDs for one penny. The recording company has lost money at this stage. But, the record company can send members a catalog of CDs each month, which are priced competitively. Over time, perhaps six months, the record company expects to make a profit on customers it acquired at a loss.[10]

Inventory or Capacity Considerations. Catalog and Internet companies that sell merchandise must consider available inventory levels when making circulation decisions. Inventory considerations may prompt these companies to mail above or below the point where unit contribution equals the cost of the contact.

The lead time for acquiring additional units of merchandise can be several months, which is unacceptably long when the products are seasonal, such as Christmas toys or trendy summer clothing. If a company knows that it cannot fulfill the orders it would generate by mailing to the point where unit contribution equals contact cost, it should mail to fewer names. Unfulfilled orders would presumably have a negative effect on customer loyalty and corporate reputation. Conversely, a company that has ordered too much inventory may have to mail more names to sell the merchandise. Similarly, service providers that use direct marketing programs to generate business should consider their existing capacity and their ability to increase capacity quickly when making circulation decisions.

Contact Strategy Constraints. A company that attempts to implement longitudinal contact strategies[11] usually does not mail to the point where unit contribution equals the cost of the mailing. Contact strategies argue against "effort-by-effort" circulation planning. They involve planning a sequence of contacts over time to achieve some goal. For example, a catalog company that sends out eight catalogs and e-mail or postcard promotions during a six-month season may want to determine which combination of contacts each customer should receive to maximize profitability over the entire season. Here, it can be difficult to estimate expected revenues because of the possible interactions between the contacts.[12]

Biased Estimates. Scoring models estimate unit contribution and response probabilities using data from a previous mailing. For example, scoring models for an upcoming spring fashion catalog are usually estimated by modeling response and unit contribution for the spring fashion catalog that was mailed during the previous year. In using data from the previous year, the modeler implicitly assumes that nothing has changed between the two years, which is often not realistic. Many factors change, including the merchandise offered in the catalog, items that are trendy during a particular year, economic conditions, competition, weather conditions, and so on. These factors can bias the predictions from a model. For example, sales of winter clothing are higher when a winter is severe. If the competition in a market is more intense this year than last, response probabilities estimated from last year's data may be systematically high. Despite these possible biases, the relative ordering of the customers from a scoring model is usually still useful.

Rate Base Constraints. Publishers of magazines usually have contracts with advertisers guaranteeing a certain paid circulation. If the circulation of the magazine falls below this figure, the publisher encounters a financial penalty. To make rate base, publishers often must mail below the point where unit contribution equals contact cost. Here, the definition of mailing cost is particularly complicated—it takes one value if the company makes the rate base, and, if not, another value that depends on the number of responders.

SAMPLE SCORING MODEL

This section gives an example of building a scoring model. It illustrates linear and logistic regression scoring models and shows how these models can be improved. The organization is a charity.

The example data set[13] is from a national veterans organization, which provides programs and services for U.S. veterans with spinal cord injuries or disease. The organization has a database of more than 13 million donors, making it one of the largest direct mail fundraisers in the United States.

A group that is of particular interest to the organization is "lapsed" donors, those who made their last donation 13 to 24 months ago. They represent an important group, because the longer someone goes without donating, the less likely they will be to give again. Therefore, reactivation of these former donors is a critical aspect of the organization's fund-raising efforts.

A large group of lapsed donors were sent a solicitation in June 1997. We built models on a sample of 95,412 from this universe. The target period begins in June 1997, and the base period is prior to this date. In total, the original data set has 478 candidate predictor variables for each previous donor, including information about previous donations (dates and amounts), previous solicitations, demographic and lifestyle overlay information, and information from the U.S. Census Bureau. The goal of the scoring model is to use this other information to estimate the likelihood of response to the solicitation in June of 1997.

To keep the example manageable, we restrict our attention to only the following variables:

1. Recency, defined as the number of days between the last donation and June 1997.
2. Frequency, or the life-to-date count of donations to greeting card solicitations. (The June 1997 solicitation included greeting cards.)
3. The size of the most recent donation.
4. The percentage of expensive homes (over $150,000) in the neighborhood.
5. The number of previous solicitations.
6. The time since first donation.

The point of this example is to illustrate some of the basic steps in building a scoring model by examining a small number of possible variables. The purpose is not to describe the best of all possible models for this data set. To simplify the problem, the models presented here consider only a small number of variables and make no attempt to model the amount of the donation.[14]

Standard Linear Regression Model

One approach to building a scoring model is to use the usual summary variables in a regression model. We shall see that this approach will not always produce an efficient model; improvements are often possible through a closer examination of the data. Here are the estimates for a simple scoring model:

$$\text{Response} = 0.11 - 0.0021\,(\text{Recency}) + 0.0026\begin{pmatrix}\text{Number previous}\\ \text{donations}\end{pmatrix}$$
$$+\,0.00020\begin{pmatrix}\text{Percent expensive}\\ \text{homes}\end{pmatrix} - 0.00096\begin{pmatrix}\text{Last donation}\\ \text{amount}\end{pmatrix}$$
$$-\,0.00014\begin{pmatrix}\text{Number previous}\\ \text{solicitations}\end{pmatrix}$$

The coefficient for "time since first donation" was not significantly different from zero, so it was dropped from the model. We can examine the signs of the regression coefficients. The effect of recency is negative, meaning that the longer it has been since a person has made a donation, the less likely the person is to donate again, a typical finding for many different industries. The sign for frequency is positive (+0.0026), indicating that the more previous donations there had been, the more likely a person is to donate again. The sign for the percentage of homes over $150,000 in the neighborhood is also positive, indicating that those who live in affluent areas are more likely to donate.

The value of the R-square is .0069, and we have seen the gains table in Table 11.1. Despite the tiny value of R-square, the gains table indicates that the model is helpful, because those people in the top deciles have lifts substantially greater than 100.

This equation could be used to assign a score to everyone in the database. Assigning scores simply means computing a predicted value with the above equation.

A More Sophisticated Linear Regression Model

Linear regression models can be improved in a number of ways, including:

- *Forming new variables that are combinations of existing variables.* We could compute a previous response rate variable by dividing the number of previous gifts by the number of previous promotions.
- *Summarizing database with a different time window.* Perhaps the donation patterns in the past two years are more important than donations over the entire lifetime. Someone who gave large amounts one

year ago may be a better prospect than someone who donated large amounts five years ago and very little one year ago.
- *Identifying transformations and interactions.* A linear regression model can be improved by modifying the functional form of the model. Some relationships are nonlinear, suggesting diminishing marginal returns to scale. For example, the difference in response likelihood between someone who has donated once and someone who has donated twice may be much greater than the difference between someone who has donated 20 times and someone who has donated 21 times. When underlying relationships are nonlinear, linear regression does not provide an optimal fit. Fortunately, it is easy to improve the fit by finding transformations and interactions of the predictor variables.

The regression model was estimated after computing the previous response rate variable and versions of frequency in different time periods. The value of *R*-squared improves to .0090, and the gains table was presented in Table 11.2. As indicated in the gains table section, this model is more efficient in finding the lapsed donors who are likely to respond.

Logistic Regression Model

Linear regression analysis was not designed for problems in which the dependent variable is dichotomous (yes/no), but logistic regression, a close cousin of linear regression, was specifically designed for this purpose.[15] The basic steps in developing a logistic regression model are the same as those for developing a linear regression model. The results of the logistic regression model are shown in Table 11.3. The performance is similar to the more sophisticated linear regression model.

On Neural Networks and Other Modern Approaches

Building a good regression model can be difficult work. It requires a lot of effort by an expensive, skilled analyst to select the right variables and identify the transformations and interactions required for a good model. Many other modern regression methods have been proposed that produce good predictions without going through all these steps, including (feed-forward) neural networks, tree-based approaches (CART, QUEST, MARS), projection pursuit regression, nearest neighbor approaches, and radial basis functions.[16] These methods tend to be computationally more intensive.

Table 11.3
"Gains Table" from the Logistic Regression Model

Decile	*Number Mailed*	*Number Respond*	*Response Rate (%)*	*Lift*	*Cumulative Mailed*	*Respond*	*Rate (%)*	*Lift*
1	9,541	920	9.64	190	9,541	920	9.64	190
2	9,541	709	7.43	146	19,082	1,629	8.54	168
3	9,541	595	6.24	123	28,623	2,224	7.77	153
4	9,542	495	5.19	102	38,165	2,719	7.12	140
5	9,541	448	4.70	93	47,706	3,167	6.64	131
6	9,541	387	4.06	80	57,247	3,554	6.21	122
7	9,542	369	3.87	76	66,789	3,923	5.87	116
8	9,541	361	3.78	75	76,330	4,284	5.61	111
9	9,541	305	3.20	63	85,871	4,589	5.34	105
10	9,541	254	2.66	52	95,412	4,843	5.08	100

Rather than having an analyst spend hours finding transformations and interactions, the idea is to have a computer spend hours, days, or even weeks estimating the model. While the details of these methods are beyond the scope of this chapter, we make several general comments:

- These methods have produced good predictions for regression and classification problems in many different fields of study. They are worth considering.
- The quality of the model depends on the skill of the modeler. A highly skilled regression modeler should be able to produce predictions that are as good as those from, for example, a neural network (the regression modeler may want to use the modern methods for identifying transformation and interactions), although it could take more analyst time. Producing a first-rate model with one of these modern approaches also requires a skilled analyst.
- Experienced users of neural networks know how to tinker, cut, and paste. They have their own ways of adjusting the number of nodes in the hidden layer to get good performance, and preventing overfitting. But most of this is folk wisdom, and there is, so far, no handbook on the mysteries of tinkering with neural networks.[17]
- Many of the modern methods produce "black-box" models that do not give the analyst any insight as to how the predictor variables

affect response. With neural networks, there are no simple ways to understand the equivalent of the signs of regression coefficients, shapes of transformations, and nature of interactions.

CONCLUSIONS[18]

In summary, the key points of this chapter on scoring methods follow:

1. Scoring models estimate the likelihood of some future behavior.
2. The quality of predictions depends on the quality of our information about our customers. It is impossible to make accurate predictions if the information available as predictors is unrelated to the behavior being predicted.
3. The quality of predictions depends on the care used in developing the model and, hence, the skill of the modeler.
4. Models assume that the new period is similar to the period used to build the model. The quality of the predictions from a scoring model may diminish if the economy, competition, fashions or values, nature of the offer, and so forth change.
5. We evaluate scoring models using a gains table.
6. Perfect data is the exception, not the rule. Expect quirky data, identify the quirks at the beginning of the analysis, and deal with them.

Finally, beware of the perfect execution of a flawed strategy. Scoring models provide a powerful way of optimizing some tactic. Many companies from different industries have found them to be valuable in deciding exactly who should receive a particular tactic. It is easy, however, to become so caught up in optimizing the tactic that we forget about the bigger picture.

For example, a credit card company found that inserting offers selling various items into their billing statements was a profitable tactic. Over time, the company became better and better at optimizing this tactic by building sophisticated scoring models to determine which customer should receive particular offers, how many offers, and so on. Later, the credit card company noticed that the customers who were responding to these offers were also much more likely to cancel their cards. The company, which was in the business of providing credit rather than selling items, was undermining its core business with this tactic. Always consider whether a tactic is consistent with the brand, mission, and values of a company. Always consider the long-term ramifications of the tactic.

Notes

1. The Knowledge Discovery and Data Mining (KDD) Competition 2000 modeled these behaviors. See http://www.ecn.purdue.edu/KDDCUP for more details.
2. See Chapter 8 by Malthouse in this volume on "Database Sub-Segmentation" for additional discussion about this kind of data.
3. See http://venus.census.gov/cdrom/lookup.
4. See http://www.claritas.com.
5. If the responses of all customers are affected the same way by a slower economy, a scoring model will still work, for example, if everyone is 20 percent less likely than they were before the slowdown to make a purchase. A problem occurs when the slowdown affects customers differently, for example, if affluent people are 10 percent less likely to purchase while middle-class people are 40 percent less likely to purchase.
6. Nevertheless, fit should be considered to be important; a model that performs well should do so because it encodes an understanding of the drivers of response and accurately represents the behaviors being modeled. Thus, it would seem that good fit is a prerequisite for these objectives. Or, consider that fit is important in estimating long-term value (LTV), or the (discounted) expected amount of money a customer will spend during a long-term period. If estimating LTV is the objective, the estimates must be made as accurately as possible.
7. A gains table is also commonly called a lift chart (or table), or decile analysis (which can have other meanings to database marketers). Other quantiles such as demideciles (20 groups) or centiles (100 groups) are sometimes used.
8. There may not be exactly 10 percent of the sample in each group because of tied score values.
9. See Saharon Rosset, Einat Neumann, Uri Eick, Nurit Vatnik, and Izhak Idan, "Evaluation of Prediction Models for Marketing Campaigns," in *Proceedings of the Seventh ACM International Conference on Knowledge Discovery and Data Mining* (2001), pp. 456–461.
10. For further discussion of LTV, see David Shepard, *The New Direct Marketing: How to Implement a Profit-Driven Database Marketing Strategy* 3rd ed. (New York: McGraw-Hill, 1999), pp. 451–476, or Mary Lou Roberts and Paul D. Burger, *Direct Marketing Management* 2nd ed. (Upper Saddle River, NJ: Prentice Hall, 1999), Chapter 9. For discussion of the history of record clubs, see Lester Wunderman, *Being Direct: Making Advertising Pay* (New York: Random House, 1997), Chapters 11–13.
11. Robert Kestnbaum, Kate Kestnbaum, and Pamela Ames, "Building a Longitudinal Contact Strategy," *Journal of Interactive Marketing* vol. 12, no. 1 (1998), pp. 56–62.
12. Lester Wunderman's "curriculum marketing programs" are akin to longitudinal contact strategies. These programs are useful when more than one customer contact is necessary to produce a sale; Wunderman, *Being Direct,* pp. 226–244 and 260–263.
13. This data set was analyzed by participants of the 1998 Knowledge Discovery and Data Mining Competition. See Stephen D. Bay, University of California at Irvine,

Knowledge Discovery and Data Mining archive, Department of Information and Computer.

14. See Bianca Zadrozny and Charles Elkan, "Learning and Making Decisions When Costs and Probabilities Are Both Unknown," in *Proceedings of Seventh ACM International Conference on Knowledge Discover and Data Mining* (2001), pp. 204–213 for discussion on modeling amounts.
15. See Paul Allison, *Logistic Regression Using the SAS System: Theory and Applications* (Cary, NC: SAS Institute, 1999) for a very readable and applied introduction to logistic regression.
16. See Trevor Hastie, Robert Tibshirani, and Jerome H. Friedman, *The Elements of Statistical Learning: Data Mining, Inference and Prediction* (New York: Springer-Verlag, 2001) or Brian D. Ripley, *Pattern Recognition and Neural Networks* (Cambridge: Cambridge University Press, 1996) for further discussion of these methods. Jiawei Han and Micheline Kamber, *Data Mining: Concepts and Techniques* (New York: Morgan Kaufmann, 2000). Chapter 7 gives a shorter and less technical introduction to these methods.
17. Leo Breiman, comment on "Neural Networks: A Review from a Statistical Perspective" by Bing Cheng and D. M. Titterington, *Statistical Science,* vol. 9, no. 1 (1994), p. 40.
18. A technical appendix is available from the author that illustrates how data-mining methods can overfit data.

CHAPTER 12

INTEGRATING MARKETING AND THE WEB

ERIC G. BERGGREN, BOBBY J. CALDER, and
RICHARD I. KOLSKY

The *real* Internet revolution is about to start. It is time to integrate the Web into your marketing efforts. Too many Web operations are predicated on the logic of the Internet bubble of the 1990s. In this article, we argue that it is time to learn from the past.

Most existing Internet operations were conceived in "Internet Space," a black hole of fertile imaginations and deep passions. Many have failed, and even the most successful face significant obstacles. Nevertheless, traditional firms, and even new dot-com firms, can create Web strategies that avoid the mistakes of the past and truly realize the potential of the Web. The path to this potential is to integrate marketing and the Web. But this integration requires that we begin to think about marketing from a different perspective—one less bound to the old media of television, print, and conventional distribution channels. To facilitate this, we introduce a concept that we call *customer space*. It is in the extended realm of customer space that the marketing potential of the Web will be realized.

THE OLD "NEW" MINDSET

The exuberance of the late 1990s, fueled by venture capital, is fading. The Information Highway is littered with road kill like Pets.com, eToys, Priceline's Warehouse Club, and DrKoop.com. The voices of the gurus preaching the rise of the "new economy" grow ever more muted. Their mantra, "They just don't get it," aimed at those who did not follow, seems self-serving at best. The fact is the utopia of the new economy was just that—a utopian bubble.

There is a revolution afoot, however. It will change the way companies think about the Internet and the way they *will* use it as part of an integrated marketing strategy. Our goal is to lay out this new marketing thinking about the Internet. To do so, it is instructive to consider how inadequate the old "new" mind-set about the Internet was.

For the most part, the original Internet revolutionaries got sucked into the mind-set of Internet space. At one time, nothing seemed cooler in Internet speak, the language of the revolution, than the notion of Internet Space. As in, "What space are you (they) in?" The Internet was imagined to be a vast stretch of territory and parts of this territory were there to be colonized by whoever could get there first.

Internet Space might be virtual, but each site's location in that space was very real and could be defined by three "coordinates," all relating to the functionality of the Web site:

1. *Content:* The process typically began by selecting an impassioned interest of the founders. This domain could be general or quite specific, covering every subject from news to search engines to weddings for left-handed couples marrying in June.
2. *Product/service:* Then, the founders decided what to offer all the traffic they were destined to attract—shall we be an information source, a store, an exchange, or some combination?
3. *Experience:* Then came the fun part—how to jazz up the site experience, with an attractive look and feel, easy-to-use interfaces, interactivity, and personalization. Will we create a virtual community? Will we remember your preferences and feed you recommendations?

The intention was to claim a space, a large space if possible, but, in any case, one that was at least your own. Internet strategies were focused on finding a space that could be yours before it was gone.

Once you had claimed it, your space defined the functionality of your Web site, subject only to the level of technology that was available and could be funded. For example, once Amazon staked out books, became a store, and enhanced the experience by providing tailored recommendations and encouraging participants to interact by posting reviews, all that remained was to work out the technical details and refinements, such as "one click ordering." The focus of the old mind-set was space, space, and space—the not terribly insightful corollary to location, location, location in the physical world.

What to do once you had claimed the space and built the site was a secondary issue but one that had to be faced. Thinking typically proceeded as follows:

- *Users will come.* The Web is exploding with growth. This growth is creating a vast group of users who are looking (surfing) for sites. Some will land on our site and use our space. We are after "eyeballs" and all we need is visibility. This thinking led to a stress on memorable addresses, search engine listings, links with other sites, aggregation, stickiness, and all the other stock-in-trade devices that came to be so commonplace: "Space plus visibility."
- *If they come, we will be rewarded.* Purchasing is increasing on the Web. Although we may not sell enough today to make a profit, some day the volume will be there and so will we. (Or at least the habit or loyalty will be there, and we can raise prices.) Alternatively, if our space does not emphasize product/service, we can still make money by virtue of the fact that people come. Subscriptions, advertising, sponsorship, resale of data: "Space plus visibility plus revenue."

But space plus visibility plus revenue did not equal profitability. Of course, in the last throes of the revolution, thinking about visibility and revenue reached new heights. Desperate advertising campaigns were added to the quest for visibility. And speculation about sources of revenue led to an expansion in the scope of sites beyond any foundation in the space owned.

Examples of the old "new" mind-set at work abound. The Parkinson brothers founded Peapod, the online grocer, because they had read that grocery shopping was second only to doing laundry as the most dreaded chore. Stores were crowded and shopping took too much time. So Peapod staked a claim to some virgin Internet Space. It focused on selling grocery products, with very narrow content (primarily easy unit price and ingredient comparison) and limited interactivity.

While Peapod was able to eliminate the trip to the store and all its aggravation, it could not give people the ability to see and touch the actual product that would arrive. Customers also had to plan ahead in placing orders and make themselves available to receive the deliveries. The majority of grocery shoppers found one aspect of their experience improved, but other aspects created even greater frustrations—not exactly a superior solution. Consequently, online grocers have thus far found few target consumers who hate the grocery store so much that they are willing to accept these inconveniences and cover the cost of system development and maintenance, as well as delivery trucks and personnel.

Case after case shows that the problem was not the Internet, but the mind-set of the Internet revolutionaries. "Space plus visibility plus revenue equals profitability" was just not the right formula. The logic was flawed at each step of the way. It was never enough just to claim an unoccupied space. The visibility of that space was never sufficient for getting more than temporary eyeballs. And revenue cannot be an afterthought; it does not automatically flow from someone's happening to land on the space. Furthermore, revenue does not automatically translate into profitability.

With the advantage of hindsight, we can see that the Internet revolutionaries were looking in all the wrong places and missing the key thing—the customer. It has always been the customer who counts, and it is customer space that matters. It is the life of the customer and the way the Internet fits into and *expands* the customer's life, what we mean by customer space, that will define the real Internet revolution. As our thinking about the Internet changes to embrace customer space, the real revolution can begin.

THE INTERNET AND CUSTOMER SPACE

So where is the opportunity on the Web? The Internet gurus thought they knew it: "It's portals . . . no wait, it's communities . . . no, it's infomediaries . . . no, it's online storefronts . . . no, it's definitely aggregation . . ." If we've learned anything in the past five years, it is that the Internet has not changed the fundamental laws of physics, economics, or marketing. The next revolution will be fought in customer space, where navigating will require a new "new" mind-set. Customer space in the world of e-commerce (just as it was before the Internet) is defined by three activities:

1. *Target the profitable segments:* from easy eyeballs to hard bodies.
2. *Maximize your value leverage:* from valuable functionality to profitable total solutions.
3. *Position for maximum life relevance:* from awareness to value and relevance.

Target the Profitable Segments

The Internet may facilitate one-to-one marketing, but it does not replace the need to identify and target specific segments. Many dot-coms developed massive and clever ad campaigns to attract the maximum number of eyeballs to their sites, figuring customers could customize their experience. But the assumption that the attracted customers would generate revenue and become profitable is fundamentally flawed. The easiest customers to attract are ready to move only because they:

- Are fed up with current providers.
- Are techies who want to try out the latest and greatest site.
- Are perpetual shoppers looking for the best price.

Typically, disgruntled customers are easy eyeballs (because they are always looking), but hard bodies to retain because the total solutions they seek are difficult to deliver. We need only look at current benefits to cost close rates to realize that attracting the dissatisfied bricks-and-mortar shopper is a lot easier than satisfying him or her. Far too many sites have paid dearly to attract these eyeballs, only to have them look elsewhere to buy.

Techies create similar problems. They always want the latest new technology, and maintaining that leadership position can be prohibitively expensive, if not impossible. In fact, techies are inherently disloyal because they live to discover the new, new thing, and inherently unprofitable because they believe that everything on the Internet should be free.

Last, the Net's perpetual price shoppers and intensive researchers are typically the least profitable and least attractive customers. They buy primarily on price, leading to lower margins on initial purchases, and then frequently switch vendors/brands for better deals, leading to lower retention. They also are sponges (even leeches) for information and other services, leading to higher costs. The Internet has not changed their behavior; rather it has given them a more cost- and time-efficient way to practice their profit-destroying behavior. It is no wonder that Priceline has struggled to create a profitable business model to serve these customers.

When considering any potential target segment, ask yourself: If the Internet did not exist, would you still want these customers? You can make money off these transactors, like Wal-Mart, but you have to have the absolute lowest costs, like Wal-Mart.

What is wonderful about the Web is the potential to get a lot more for a lot less. Therefore, it is time to move from easy eyeballs to hard bodies. If not the price shoppers, techies, and whiners, then who is the B2C target? The answer is: segments with significant potential for *value leverage.* You will have the greatest leverage with segments for whom the perceived

Priceline and the Paradox of Internet Space: Even When You Win . . . You Still Lose

Priceline successfully claimed Internet space and generated huge volume without building a sustainably profitable business. Initially, Priceline had to subsidize consumer purchases. It bought and resold airline tickets to improve the customer's chance (originally less than 10 percent) of getting the ticket. Later, it got a major airline (Delta) to participate by offering warrants to purchase 15 million shares in Priceline (worth $1 billion at one point). In other words, its customers are so unattractive that Priceline had to bribe the provider with $1 billion to participate. Perhaps Henny Youngman should have replaced spokesperson William Shatner: "Take my customers . . . please!" Now that the warrants are worth significantly less, the airlines have looked at what Priceline brings to the party and concluded that they can get rid of their excess inventory on their own. All the major airlines have banded together to form a rival service.

How did Priceline respond? It tried to colonize another dark planet in Internet Space—expanding the scope of the products and services it offered. But just because a consumer conducted a transaction with you online does not mean you have an intimate one-to-one relationship that will transcend product boundaries. For example, if I were willing to stop overnight in Iceland to save $41 on my European vacation, does that mean that I'd tolerate adding an hour to create a shopping list and then have to settle for off-brands in my grocery shopping, or go out of my way to save $1 the next time I fill up? Where's the disappearing gas and grocery inventory that provided the "cost" opportunity for airline tickets? Is it any wonder that Priceline's forays into gasoline and grocery shopping failed? As Priceline learned, B2C sites should not assume that cross-selling will be easy or economical. Priceline has mastered Internet space, but it is losing in customer space.

benefits of the total customer experience exceed your costs by the largest amount. Contrast Schwab with E*Trade. The price shoppers who use E*Trade are the easy eyeballs, but they represent low customer value because they perceive little benefit from anything but executing the trade; they are not willing to pay much for service. E*Trade can make money from them, but it will have to have the lowest costs.

For the vast majority of investors, however, executing a cheap trade is not terribly meaningful or relevant to achieving their overarching objectives—managing their wealth or ensuring their lifestyle. Schwab has gone after these hard bodies in online investing. Schwab's customers get a good, but not the best, price; however, they also get access to analysts' reports, integrated statements, decision-making tools, wealth management expertise, and infrastructure (like OneSource for mutual funds, AdvisorSource for investment/estate planning, branches for face-to-face service, etc.) that E★Trade can't match. Interestingly, E★Trade has bought an Internet bank and is adding other products and services in an effort to occupy more Internet space! However, it is still focusing on the "price shopper" with services that are transactional in nature, only this time without a clear cost advantage—a potentially deadly combination.

Schwab's leverage with its target customers is significantly higher. Yet, while Schwab benefits from a cost advantage now that 80 percent of its transactions are electronic, 70 percent of its customers still want to open their accounts face-to-face in a branch. Because Schwab's target customers are more attractive, and its solution more complete, its market value per customer (at the end of the year 2000) was almost 8 times E★Trade's. See Figures 12.1 and 12.2 for comparisons on these companies' figures.

Maximize Your Value Leverage

Forget Internet space and start with the right question: What is the customer trying to accomplish, and can you improve that experience profitably by using the added dimension of the Web?

Amazon has created a total solution for the book-buying experience. What benefits are the dual-income, time-poor, overeducated consumers of

Figure 12.1
Schwab and E★Trade: Numbers of Accounts

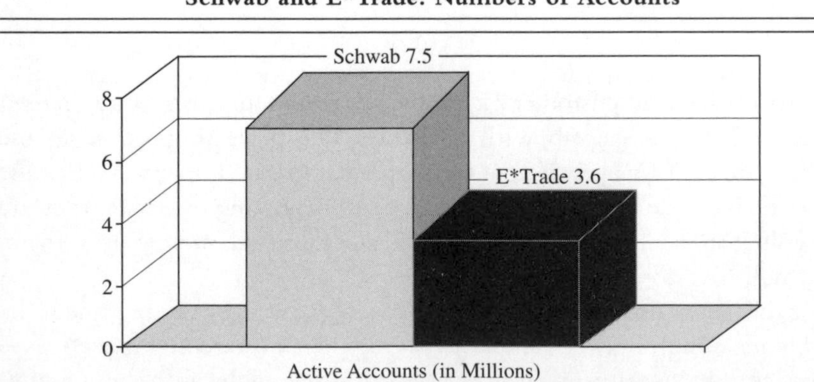

Figure 12.2
Scwab and E*Trade: Values

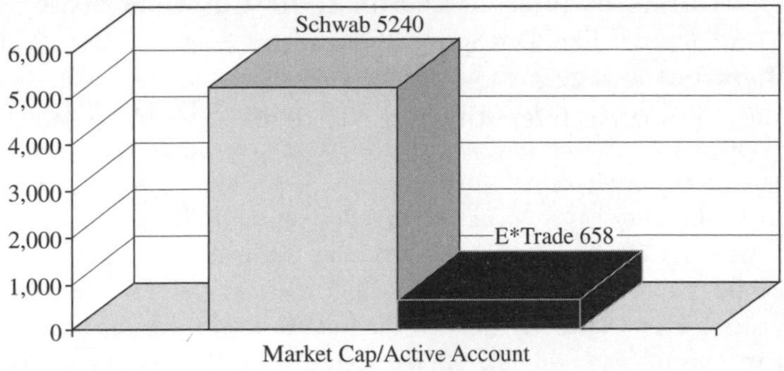

today looking for when purchasing books? Quite simply: variety, availability (in a reasonable time frame), and objective advice without the waste of a lot of their precious time. Amazon has taken each of these benefits to new heights online with a significantly more comprehensive inventory, simple search capabilities, editorial and customer reviews, recommendations based on customers' individual tastes, and a patented one click ordering system. Buying a book has never been easier. When we have asked Amazon consumers why they use Amazon, the answer is rarely price; instead, customers talk about the convenience of not having to go to the store only to find that the book is unavailable. In fact, Amazon has finally reached the conclusion that it has a better solution that customers are willing to pay for; it has recently raised prices by 10 percent on best-sellers. By pricing for the value that it creates, Amazon is finally turning the online book business profitable.

eBay has also done a masterful job of delivering a total solution that dramatically improves virtually every aspect of the target customer's experience while reducing the cost of the traditional distribution system. In the coming revolution, a total solution will be necessary—but insufficient by itself—to owning and prospering in your customer space.

Strive for Maximum Life Relevance

No business concepts have been more abused online than branding and one-to-one relationships. First, in their drive for visibility, most e-tailers have confused name recognition for brand. A brand is not a name or logo

Despite Its Success in Internet Space, eBay Will Ultimately Need to Dominate Its Customer Space

Most Internet strategy starts with the wrong question: "How can the Net's functionality improve the customer's experience?" This question can lead to a successful business only if that functionality can deliver significantly enhanced customer value with minimal cost. Take eBay and its auction functionality. For hard-to-find items, eBay dramatically lowers search costs and increases effectiveness by eliminating the need to spend your entire weekend browsing garage sales or reading thousands of "for sale" classifieds or visiting every hardware store in the state to find a missing part. For expensive second-hand durable goods, such as camera equipment, eBay can match buyers and sellers who can then share 50 percent to 75 percent reseller margins. It also ensures recourse for items purchased from strangers. Last, it has made shopping on the Net entertaining by introducing the thrill of bidding into the buying process.

eBay was skillful enough to hit a home run with a well-orchestrated combination of Net functionalities, but its bigger challenge is, "What next?" In Internet Space, eBay has a dominant share of consumer auctions, and, thus, it is unlikely to grow by stealing share. It can:

- Sit tight and grow with the Internet user population, but that's not an exciting story to tell Wall Street.
- Develop a new Net functionality, but which one?
- Reach out to new types of customers, but which ones?
- Expand the types of products/services that it offers, but which ones?

How should eBay allocate its resources across these opportunities? Others have already stumbled at this point in their conquest of Internet Space because they didn't understand customer space.

What does eBay look like in customer space? First, what segments should it target? Today, eBay has become a destination site for consumers looking for a specific item or interested in browsing for something that might pique their interest. In fact, the classification system in eBay is tough to navigate. Customers revisit the site because they had fun the last time and know that eBay is the most likely place to find what they're looking for—if not the easiest place to find it.

Second, can't eBay go further in helping to improve customers' lives and, therefore, become more meaningful and relevant? For example, it already implicitly targets "nostalgia-holics," or those people who try to recreate the past. What if it were to truly create a life-transforming experience, rather than simply a series of fun transactions? For example, consider all of the

Despite Its Success in Internet Space, eBay Will Ultimately Need to Dominate Its Customer Space (*Continued*)

vintage Coke bottles sold on eBay. Is there a group of customers looking to create the 1950s feel for a family room in their homes, complete with leather chairs, vintage movie posters, and an authentic jukebox?

Last, what is the total solution that would extend that customer relationship? For example, could eBay:

- Help to (or partner with other organizations to) create more interest in the era or topic?
- Give consumers new ideas for nostalgic items that might be unique and/or appreciate in value over time?
- Allow consumers to find and purchase those items faster (the site's their main benefit today)?
- Teach consumers how to use and care for their new items (and sell the necessary supplies)?
- Show consumers the best places to repair those items if they break (borrowing a page from Sears' success in the 1950s)?
- Enable those customers to sell those items (perhaps at a profit) when their tastes change? Could eBay become the GE Capital of nostalgia leasing?

In other words, eBay should be looking for creative ways to build on its strength, yet be open to building fundamentally new capabilities to solve the broader customer problem. Is this segment one of the most attractive for eBay? We don't know because we have not analyzed the economics of the business model for this example. Nevertheless, this solution is undoubtedly more complete and meaningful to this target customer than eBay's internally driven classification of products.

or clever slogan. A brand is an idea in the mind of a customer—it is what your company or your particular solution means to them. A great brand is an idea that is meaningful, relevant, and valuable to the customer's life. For example, in the 1990s, the "big idea" of the Microsoft brand was the perception among consumers that its software was ubiquitous. This ubiquity was essential to the lives of consumers who were paranoid about being able to integrate information across applications on their desktops and share that information with other computer users. Consequently, Microsoft was able to take over the spreadsheet, word processing, and presentation software markets even though it had technically inferior product offerings. Unfortunately, the brand meanings for many of the e-tailers lacked sufficient "life relevance" to be a powerful motivator for consumers to buy without significant price breaks, resulting in unsustainable profit models.

Second, once armed with brand awareness and a couple of price-based transactions with customers, many e-tailers expected to easily cross-sell them additional items. In reality, when you start off with a freebie or price-based transaction, a long-term relationship is unlikely to develop, in part because the "brand meaning" is transactional and in part because the consumers are self-selected transactors.

The key to extending the product and service scope of any relationship is to solve more important problems for the customer. In other words, you have to earn the right to have a relationship with your customers. This must be done with both a series of total solutions and a supporting "brand meaning." Schwab started out as a simple discount broker; the equivalent of today's E*Trade. It could have focused on executing low-cost transactions; instead, it continued to create more comprehensive solutions to its target customers' wealth management issues (from creating OneSource to buying US Trust). The Schwab brand has laddered up from being a *cheap trade* to being a *trusted source for helping me invest and manage my money smarter,* which is more meaningful and relevant to their targets' lives, and gives Schwab the ability to cost-effectively cross-sell. For example, when they launched annuities (a product traditionally sold by untrusted insurance agents), Schwab generated $1 billion in sales with virtually no advertising cost.

WHAT YOU CAN DO TODAY

Brick-and-mortar companies that have made unsuccessful e-commerce efforts can take heart. Despite the rhetoric about the dot-coms coming in and destroying all existing businesses, the "hard (but most profitable) bodies" are still customers of old-economy companies, and those firms have the breadth of capabilities to more effectively deliver meaningful and relevant total solutions. In customer space, the dot-coms may be at a disadvantage. For example, Wingspan (BankOne's Internet-only bank) attracted only 100,000 customers after spending more than $100 million on advertising and promotion, while BankOne's clicks-and-mortar service signed up more than 500,000 accounts at a fraction of that cost.

The good news is that customer space is navigable, if you take the following steps to create and dominate the next B2C revolution:

1. Analyze one customer at a time to understand your target market's needs and to identify the most meaningful and relevant imperfections in the customers' current experience. Total solutions cannot be derived from superficial, incomplete views of your customer generated from phone surveys. Rather, the most useful insights are created the old-fashioned way: one customer at a time. Go in-depth with individual customers and analyze their entire experience from need identification to action to the results of their current solution.
2. Develop total solutions that address the most meaningful and relevant imperfections and measure the resulting customer value against the costs of delivering that value. View the solution as it fits into the life of your target market from customer space, rather than the Web experience of an alien content expert from Internet space!
3. Segment and prioritize customers based on your customer value leverage (customer value created minus your cost to deliver). Be selective, find the hard, sticky bodies, and avoid the temptation to chase the easy eyeballs.
4. Reposition your brand for your chosen targets. Strive for maximum life relevance and customer value leverage by rigorously defining the winning value proposition and delivery strategy for each target. Integrate every potential brand contact (beyond simple marketing communications) to reinforce this new brand meaning.

Today is the perfect time to build a profitable and defensible business using the Internet. Yesterday's conventional wisdom said that whoever was first to stake a claim to Internet space would generate previously unimaginable wealth, but today the belief is that "profitable" and "defensible" businesses are difficult, if not impossible, to create on the Net. It is difficult offline, so why wouldn't it be difficult online? But it is impossible only if your strategic thinking languishes in Internet space.

CONCLUSION

The irony is that all businesses now operate in customer space, whether they know it or not. The Internet is here to stay. It is a part of the lives of most consumers. As new generations come of age, it will become a bigger dimension in the consumer's life. Internet hysteria distracted otherwise smart managers from addressing the real issue of how the Internet really changes the consumer's life. This is where smart companies will focus in the future.

CHAPTER 13

AN ILLUSTRATION OF INTEGRATED MARKETING

BOBBY J. CALDER

The goal of integrated marketing is to create a consumer, or customer, experience that is as meaningful and relevant as possible. That experience comes from a set of contacts or touchpoints with a product/company over time. Some of these contacts are ideally customized to specific sub-segments of consumers. The entire set of contacts is managed so that they form a single integrated experience from the point of view of the consumer.

In what follows, I describe the development of an integrated marketing program as a case illustration. The product is the daily newspaper. Most newspapers in the United States currently follow the classic functional approach to marketing. They seek to associate their news coverage with the benefit of being local and a part of the community or with some other benefit such as providing a high level of expertise and trustworthiness. They promote the benefit of the newspaper with advertising messaging and attempt to orchestrate this with editorial decisions about content (product) and pricing and distribution decisions. As can happen all too easily with such a functional approach, the marketing benefit that newspapers focus on is typically too vaguely conceived and too broadly targeted. In addition, from the point of view of consumers, advertising is hard to relate to the content of the newspaper. Likewise, pricing is likely to revolve around discount offers.

How could a newspaper profit from integrated marketing?

THE PROCESS

Integrated marketing begins with a strong connection to corporate strategy. Almost all newspaper companies in the United States face a similar strategic problem. Whereas there are many heavy readers of newspapers, heavy readers tend to be older and part of a generation that is less attuned to other media as a source of news and more imbued from an early age with the habit of reading the daily newspaper. An explicit strategy for dealing with this situation is a necessary first step in developing an integrated marketing plan.

Once a strategy is in place, we must think through the consumer's experience of the product. What is the experience now of reading the newspaper? How will the experience have to change for the strategy to be successful? For this, we must analyze not just the benefit of various attributes of the newspaper, but the consumer's life more generally. How does/could the newspaper fit into the lifestyle of the consumer and the culture that the consumer is part of?

It is necessary to develop a concept or idea of what the consumer's experience must be to be meaningful and relevant. We can then use this concept to design contact points or touchpoints aimed at creating the desired experience. The product itself is, of course, the prime platform for such contacts. What can we do in the newspaper to create the experience that we have conceptualized for the consumer?

Beyond the product platform, there are ordinarily other contact points that occur both before and after use of the product itself. These may relate to the acquisition or retention of consumers (i.e., sales contacts). More generally, however, these contacts are intended to extend the experience beyond the product platform itself or to reinforce the experience. Contacts should span a range of communication opportunities. Advertising media may play a role but should not be limited necessarily to message exposures. Some contacts may involve communication among consumers and represent viral marketing efforts.

Attention should also be given in the integrated marketing process to the possibilities for customer relationship management. If the original segment of targeted consumers can be sub-segmented into groups for which special contacts are relevant, it may be possible to establish customized relationships in which consumers feel that the experience is being tailored to them. Beyond this, if specific contacts (such as cross-selling) are repeated over time, these contacts can be evaluated with scoring models so that only consumers who are likely to respond are contacted. The use of scoring models, as with sub-segmentation, can add a relationship quality to the consumer's experience.

THE STRATEGY

Return to the situation facing newspapers. Newspaper companies have a variety of strategic options. They could concentrate on current heavy readers and seek to exploit this base. Another strategy would be to go after light readers to increase their market penetration. Light readers are people who read the newspaper but who do so infrequently, or they do not spend much time with the newspaper or complete much of it. The light reader may get the newspaper by buying a single copy or by reading a copy passed along by someone else. (Even pass-along is valuable because of advertising revenue.) And even subscribers can be light readers. They simply do not get to all of the issues delivered to them, or they read the issues in a very incomplete way. These light readers are highly likely to "churn" at renewal time.

The strongest characteristic of light readers is that they are younger. Both Generation X and Y are more likely to be light readers. They have grown up with both television and the Internet.

Let's say the explicit strategy of a newspaper company is to increase readership (frequency, time, and completeness) of these light readers. We now have the direction for an integrated marketing plan. The goal is nothing less than to create an experience of reading the newspaper that is meaningful and relevant to these readers.

THE EXPERIENCE

We must first consider the current experience of light readers. We need to develop an idea, a concept, of how this experience could be more meaningful and relevant. Here are some of the reactions that many light readers now have to the news in general and to newspapers in particular:

"I feel drowned by the news."

"I already know what is going on without having to read the paper—repetition is boring, plus the news can be depressing."

"Much of the paper is uninteresting, and I feel my time has been wasted after I read it." (Subscribers: "But if I don't, I feel bad that they pile up unread.")

"I do not have time in my day to sit down and *read* the paper."

Light readers tend to feel overwhelmed by information. They express this with words such as "drowned" or "flooded" or the like. There is so much information, but so little seems really new. Much of this flow of information is just the reporting of events that seem repetitious and not worth thinking about or talking about to others. And this sense of being awash in information is all part of a larger busy lifestyle that already seems out of balance with things that must get done but are not very personally stimulating.

Light readers do value being informed and keeping up. They especially do not want to be seen by others as someone who does not know or care about what is going on. The newspaper is not irrelevant to them. But they do not feel that they can get enough out of the newspaper without spending far more time reading, and perhaps not even then. They do not come away from the newspaper with a sense of what is interesting and worth thinking and talking about.

Integrated marketing requires that we come up with a concept that can make the consumer's experience more meaningful and relevant. For the marketer, this is a branding idea. For the light reader, it is simply an idea of how the newspaper is more stimulating.

Here is one such concept: The newspaper not only brings you the news of the day but also asks the questions behind the news. In every issue, questions are raised that are worth thinking and talking about to others. The questions are made more interesting by using information to show how a person might answer the question in different ways. There is, however, no attempt to resolve the question or even to debate it. The emphasis is on showing how provocative the question is—on why it is stimulating to think about the question and perhaps talk to others about it. For Generations X and Y, the question is even more intriguing if it leads to an ironic take on current events or life in general.

Per our illustration, this concept might be described more concretely, but still in concept form, as shown in Figure 13.1. In qualitative interviews, light readers readily grasp this concept and anticipate that their experience of the newspaper would be much more positive.[1]

PRODUCT PLATFORM CONTACTS

The brand concept serves as a guide to delivering the desired experience for the consumer. We now need to design into the product the content of the newspaper in our illustration—contacts or touchpoints that would in fact result in the desired experience. In the case of the newspaper, one obvious possibility is the use of stories that pose stimulating questions.

Figure 13.1
A Concept for Light Readers

The newspaper that features stories that arouse your curiosity, make you think – and want to talk to others

Scratch your head

Think to yourself

Talk to others

DID YOU KNOW

Figure 13.2
A Front-Page Contact Point

The Daily Paper

TUESDAY, JANUARY 29, 2002

www.newsobserver.com

FINAL EDITION
50 CENTS

Detainees are killers, Bush says

President promises help for Afghanistan

BY RON HUTCHESON
KNIGHT RIDDER NEWSPAPERS

WASHINGTON — President Bush said Monday that detainees captured in Afghanistan are terrorist killers — not prisoners of war — but he left open the possibility that the United States would adhere to international rules governing the treatment of battlefield captives.

Wading into a dispute that has roiled his Cabinet and divided world opinion, Bush said he will decide soon whether captured al-Qaeda and Taliban fighters will receive protections under the Geneva Convention. But Bush also made it clear that he has no intention of granting the detainees prisoner of war status, a designation that would give them the highest level of protection.

"They will not be treated as prisoners of war. They're illegal combatants," Bush told reporters at a brief joint news conference with Hamid Karzai, the head of Afghanistan's

INSIDE

RAID: U.S. special forces help end a standoff at a Kandahar hospital. ▶6A

Catching Bin Laden: Spare lives or accomplish the mission?

DEBATABLE

Are we trying too hard to prevent U.S. casualties?

Nearly two months after the last major battle in Afghanistan, Osama bin Laden's location is as mysterious as ever. Some intelligence sources think they can pinpoint the period when bin Laden slipped away and cite a military misjudgment. This episode raises questions about how the United States conducted this war and how it should conduct future wars.

The incident in question is the decision to call a brief cease-fire at the height of U.S. bombing in Tora Bora. Al-Qaeda fighters were holed up in cave complexes in the region that borders Pakistan, and intelligence indicated bin Laden might be with them. U.S. bombers were blasting the cave complexes, while anti-Taliban allied conducted the ground fighting. U.S. and British commandos had not yet arrived in large numbers to lead the hunt for bin Laden.

Rebels under the command of warlords in Tora Bora called a surprise cease-fire at the peak of the bombing and U.S. commanders agreed to the request. Intelligence officials now say the cease-fire was called to allow al-Qaeda forces to escape, probably across the mountains into Pakistan. "Plain and simple, the United States was hoodwinked," said Sohab Qadri, intelligence chief of the anti-Taliban forces in Tora Bora.

The real issue is the reliance on proxy forces in Afghanistan to conduct the ground war in the early stages. When you have allies on the ground, you have to cooperate on tactics, including cease-fires, Pentagon officials say.

Another strategy involving large numbers of U.S. ground forces earlier in the fighting might have made Bin Laden's capture more likely but would have been far bloodier than the Afghanistan war.

Relying on proxy forces in Afghanistan —rather than a large force of our own—ensured that the hunt for bin Laden would fall to the bottom of the priority list. Opposition fighters had one major goal: seizing power from the Taliban. Once that was realized, they had little interest in doing the United States' bidding.

The question for U.S. officials—and for the country – remains whether sparing American lives at the expense of letting bin Laden slip away was a reasonable tradeoff.

Fleeing fire, 500 drown

STATE OF THE UNION

TIME: 9 p.m. today
TV: On most major networks
AT GOP HEADQUARTERS: Watch with Republicans at 1410 Hillsborough St. in downtown Raleigh.

TOWN HALL MEETING

TIME: 2:30 p.m. Wednesday
WHERE: Lawrence Joel Coliseum, Winston Salem
TICKETS: A limited number are available through the state Republican Party. Call (919) 828-6423.
INSIDE: Bush expected to address education, terrorism issues. ▶7A

State

Figure 13.3
A Business Page Contact Point

WEDNESDAY, JANUARY 30, 2002

DOW 247.51 at 9,618.24	NYSE 14.70 at 564.93
NASDAQ 50.92 at 1,892.99	S&P 500 32.42 at 1,100.64
AMEX 7.13 at 826.69	10-YEAR NOTE YIELD 4.942%, down from 5.073%

The Daily Paper

Business

D

SciQuest: Company posts a loss that was less than analysts had expected. **Page 2D**

Local banks: Interest rate cuts have hurt their earnings. **Page 2D**

Sept. 11 victims' fund: What price to pay for a human life?

DEBATABLE

How much should the U.S. government compensate terror victims' families?

How much is human life worth? Some would say it's priceless; other may offer more concrete figures. It all depends on whom you ask.

But would you ever expect to get the answer, "Depends on how they died"? That's the answer we seem to be getting from the U.S. government.

The debate: A federal commission has written the final rules for death benefits to compensate those who lost family members in the World Trade Center and Pentagon attacks on September 11. The multi-million dollar awards going to these families far exceed the standard death benefits – an average one-time payout of $6,000 plus monthly stipends - for military personnel killed in combat, and many Americans are asking why.

To add to the debate, those who lost family members to the Oklahoma City bombing and on the U.S.S. Cole are now demanding federal compensation. All this causes us to ask the questions "How much should the government give to compensate for the loss of life and where does it draw the line on whom should be compensated?"

Setting a standard?: According to the Victim Compensation Fund for the families of the nearly 3,000 people killed in the Sept. 11 attacks, the cost of a human life is, on average, about $1.8 million. While no money can truly compensate Trade Center victims' families, a federal commission has developed a complex process for determining a nominal compensation that's based upon lifelong earnings potential, number of children and so on. Special Master Kenneth Feinberg, the fund's administrator, says there is no minimum award amount or "cap" specified in the final rules released this week but compensation will range somewhere between $250,000 and $4 million per person. So far, about 370 people have filed for compensation from the fund.

Again, the compensation drops dramatically if you're a soldier and die fighting for your country. The U.S. Armed Forces awards a $6,000 death benefit, plus $250 per month per spouse and dependent child – but only until the spouse is remarried. Some claim that this benefit is not out of line because soldiers know the risks involved and are paid a salary to put their lives on the line. Others claim that because of their noble efforts, soldiers' families should be paid more - not less - than those who lost loved ones in the Sept. 11 attacks.

Forgotten fallen: What of the families of those who were killed at the Oklahoma City bombing? Beyond the Social Security system's relief payouts, they received nothing extra from the U.S. government for the loss of their loved ones. Just like those who died on Sept. 11, those who died in Oklahoma City were victims of terrorist atrocities, albeit at the hands of U.S. citizen Terry McVeigh.

Although it is not surprising that the survivors of the dead in Oklahoma City are now calling for similar compensation, these actions make some government officials worry that the U.S. is on a slippery slope. What types of tragedies should the government be held accountable for?

The seeds of greed: Families of those killed in either attack insist that they are not trying to get rich, but that they want to make sure that their children are provided for and that the government is held accountable. "Here we are pitted against justifying ourselves to the nation. We deserve accountability from the government," said Loreen Sellino, mother of Matthew Sellitto, 23, who died in the Sept. 11 attacks. "This is not just about the money."

Fund adminstrator Kenneth Feinberg said: "These are people, families, American citizens for the most part, who have suffered a horrible loss, months ago -not years ago, months ago - and they are trying as best they can to value a lost loved one. I do not believe it has anything to do with personal greed. It has everything to do with valuing a lost loved one." But with a federal valuation that claims to be fair, yet proves to be inconsistent, accountability becomes a much larger issue.

Biotech CEO Barry dies suddenly

FLOORING MAKER | GETTING STEPPED ON

IBM chooses successor to Gerstner

In every issue of the newspaper, there could be stories with headlines featuring questions. The questions would not relate to specific events of the day but would be relevant to the flow of the news. They would raise a provocative issue underlying the news, one that light readers would be unlikely to think of themselves. The question would not be raised for debate or editorial comment. The question is interesting because it can be seen in different ways and is, therefore, interesting to think about. The story itself helps the reader to see why the question is worth thinking about. The stories must be subbranded so that they stand out in the newspaper. We might call the stories *Debatables* and identify them with a symbol of people talking.

Figure 13.2 on page 273 illustrates this in-paper contact with a story raising the question of whether the military should try to catch the terrorist Bin Laden, no matter what the cost in lives, or hold back to save lives. The question is stimulating in that it forces the reader to think about the cost of a strong response to terrorism versus the cost of not responding. Out of a sea of stories about terrorism, the reader now comes into contact with one that seems different and stimulating.

Similar contact points could be embedded in the paper at different points. As shown in Figure 13.3 on page 274, the business section might raise a question about funds for the victims of disasters. Some victims receive considerable amounts of money; others receive less even though their loss may be the same or greater. There are reasons for this that can be explained, but it still raises a provocative question of fairness.

The presence of these contact points in the newspaper can be reinforced with another contact point that flags two or three of the key *Debatables* in an issue on the front page. This is not simply a promotion because the item itself, as illustrated in Figure 13.4, poses the questions and invites the reader to think about them.

Figure 13.4
Another Contact Point on the Front Page

Other contact points could be created with smaller stories that would appear more at random in the paper. These could pose less serious questions and even humorous questions. They would be the kind of contacts intended to surprise or delight readers. An example is a one-inch story headlined: "Now what would this taste like?" The story is about researchers who have inserted the genes of spinach plants into pigs.

CONTACTS OUTSIDE THE PRODUCT PLATFORM

One of the strengths of an integrated marketing approach is to recognize that the consumer experience can be created by contacts outside the product itself. Even what conventionally would be thought of as an advertising exposure can be turned into a touchpoint with the brand concept. Suppose we have an ad such as the one in Figure 13.5 for our newspaper concept. The ad copy mimics the question format used in the paper and communicates that the concept is to stimulate the reader.

The ad in Figure 13.5 could run in a variety of media. With an integrated marketing approach, we would also try to make the ad more a part of a touchpoint. When might our light reader be in a situation where he or she is a little more reflective? One situation might be while waiting in a subway. There is very little else to do, especially for a light reader, other than to look around and let your mind wander. The transit display shown in Figure 13.6 is not just an advertising exposure in this case. It is a chance to enhance the person's experience of being more reflective.

Now suppose the light reader is waiting for a bus. Most people spend their time at a bus stop looking for buses. The ad on the side of the bus in Figure 13.7 is intended to make the reader stop and wonder about what is new with the paper. This sets up the experience of waiting for the bus, again with a chance to reflect, and noticing the ad in Figure 13.8. This is turned into even more of a contact point because there is a holder on the ad that contains cards with *Debatable* stories reprinted from the newspaper. Therefore, even without the newspaper, the light reader can experience the concept of being stimulated by the newspaper.

A similar contact point can be created for the light reader stuck in traffic. The person has nothing to do but look around and think about things. Our ad appears on a billboard. An even stronger contact can be created if there is an electronic display (see Figure 13.9), showing a question posed in the newspaper that day. In the absence of such a display, an extension

Figure 13.5
A Basic Advertising Communication

Figure 13.6
Subway Ad Contact Point

Figure 13.7
Bus Ad Contact Point #1

Figure 13.8
Bus Ad Contact Point #2

Figure 13.9
Stalled in Traffic Ad Contact Point

attached to the billboard could be used to show a question. This could be changed weekly so that, again, there is an experience of the concept.

Newspapers are often sold near the checkout lines in supermarkets. This, too, could be turned into a contact point. A blow-up of the *Debatable* question and story of the day (see Figure 13.10), could be displayed so that people have a chance to read it while they wait.

Additional contacts could involve other product platforms. For instance, the best *Debatable* questions and stories could be collected in book form. The book could be sold (a cross-selling contact), or it could be offered as an incentive to attract new light reader subscriptions (an acquisition or retention contact). It could also be placed in waiting rooms as an additional contact point opportunity.

VIRAL MARKETING CONTACTS

Still other contacts can be initiated to increase the chance that light readers actually discuss the content of the newspaper with other people. Thus, we might place cards with the *Debatable* question and story of the day in places where younger readers are likely to eat. This could be as simple as putting the cards in holders on tables as shown in Figure 13.11.

Being stimulated to notice and talk about a question at lunch is a powerful experience in itself. Once a person has talked about something with one person in a conversation, he or she is very likely to have the same conversation with someone else. The restaurant contact could thus trigger a viral chain of contacts that spread beyond the original people having lunch.

A similar contact could take advantage of the desire by many women to stimulate dinner conversation among the family. Cards containing a *Debatable* question and reprinted story could be mailed to selected households likely to be light readers. The card would invite people to talk about the question at dinner, as shown in Figure 13.12.

Given a successful dinner conversation, it is to be expected that both the husband and wife would repeat what they said to other people. The original mailing could even be targeted at people likely to be tastemakers in their neighborhood or even at people likely to be interested in a topic (perhaps using magazine subscription lists to identify likely topics of interest). In this way, the viral flow of contacts with relatively influential people resulting in contacts with many others might be enhanced.

Figure 13.10
A Checkout Line Ad Contact Point

Figure 13.11
A Restaurant Viral Marketing Contact

Figure 13.12
Dinner and a Conversation Viral Marketing Contact

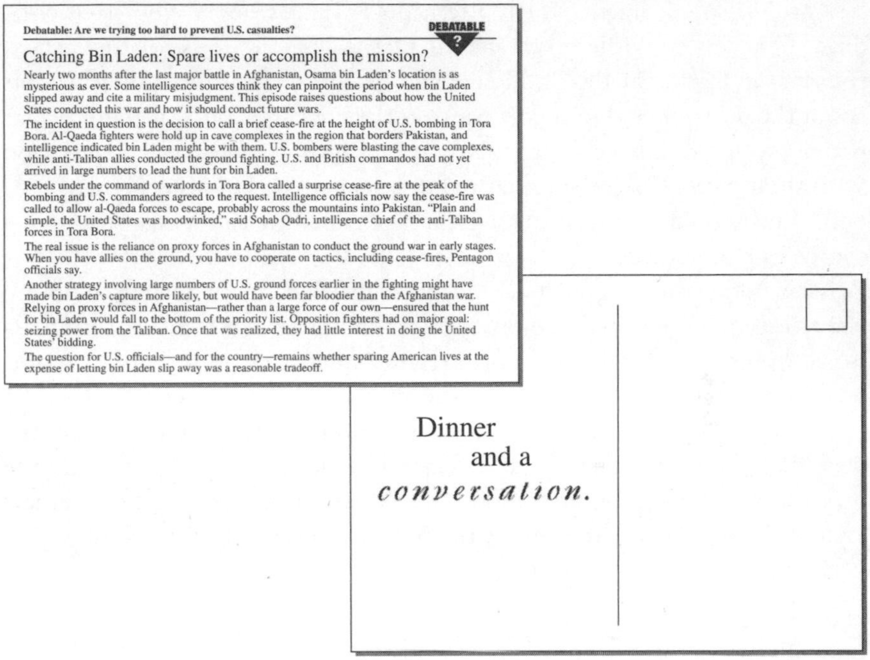

Debatable: Are we trying too hard to prevent U.S. casualties?

DEBATABLE ?

Catching Bin Laden: Spare lives or accomplish the mission?

Nearly two months after the last major battle in Afghanistan, Osama bin Laden's location is as mysterious as ever. Some intelligence sources think they can pinpoint the period when bin Laden slipped away and cite a military misjudgment. This episode raises questions about how the United States conducted this war and how it should conduct future wars.

The incident in question is the decision to call a brief cease-fire at the height of U.S. bombing in Tora Bora. Al-Qaeda fighters were hold up in cave complexes in the region that borders Pakistan, and intelligence indicated bin Laden might be with them. U.S. bombers were blasting the cave complexes, while anti-Taliban allies conducted the ground fighting. U.S. and British commandos had not yet arrived in large numbers to lead the hunt for bin Laden.

Rebels under the command of warlords in Tora Bora called a surprise cease-fire at the peak of the bombing and U.S. commanders agreed to the request. Intelligence officials now say the cease-fire was called to allow al-Qaeda forces to escape, probably across the mountains into Pakistan. "Plain and simple, the United States was hoodwinked," said Sohab Qadri, intelligence chief of the anti-Taliban forces in Tora Bora.

The real issue is the reliance on proxy forces in Afghanistan to conduct the ground war in early stages. When you have allies on the ground, you have to cooperate on tactics, including cease-fires, Pentagon officials say.

Another strategy involving large numbers of U.S. ground forces earlier in the fighting might have made bin Laden's capture more likely, but would have been far bloodier than the Afghanistan war. Relying on proxy forces in Afghanistan—rather than a large force of our own—ensured that the hunt for bin Laden would fall to the bottom of the priority list. Opposition fighters had on major goal: seizing power from the Taliban. Once that was realized, they had little interest in doing the United States' bidding.

The question for U.S. officials—and for the country—remains whether sparing American lives at the expense of letting bin Laden slip away was a reasonable tradeoff.

Dinner
and a
conversation.

SUB-SEGMENTS AND RELATIONSHIP CONTACTS

Light readers can be further segmented into any number of different sub-segments. Contacts designed especially for these sub-segments can provide a more customized experience and facilitate a sense of having a relationship with the newspaper. Because the newspaper understands and relates to them in a special way, the consumer feels more of a relationship tie-back to the newspaper.

Some light readers are health and fitness conscious. They are likely to frequent health clubs. The experience we are after can be customized to these people. Many use machines to exercise that allow them to read at the same time. We could make *Debatable* questions and stories that concern health and fitness available near these machines. Again, cards in a holder attached to an ad could be used; see Figure 13.13. Because people talk a lot at health clubs, this contact can also be viewed as having viral marketing possibilities. It might even be possible to identify leaders or role models and design special contacts for them.

Another sub-segment worth attention is light readers who have children. Teachers could be given special *Debatable* questions for their classrooms as in Figure 13.14. Children could be assigned to talk to their parents about the question and to report back on the conversation. The light reader parents would thus have a particularly meaningful contact, the conversation with their child, and a sense that the newspaper is relating to them as parents. This should in turn foster a greater personal tie to the newspaper as a source of stimulation.

Many other sub-segments could be identified. Light readers who are heavy Internet users might be offered chat rooms geared to *Debatable* questions. Sports fans might see sports-related questions on a stadium scoreboard or on radio or television talk shows. These contacts would not dilute the basic concept we started with. They would customize the concept in a way that different groups could relate to even more. This fulfills the promise of integrated marketing to appeal to a large group of consumers and, at the same time, to achieve the power of customized targeting.

SCORING MODELS

A successful integrated marketing effort presents many opportunities for making additional offers to consumers. An example is our newspaper's hosting an event aimed at light readers. This might take the form of a TV talk show where the audience could listen to celebrities talk about *Debatable* questions. A local show could even invite consumers to be part of the audience.

In contacting consumers with an offer such as this, where the same or similar offers are to be made over time, it is important to use scoring models to evaluate the results. For obvious cost reasons, we want to confine the offer to consumers who are likely to respond. Just as important, we want such offers to be perceived as part of the consumer's relationship with the brand concept.

If a consumer repeatedly receives offers that are of no interest, this decreases the sense of relationship with the brand. By scoring responses and not contacting those who are not interested, and whom we may be annoying, we can further a sense of relationship with the consumer. We are providing the consumer with offers that reflect an understanding of them.

Figure 13.13
A Health Club Relationship Contact

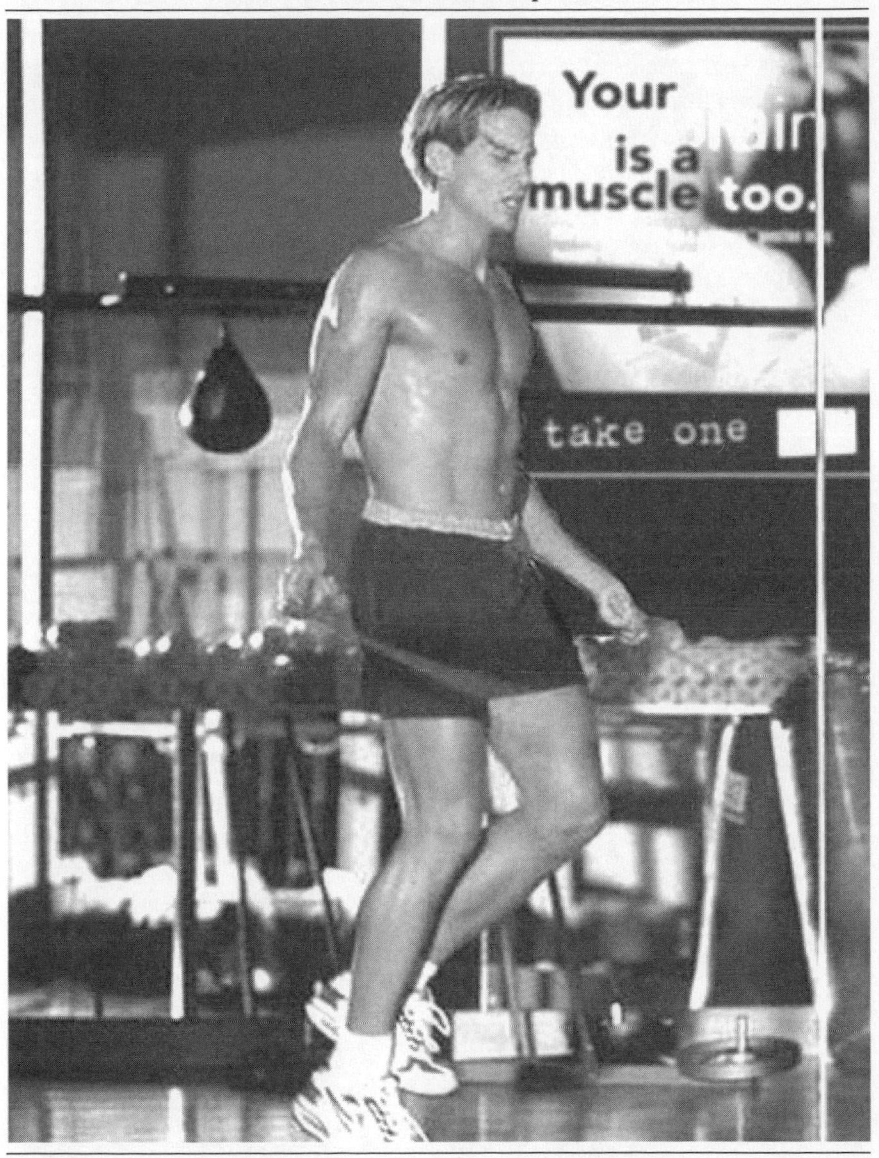

Figure 13.14
A Parent Relationship Contact

CONCLUSION

We have illustrated an integrated approach to marketing planning. At its core, an integrated marketing plan flows from a strong concept of how to create a more meaningful and relevant experience for the consumer that is delivered through contact points both within and outside the product platform itself. Ideally, this experience is augmented by the use of subsegmentation and scoring models to customize the experience and foster a sense of relationship.

Beyond this, I hope this illustration also shows that an integrated marketing approach opens many creative and cost-effective paths to satisfying consumers. It should be difficult to read the example given here and not think of more contact points that could make the desired consumer experience even richer.

Notes

1. Bobby Calder, "Understanding Consumers," in *Kellogg on Marketing* (New York: Wiley, 2000); Bobby Calder, "Qualitative Marketing Research," in *Handbook of Marketing Research* ed. R. Bagozzi (London: Blackwell, 1993); and Maria Flores, Charles Spinosa, and Bobby Calder, "Taking An Expanded View of Customers' Needs: Qualitative Research for Aiding Innovation," *Marketing Research* (winter, 2000), pp. 4–11.

CHAPTER 14

REFLECTIONS ON BECOMING A GREAT MARKETING ORGANIZATION

STEPHEN BURNETT

As compared to other chapters in the volume, this contribution is personal in nature in that it draws exclusively on the author's 20 years of experience in helping a dozen major companies become better at marketing. Most of the companies on which the experience and this chapter are based approached the Kellogg School (a few were private clients of the author) with the request to help them significantly improve the quality of their marketing efforts. All the companies were already leaders in their industries, and, in some cases, they held the top market share position by a considerable margin. Based on this observation, you might conclude that they were already accomplished marketers, at least historically, and against their industry competitors. But their motivations for embracing marketing were remarkably similar:

- They realized that their marketing was exceptionally weak compared to best-in-class marketers found in other industries. While this epiphany had different sources, they were all external in nature: a new CEO or other senior executive hired from outside the industry, a consulting firm working with the company on various projects, or even a number of executives attending one or more Kellogg School marketing executive programs and purportedly finding the marketing "religion."
- Better financial performance was the prime objective of improved marketing decisions. While all the companies were profitable, margins were under pressure or returns on invested capital were meager, and management believed (correctly) that marketing effectiveness was a

principal driver of profitability. That is, they were not ever going to deliver much to shareholders unless they first delivered to their customers.

- The future did not look as bright as the past. There was a growing uneasiness that future competition was going to be far tougher and that the skills and strategies that had gotten them to leading positions were not adequate for this uncertain, but certainly challenging, future state.

The role of the Kellogg School of Management in helping these companies improve their marketing skills was to teach marketing to hundreds of their managers, drawn from all functions, divisions, geographies, and levels of responsibility. Countless sessions on segmentation, targeting, positioning, communications, channels, sale force management, product strategy, and pricing were taught, often over a decade or more. There were marketing planning workshops for executives to practice applying course concepts to their businesses and marketing simulations to demonstrate the profit consequences of marketing decisions. To show best-practice marketing in the context of client companies, case studies were written and company executives lectured on success stories and the lessons learned.

The purpose of this chapter is twofold. The first task is simply to report on what happened. Were these companies able to substantially improve the effectiveness of their marketing based on large-scale educational initiatives? A caveat: This was not a formal study with a carefully chosen sample and scientific measurement of results. These were custom executive program clients of the Kellogg School, not research subjects; and, as such, they tended to be very large multinational companies, professionally managed, with famous brand names and considerable resources. The odds of their improving the quality of their marketing were far greater than for the typical company. Our objective was to educate them, not study them, so the results reported here are impressionistic. Stories will be told, rather than data presented, to support conclusions.

Second, and of special importance to this effort, is a discussion of what the faculty learned—about marketing in general and specifically about how to be better at it, both now and in the future. We came to know these companies extremely well at all levels and over many years; and as a result, we had the unique privilege of witnessing up close the perils and opportunities of organizational transformation.

So what happened? Here are some general impressions: It would be gratifying (and fee-enhancing) to report that every single one of our marketing-embracing clients is now a best-in-class marketer with a market capitalization that is the envy of its industry and beyond. This is decidedly not the situation. The results were variable. At one end of the scale, there was a company that designed and test-marketed a highly innovative, customer-driven strategy within a year with spectacular financial results. This same company, in the aftermath of a merger and changes in leadership, appears to have reverted to the old behavior of simply trying to sell what it chooses to make. Another "success story" made superb progress in about three years, especially notable given its tremendous size and strong manufacturing culture. Currently, this company is working on segmentation schemes, conducting far more and better marketing research, designing a corporate brand strategy, and enjoying incremental profits from improved marketing in a few documented situations in which it identified and solved priority customer problems and profited from the effort.

The anchor at the opposite extreme is represented by a company that recently asked the Kellogg School to conduct a marketing program for its top management group because its new CEO (from outside the industry) had immediately perceived marketing practice and skill deficiencies. Some 10 years earlier, we had delivered a series of custom marketing programs for the same company. In designing the new program, our due-diligence interviews revealed a well-defined and classic set of marketing problems to be addressed. Astonishingly—and you probably guessed it—the firm's marketing problems today were identical to what we had witnessed and tried to correct a decade earlier. At the conclusion of the seminar, the CEO made an ominous, yet entirely appropriate, prediction that if the company had to mount another seminar on the same subjects 10 years hence, the executives in the room today, including himself, would not be attending.

Between the extremes, companies made varying degrees of progress in various forms: better integration of communications, improved customer service, revised planning processes to include target segment definition, greater use of databases to track and understand customers, larger market research budgets, more customer input in new product design projects, and so on. Sometimes *progress* was defined as having a formal marketing department for the first time. What was striking, however, was the fantastic amount of time it took to improve the quantity and quality of basic marketing activities, much less to have those activities yield measurable financial results. On embracing the marketing "religion," the firm would follow with a burst of activities. Then the momentum was often lost as people or the situation changed (an industry recession shifted attention from the customer exclusively to cost reductions, for example). The most persistent company, now 14 years into its quest for great marketing, still has glaring marketing weaknesses, although considerable progress has been made. What is significant here is not the remaining challenges or the progress, but the time frame—14 years and counting!

Yes, there were lessons learned. The charm of variance is that it just begs to be explained. Why did some companies make rapid gains and then appear to lose interest? Why is the process so lengthy in the best of cases? Even modest improvements in basic activities spanned years. Here are some thoughts from years of toiling with our client companies in the customers' vineyards.

YOU CAN NEVER BE TOO RICH, TOO THIN, OR TOO GOOD AT MARKETING

While it is troubling to admit it, marketing is just plain hard to do. It is infinitely more difficult to implement the marketing concept than to talk about it (this observation explains why the author loves to teach marketing). Perhaps this is true of many things, but it is especially the case with marketing. If you think about classic marketing decision categories, there are many of them—identification of segments, targeting, crafting a positioning statement, product and service offerings, pricing arrangements, marketing communications of all sorts, channel design and management, pricing arrangements, and sales force decisions. Under each of these categories, there are dozens of specific decisions, each with numerous options. (Under the rubric of sales force decisions, for instance, there are issues regarding size, composition, compensation, training, territories, allocation of effort by product, etc.) The challenge of marketing (and the theme of this volume) is to integrate or coordinate literally hundreds of decisions so that target customers perceive that the most important problems in their lives or businesses are well satisfied. Add to this complexity multiple target markets across multiple sister businesses, owned by a parent corporation that has its own brand (whether it wants one or not) and must market itself to investors; society; regulators; vendors; and prospective, as well as, current employees.

Moreover, as if marketers did not have enough problems already, to implement the marketing concept requires that you understand, predict, and influence human behavior in group and individual settings, which just also happens to be the collective challenge of all social sciences (marketers are in good and ample company). People are frustratingly complex, often blind to their motivations and perceptions, diverse, and—especially troublesome for marketers—dynamic. The degree to which customers understand their needs and judge potential solutions is directly influenced by the quality of marketing. If you do a superb job of understanding and satisfying your customers' needs, they reward you with even higher expectations and greater demands. No good deed goes unpunished! Delivering consistently mediocre fast food in a warm, caring, clean environment built McDonald's Corporation. To continue to do so will ultimately destroy it. Fast food today must be consistently fresh, delicious, healthy, custom tailored, and constantly varied, while being delivered in an entertaining, clean, warm, caring environment. You can also add to this that standard menu items (a basic cheeseburger) should be practically free of charge. The better you are at marketing, the better you have to be.

So marketing, even ordinary marketing, is an extraordinarily difficult task. This observation implies that marketing must be about the proverbial journey because the destination is only temporarily achievable, if at all. Nirvana will always be over the next hill. Companies aspiring to improved marketing must understand this or they are doomed to frustration and ultimately abandonment of a fundamental quest. *Great marketing* means that you constantly strive to be better—to have a clearer concept of who is and is *not* your target customer, to understand more deeply priority customer problems (and how these are different for different customers), and to solve customer problems far better than currently possible. The quality of an organization's marketing can and should be measured (through customer satisfaction tracking, trends in profit growth by market segment and product/service line, etc.). Progress can be fast or slow (more on this later). But desired improvements in marketing are never the flavor of the month; better marketing should never be an initiative with a beginning and an end. Returning to our client company, the one 14 years into the journey, our advice is to be more aggressive in your pursuit of marketing excellence, accelerate your progress, measure marketing effectiveness, set milestones, but we all should stop counting the years!

MARKETING IS PHILOSOPHY OF MANAGEMENT

That marketing is a philosophy of management is best illustrated by a recommendation from a keen and alert observer of contemporary customer behavior, Pulitzer prize-winning humorist Dave Berry:

> On the one hand, we have telemarketing people constantly calling us, despite the fact that everyone hates them and, to my personal knowledge, nobody in the history of the world has ever bought anything from them; on the other hand, when we want to reach Customer Service, we can never get

> through. Obviously, what corporate America needs to do is round up all the employees in the Telemarketing Department, march them over to Customer Service, and order them to step over the bodies of the Customer Service employees, all of whom apparently passed away years ago, and ANSWER THE PHONE, OK?[1]

Professor Berry may or may not understand contact mapping, customer relationship management, and integrated marketing, but he certainly sees the world through the eyes of the customer, and, for marketers, this is our reality. The telemarketing department is trying to sell us something (and we hate them); the customer service department solves our problems (and we need them). The extent to which we solve our customers' most important problems, and whether they perceive that we do, is only marginally related to decisions made in the formal Marketing Department.

Indeed, a telling question is the following: Of all the decisions that affect your customers each and every day, what percentage are made by people in the marketing department? While the answer is not generally known and perhaps not precisely knowable, we are certainly safe in hypothesizing that the number is in the low single digits, even for companies particularly talented at marketing.

The goal of marketing—to deliver profitable solutions to the priority problems of target customers—is ultimately a function of actions that every employee of an organization takes every day. Even accountants have enormous impacts on our customers (admittedly a truly frightening thought). How often have you heard this comment: "Why do we do things that way?" "Because that is how we keep the numbers"? Accountants do rule! Whom you hire and how you acculturate, train, compensate, develop, and motivate them have powerful implications for customers because your people take the actions and make the decisions that affect customers. In other words, the way an organization thinks about and treats its people heavily influences how it thinks about and treats its customers.[2]

Thus, to view better marketing as a marketing department issue totally misses the point and will inevitably thwart attempts, however needed and sincere, at improved marketing. Indeed, the single most important predictor of whether a Kellogg client company made substantial and rapid improvements in marketing was who owned the problem. If better marketing was viewed as a marketing department problem, then almost nothing changed. And why should it, as the formal marketing staff controls very few of the decisions relevant to customers? Conversely, if better marketing was perceived to be a total organizational issue and, therefore, the responsibility of all managers—general managers in particular—improvements were significant, rapid, and sustained.

Of all the companies that Kellogg School faculty have worked with to improve their marketing, one has clearly set the standard over the past three years because it correctly perceives improved marketing as a total organizational change process rather than a functional skill problem. To illustrate, of the 50 executives attending the inaugural program for this company, there was one marketing person present (the head of corporate marketing). The class was composed of the CEO, the heads of corporate staff functions (finance, people, manufacturing, legal, marketing, technology, etc.), and the company's most senior general managers (group executives, division presidents). The topic was marketing, but the audience was general managers and the corporate staffs supporting them. The CEO summarized the seminar by saying that his intent was to manage the entire corporation from the perspective of target customers, and this is precisely what the firm has been striving to do. Yes, traditional marketing activities are being upgraded, but that is only a small part of a total change process that encompasses numerous elements:

- Fundamental changes in corporate-level strategy (mix of businesses, vision, guiding principles, etc.), all of which are designed to favor a stronger corporate brand and customer leveraging across sister business units.
- Changes in the behavior of top management in terms of the way they allocate resources, the questions they ask in meetings, and the activities they wish to model (senior executives now routinely visit customers and ask their subordinates how many customer visits they have made).
- Realignment of the company's people strategy to fit better with a customer orientation (definition of the desired culture, people selection and development practices that are consistent with the culture, policies to promote greater responsibility and accountability for customers, etc.).
- Better information, not only about customer needs, but also about customer and product profitability as inputs to more intelligent targeting decisions.
- A balanced scorecard approach to executive compensation that captures several marketing quality variables.

Our advice to those in search of great marketing: Always remember that marketing deficiencies are not just a marketing department problem any more than customers belong exclusively to marketing and salespeople. While you may need better educated and experienced marketing people and more contemporary marketing practices, these actions are modest steps in a total organizational change process. All available change levers must be pulled forcefully and frequently—strategy, management behavior, culture, people, organization structure, rewards, and information—ideally in an integrated fashion. Not surprisingly, marketing staffers are an integral part of the change process and do most of the heavy lifting when it comes to customer understanding, but general management must see marketing effectiveness as their issue. Marketing executives, no matter how senior and charismatic, cannot unilaterally change business strategy, organizational culture, reward systems, or human resources policies.

MARKETING IS A CROSS-FUNCTIONAL FUNCTION

It is plausible that some marketers (specifically, managers in formal marketing positions) could use the notions that better marketing must be a general management issue and a total organization change process as convenient excuses for all sorts of sins and nasty behavior. In addition, it is always convenient and comforting to blame the general manager and other functions for marketing deficiencies. Perhaps the following comments are familiar:

- "The advertising campaign we created was brilliant, but those jerks on the (executive) floor cut the recommended budget by half, so don't blame us for first-quarter results."
- "Sure, we can grow sales by 40 percent, but not with fewer salespeople; with the current headcount restrictions, there's not much we can do; this goofy company apparently prefers to make less money than more money."
- "The product that we requested was perfectly calibrated to what customers said they wanted; unfortunately, that is not the product we actually manufactured, not to mention that it was over a year late to market; those engineering types, for all their brains, just don't get it."
- "Customer service positions are the lowest paid in the company, with the highest turnover rate; their training is nonexistent, and then everyone is surprised when customer satisfaction ratings decline; this place is managed by wolves."

It would be hopelessly naïve to believe that marketers, even in organizations where marketing is a philosophy of management and all decision makers are sensitive to customer problems, will ever be completely free of constraints and compromises from other functions. Nevertheless, marketers must understand that marketing, as a function, is inherently cross-functional in nature. Financial, operations, and people managers have their own unique objectives, models, and vocabularies, as do marketers. The managers of these functions do not naturally embrace the precepts of marketing any more than marketers eagerly anticipate the latest ruling by the Financial Accounting Standards Board. Therefore, if marketing is to be a philosophy of management, marketers must be comfortable working across organizational boundaries as they assist their sister functions in understanding the priority problems of target customers and adapting their function's policies and practices accordingly. To do this, marketers must have the "right stuff" in two regards.

First, marketers have to continuously and credibly invoke the voice of the target customer throughout every nook and cranny of the organization. Even intellectually challenged managers listen when someone stands up in a meeting and demonstrates with supporting data (as opposed to tribal wisdom and mythology) how cherished customers are likely to react to the decision being discussed. The practical power of marketers to influence decisions stems from their ability to show the ramifications for customers rather than from the vaulted position of the marketing department in the corporate hierarchy. If marketers cannot credibly speak for customers, they have no power, and they deserve to have none. Having excellent customer insight to influence cross-functional decisions and activities is of limited use if it is not amply shared throughout the organization. Here is a quiz for marketers to determine whether they are adequately communicating customer perspective:

- Could the lowest-paid, most newly hired employee tell his or her friends the sorts of customers your company wants and what the most important problems are in the lives or businesses of these customers?
- On any given day, how many customers can be found visiting corporate headquarters, sales offices, and manufacturing facilities so that employees of all stripes and flavors can meet and listen to customers?
- Do nonmarketing employees routinely accompany salespeople on customer calls?
- Are customers featured guest speakers at company conventions and management conferences?
- If a target customer walked into a typical meeting at your company, sat down, and listened carefully, would he or she find the discussion meaningful?

If the answers to many of these questions are generally negative, marketers are simply not doing their jobs. Moreover, marketing is not likely to ever be a philosophy of management. It is viewed as one of many functions, and not particularly important in the grand scheme of things.

The second implication for marketers is that they must be extremely comfortable and effective working across functional boundaries. To illustrate, one of Kellogg's client companies decided that the way to supercharge its trajectory on the path to great marketing was to hire experienced marketers (at substantial salaries) from outside its industry and to place them in senior marketing positions. They all had proven track records at companies well regarded for marketing. Their average tenure was approximately 11 months. They were either fired or ran from the building muttering incoherently about the actuaries. The nature of this company's business was such that the product was designed and priced by actuaries, who are highly trained applied mathematicians. The problem here is immediately obvious—if you are a marketer in such a company, you have to work closely with the actuaries (they do control your product and its price). To do this requires that you have an appreciation for the way they are trained and think, and the methods they use. Our hotshot marketers were clueless about actuarial science and apparently had no interest in learning. They did not work collaboratively with actuaries (who were important and powerful people in this company), and, consequently, they were ineffective and frustrated. Today, we simply teach marketing to the actuaries—it works much better.

The point is that marketers must be marketing wizards, but they also must possess a solid working knowledge of corporate finance, accounting, manufacturing, people management, R&D (in their industry), information technology, and the unique role and challenges of being a general manager. Also, and of equal importance, by way of education and personality, marketers must be comfortable interacting with people most unlike themselves. Accountants help marketers understand where and how they make money. Financial managers assist in measuring the financial consequences of marketing decisions and thereby gain the needed resources. You must rely heavily on technical managers for products and operations managers for services. You ask people managers to attract, retain, and develop the right people to serve target customers. Information technology managers are critical to understanding and developing relationships with customers. At the end of the day, marketing must deliver to the general manager's bottom line. Our advice: Know all kinds of different functional managers and general managers, appreciate their tasks and views of reality, and hug them regularly—you need their help if you have any hopes of being good at marketing.

JUST SAY NO, PLEASE

The final lesson from our years of helping companies in their search for better marketing is succinctly captured in an old but still keenly insightful saying about strategy: "Strategy is more about what you don't do, than what you do."

When companies receive the marketing "religion," a common first action is to commission an elegant market segmentation study with a large sample of customers and prospects. Dozens of behavioral, attitudinal, and demographic variables are captured and then factor- and cluster-analyzed to yield a segmentation scheme. After labeling each segment with a cute and descriptive name, the company goes about determining precisely what it should do to ensure that it fully meets the needs of every single segment. You can hear the deck chairs on the Titanic being rearranged. The company has forgotten that after this concept called *segmentation* comes *targeting,* the single most strategic decision of the marketing planning process. The essence of marketing is knowing that to integrate all organizational decisions around the perceptions and priority problems of customers, you must be highly selective and clear about which customers you want and which ones you do not want. To serve all is to serve none particularly well in the highly developed, intensively competitive markets of North America, Europe, and Japan. When it comes to targeting, companies have some terrible natural aversion (we call it the "dark side") to saying "no thanks" to a potential sales opportunity, though that opportunity may be decidedly unattractive, a horrible fit with their skills and resources, and even destructive of their brand image. The logic is this: If there is a sale to be had, we must go get it; gosh, you certainly don't want to lose a sale, even if you have zero chance of getting it and there are far better opportunities.

As an example of this apparently DNA-based tendency, one of our client companies determined that a new family of products was needed for the future and, accordingly, launched a new product development project. Having heard the marketing sermon from Mount Kellogg, the firm made its first step to segment the market for this product and to conduct an elaborate Market Attractiveness–Business Position Assessment.[3] Because this company operated in all regions of planet Earth and there were multiple and radically different uses for this product, some 84 segments were evaluated for attractiveness and company fit. While many segments were designated as *nontargets,* one nontarget segment was especially noteworthy. Let's call it the XYZ business.

The company currently enjoyed a 50 percent market share of good old XYZ with profit margins that can best be described as obscene. Furthermore, XYZ was projected to grow at planetary GDP + 2 percent. The decision was taken that XYZ would be designated nontarget and, therefore, no research would be conducted on this segment, the new product would not be designed to appeal to this segment, and no resources would be devoted to attracting XYZ customers. If the new product accidentally appealed to XYZ customers, we might lower ourselves to selling the product to them, assuming capacity was underused, they begged us for it, and the price was in the "offer you can't refuse" range. This appears to be a bizarre targeting decision until you add a simple fact: All the potential customers for XYZ applications could fit into a small conference room. This was a tiny market. Target segments were a thousand times larger, with equivalent margins, and growing at planetary GDP + 10 percent. To devote resources to XYZ was to deny resources to truly massive opportunities. The targeting decision regarding XYZ was sound.

The project proceeded with hour-long, in-depth interviews conducted with target customers in seven languages in all regions of the planet (XYZ customers were not interviewed). Customers were asked about the most important problems in their businesses, which served as input to product specifications. Then came the meeting during which the engineers were to present preliminary product design ideas. The following words were spoken during that fateful presentation: "But to accommodate the XYZ market, we will have to modify the base product. . . ." The Dark Side had reared its ugly head. They were reverting to the old thinking, the old ways, a sales-driven view that any customer was a good customer.

Among the pitfalls that can derail a company's quest for better marketing, lack of discipline in selecting and serving target markets is unfortunately common and uniformly deadly. It is also responsible for causing tension between sales and marketing staffs. For example, good salespeople see themselves as advocates for individual customers, and rightfully so. They often argue that they can secure a particular account if certain modifications are made to the offering—different service arrangements, product modifications, price reduction, and so forth. From a marketing perspective, this opportunity would be viewed far more skeptically. Most importantly, does this account fall within one of our high priority target segments? If not, it would be foolish to devote time and introduce additional costs and complexity in attempting to serve it. Indeed, it would be a distraction from our focus on target segments. Suppose the account *is* consistent with the desired target segments. There is still an issue—are its requirements unique, or might other target customers need similar adjustments? If the requested adjustments to the offering are idiosyncratic, we could conceivably compromise our ability to serve other target customers by accommodating this single account. This is the classic dilemma faced by Federal Express and all network operators. They want to respond to special requirements of large customers, but Federal Express is running a complex network system that cannot deliver perfect reliability (what all target customers demand) if thousands of exceptions are being made to the system every day. To satisfy one customer (even a target) may jeopardize the firm's ability to serve all target customers.

The issue of maintaining discipline can be attacked on several fronts. First is the obvious need for the market strategy to be widely and continuously communicated throughout the entire organization, so that all employees understand who is and who is not a target customer and what the most important needs of target customers are that are being satisfied. Beyond this, there should be specific guidelines for how nontarget business will be treated. At one extreme, you can simply refuse to do business with nontargets (this would be difficult to strictly enforce in a consumer marketing setting). Or, you could devote absolutely no time and resources to attracting nontargets but accept these customers to the extent that the offering designed for target customers appeals to them. This is the approach used by Southwest Airlines in that its offering is designed for the short-haul frequent traveler even though many different types of travelers undoubtedly fly Southwest. There is also the option of setting specific conditions under which nontarget business is accepted (capacity must be available, customers must buy at list prices and order minimum quantities, there are no special product or service modifications, etc.).

To address sales versus marketing conflict, management can structure sales force compensation and training to recognize the importance of target segments. Measures of market share, growth, and profits also should be on a market segment basis. More generally, sales and marketing people have to understand and accept the reality that there will always be issues about the desirability of serving specific customers. Harmonizing sales force strategy with the overall market strategy should reduce screaming, yelling, and bloodshed; but sales and marketing people are likely never to see the world exactly the same way. Conflicts over who is and is not a target customer are inevitable by-products of trying to have target customers, and what is really important is that individual cases are intelligently discussed and debated.

SUMMING IT UP

After thousands of executive students and hundreds of class sessions, what can we definitively say about great marketing? Today, great marketing is all about integrated marketing, a philosophy of management in which the challenge is to drive the target customer perspective through all decisions. Great marketing tomorrow may be something different. Do not forget—great marketing is a journey with a moving destination. There is no doubt that companies can improve the quality of their marketing, even to the point of approaching some measure of integration. The task, however, takes enormous dedication of time, effort, and talent. It is technically complex and requires transformation of the entire organization, and without target market discipline, it is simply impossible. Marketers who dream of starting their organizations on the journey must first prepare themselves for the task ahead. Have you segmented and targeted? Do you truly understand the voice of the target customer? Are you prepared to talk about customers with anyone who will listen, especially people who do not know the secret marketer's handshake; speak in codes; and are inclined to reject; at least initially, your entire thought process? If you think you are ready, call us. But please do not be offended if your company is not a target customer—it's nothing personal, just great marketing.

Notes

1. *The Dave Barry 2002 Calendar* (Kansas City, MO: Andrews McMeel Publishing, 2001).
2. For a thorough presentation of how people decisions drive overall financial performance, see Jeffrey Pfeffer, *The Human Equation: Building Profits by Putting People First* (Cambridge: Harvard Business School Press, 1998).
3. George Day, *Analysis for Strategic Market Decisions* (St. Paul, MN: West Publishing, 1986).

About the Contributors

Eric G. Berggren is a cofounder and managing director of Axios Partners, LLC. Throughout his 17 years in consulting, Eric has grown his clients' revenues and profits through superior customer value innovation and management. In addition to his consulting, Eric has taught in several executive education programs at the Kellogg School of Management, where he received his MBA. Eric's previous marketing publications have been in the areas of new product development, marketing research, and organization design.

Stephen Burnett joined the faculty of the Kellogg School in 1981 and is currently professor of Strategic Management. His teaching, research, and consulting interests focus on the interface of corporate, business, and market strategy. As the member of the Kellogg faculty whose primary responsibility is the school's executive education mission, Steve is involved in a full range of Kellogg executive offerings. He is faculty director of the Advanced Executive Program, Kellogg's oldest and most senior management program. He founded and directs the Kellogg Management Institute, the school's newest general management program. For 20 years, Steve has played an active role in developing and popularizing the notion that custom or company specific executive programs can be powerful forces for implementing organizational change. In addition to writing and speaking about custom programs, he has designed, directed, and taught in dozens of Kellogg custom offerings for such companies as Brunswick, British Petroleum, R.R. Donnelley, Ernst & Young, General Motors, Goodyear, International Paper, Motorola, Sears, Spiegel, USG Corporation, and the Zurich Insurance Group.

Bobby J. Calder is the Charles H. Kellstadt Distinguished Professor of marketing and professor of psychology at the Kellogg School of Management, Northwestern University. He is also a professor of journalism in the Medill School of Journalism. His work is primarily in the areas of marketing strategy, media, marketing research, and the psychology of consumer behavior. Previously, he has taught at the Wharton School, University of

Pennsylvania, and the University of Illinois and has been a consultant for Booz Allen and Hamilton. He is a graduate of the University of North Carolina at Chapel Hill. Presently he also serves as director of research for the Media Management Center at Northwestern and is codirector of the media MBA program at Kellogg. He has been a consultant to many companies (including Aetna, Baxter, Bristol-Myers Squibb, Cemex, Coca-Cola, General Electric, General Motors, Hearst, McDonald's, Motorola, and Prudential) and to government and not-for-profit organizations (such as the Census Bureau, the Environmental Protection Agency, the United Way, and the U.S. Army).

Tom Collinger is Associate Professor of Integrated Marketing Communications and Director of Direct, Database & E-Commerce Marketing in the Medill School of Journalism at Northwestern University. Tom joined Medill's IMC program in 1998 after over 25 years in the workforce, most recently, following his ten years at the Chicago-based Leo Burnett Company, where Tom served as senior vice president, director of direct and promotion marketing. Prior to that, he served as vice president, general manager of Ogilvy & Mather/Direct's Chicago office, and as general manager of Ayer Direct/Chicago. Prior to this, Tom developed a business, which he subsequently sold to Time-Life Books, Inc.

Tom also serves as president of his own marketing consulting practice, The TC Group, with a select group of client organizations, including: Advanta Corporation, Discover Card, Sony, and Walt Disney World. Tom also serves as a member of the board of directors of Learning Curve International, and the advisory boards of Performics, as well as vice president of the board of directors of The Cancer Wellness Center.

Adam Duhachek is a doctoral student in marketing at the Kellogg School of Management. His research interests include marketing relationships, consumer dissatisfaction, and experiential consumption. He also enjoys investigating a variety of methodological issues, including both interpretive inquiry and psychometric methods. He has extensive experience as both researcher and consultant in the market research industry.

Lisa Fortini-Campbell owns and operates The Fortini-Campbell Company, a marketing consulting firm in Evanston, Illinois. She works with clients to develop marketing and communications strategies that focus on consumer insight and integrated marketing communications principles, as outlined in her book *Hitting the Sweet Spot*. She runs training seminars based on these principles for organizations such as Hewlett-Packard, Kraft Foods, Ford Motor Company, Spiegel, Emerson Electric, Agilent Technologies, John Nuveen & Co. The Seagram Beverage Company, Tropicana, and Reebok.

Lisa has also been an associate professor in the Integrated Marketing Communication graduate program at the Medill School of Journalism, Northwestern University. At Medill, she works with students from around the world in communications theory, research methods, consumer insight, and account planning. She also conducts the Communications Strategies program at Northwestern's Kellogg School of Business Executive Programs.

Before joining Northwestern, Lisa spent 10 years working in the advertising industry, beginning as an analyst in the research department at Leo Burnett and moving to Young & Rubicam in Chicago where she served as research director for five years. In the last two years of her agency career, she managed the Chicago office of Hal Riney & Partners, a San Francisco-based advertising agency. Lisa earned her doctorate in Mass Communications from the University of Washington in 1980. She holds a master's degree in journalism and a bachelor's degree in psychology, both from Ohio State University.

Nigel Hopkins is president and CEO of Clariom, Inc. (http://www.clariom.com). He is an established expert in the convergence of the fields of market research, management science, and information technology. Nigel has more than 15 years of experience in assisting Fortune 1000 companies leverage market and customer data to optimize the performance of their businesses. He has published in several leading journals including the *Journal of Marketing Research* and the *Journal of Business to Business Marketing*. He holds BCom and MCom degrees from the University of Auckland in New Zealand and received his doctorate in marketing from the J. L. Kellogg School of Management at Northwestern University.

Dawn Iacobucci is the Coca-Cola Distinguished Professor of Marketing and head of the Marketing Department at the University of Arizona in Tucson, where she moved after serving 14 years as professor of Marketing at Kellogg. She teaches service marketing, marketing research, and multivariate statistics. She edited *Kellogg on Marketing* and is co-author of the lead *Marketing Research* text with Gilbert Churchill. Her research has appeared in the *Journal of Marketing, Journal of Marketing Research, Journal of Consumer Psychology, Harvard Business Review, Journal of Service Research,*

International Journal of Research in Marketing, Journal of Interactive Marketing, Journal of Advertising Research, Sloan Management Review, Psychometrika, Psychological Bulletin, Journal of Personality and Social Psychology, Social Networks, and *Multivariate Behavioral Research.*

Richard I. Kolsky founded Kolsky & Co. in 1991, a consulting firm dedicated to helping companies take marketing to the bottom line. Richard has spent the past 19 years helping clients convert many of today's fads—such as strategy innovation, core competencies, making mergers work, target marketing, reegineering distribution, relationship selling, and "rightsizing"—from simple buzzwords to bottom-line reality in markets as diverse as infant formula, life insurance, and earth-moving equipment. Among Kolsky's clients are Aetna, Allstate, American Express, Bristol Myers, Caterpillar, CIGNA, IBM, J&J, MasterCard, Motorola, Smuckers, and The Zurich.

In addition to his consulting engagements, Richard is a faculty member for a number of company specific and Northwestern University executive education programs. He has published numerous articles and been keynote speaker for conferences on a range of subjects including "Break the Rules to Compete for the Future," "Making Mergers Work," "Distribution: From Landmine to Competitive Advantage," and "Tossing Out the Pink Slips," a cover article for Best Review.

Prior to starting Kolsky & Co., Richard worked in the White House, was a consulting partner for The MAC Group and Peat Marwick, and taught economics and consulted at Yale. He holds a bachelor's and master's degree in Economics and Engineering from Brown University and doctorate in Economics from Yale University.

Maria Flores Letelier has dedicated her career to investigating the phenomena of change in values and the application of value change to marketing and innovation. Maria's expertise consists in listening profoundly to customers in order to generate insights into future behavior that will form the basis for innovative offers. Maria has led client engagements through the entire market expansion process, starting with generating unique consumer insights and designing innovative product concepts to designing customer experience/interaction points, and then to developing new business models and ramping up the businesses. She has developed a particular expertise for working with culture segments, including Latino market and the culture industries of music, media, and fashion. By working through the entire innovation process, Maria's engagements have resulted in the creation of new market categories, increased market-share, high customer loyalty, and brand differentiation.

Maria has worked with the following companies: Time Warner Inc., Calvin Klein Inc., the *San Francisco Chronicle,* Conde Nast's *Self* magazine, American Century Investments, newScale Inc., CVS Pharmacies, CEMEX (the third largest cement producer in the world), Grupo Alphas Sigma Alimentos, Grupo BBVB/Bancomer (Mexicos largest bank), Banco Santander Central Hispano (the largest Spanish bank), and KSTS-TV Telemundo Group.

Maria received her bachelor's degree with highest honors distinction in Philosophy from the University of California at Berkeley. She later received her MBA from the J. L. Kellogg School of Management at Northwestern University where she majored in Marketing and Strategy.

Edward C. Malthouse is an an assistant professor of integrated marketing communications at the Medill School of Journalism at Northwestern University, where he teaches courses on research methods, customer contact management, and data mining. He also co-teaches the Kellogg course on media marketing, teaches database marketing in the communications systems executive program, and teaches MBA and graduate advertising students at Aoyama Gakuin University. He won the teacher of the year award at IMC and paper of the year award from the Direct Marketing Education Foundation. He is the senior research statistician at Northwestern's Media Management Center. His research is in the area of database marketing, on customer equity, segmentation, and targeting. He received his doctorate in statistics from Northwestern University, an master's degree in operational research from Southampton University, and a bachelor's degree in mathematics from Augustana College.

Francis J. Mulhern is associate professor and chairman of the Department of Integrated Marketing Communications at the Medill School of Journalism, Northwestern University. He specializes in research on customer database analysis and promotion marketing. He earned his doctorate in marketing at the University of Texas at Austin.

Lisa A. Petrison is a marketing consultant and adjunct professor at Northwestern University, where she teaches advertising and database marketing. Her PhD is in marketing from the Kellogg School of Management, Northwestern University.

Andrew J. Razeghi is a speaker and advisor on innovation, creativity, and growth strategy. He is a guest lecturer at The Kellogg Graduate School of Management at Northwestern University, an adjunct faculty at Loyola University Chicago and a Thought Leader with The Financial Times Knowledge Dialogue. Andrew advises organizations on product development, strategy, and innovation. He works with clients looking to exploit their core competencies, identify new markets for existing products and new products for existing markets. He helps organizations accelerate the time between ideation and action. He's worked with the world's leading innovators, rule breakers, and household brands in formulating strategic direction and translating unconventional ideas into unconventional returns on investment.

Andrew has been listed as "One of America's Most Powerful People" by *Swing Magazine* and one of "Chicago's Most Influential" by the *Chicago Sun-Times,* As founder of StrategyLab, Andrew has worked with clients in industries as diverse as aerospace, consumer products, food, healthcare, retail, and media. He has helped clients create such innovative concepts as GPS-enabled automobiles, healthy fast food, funeral homes without walls, junkless junkmail, and healthcare with a Disney flair.

Don E. Schultz is professor (Emeritus) of Integrated Marketing Communications at the Medill School of Journalism, Northwestern University. He is also president of the consulting firm, Agora, Inc. in Evanston, Illinois.

Following his graduation from the University of Oklahoma with a degree in marketing/journalism, Don began his career as a sales promotion writer for trade magazine publishers in Dallas. From there, he moved into publication sales and management, and was advertising director of a daily newspaper in Texas. He then joined Tracy-Locke Advertising and Public Relations in Dallas in 1965. He was with the agency for almost 10 years in its Dallas, New York, and Columbus, Ohio, offices as branch manager. He served as management supervisor for a number of national consumer product, service, and industrial accounts.

In 1974, Don resigned as senior vice president of Tracy-Locke to launch a career in academia. He obtained a master's degree in advertising and a doctorate in mass media from Michigan State University while also teaching in the Department of Advertising. He joined Northwestern in 1977.

Don has consulted, lectured, and held seminars on integrated marketing communication, marketing, branding, advertising, sales promotion, and communication management in Europe, South America, Asia/Pacific, the Middle East, Australia, and North America. His articles have appeared in such publications as: *Advertising Age, Journal of Advertising Research, Journal of Advertising, Journal of Direct Marketing,* and *Journal of Database Marketing.* He is author or co-author of nine books, including: *Strategic Brand Communications Campaigns* (5th ed.), *Essentials of Advertising Strategy* (3rd ed.), and *Essentials of Sales Promotion* (3rd ed.), and the recent *Communicating Globally,* and *Raising the Corporate Umbrella.* His book *Integrated Marketing Communications* was the first text in this emerging field. He was the founding editor of the *Journal of Direct Marketing* and is a regular columnist for *Marketing News.*

Don was selected the first Direct Marketing Educator of the Year by the Direct Marketing Educational Foundation in 1989 and was named Educator of the Year by the Chicago Chapter, Sales and Marketing Executives Association, 1996. He was named Distinguished Advertising Educator of the Year by the American Advertising Federation in 1992. Don also serves on the advisory boards of several organizations.

Charles Spinosa has been engaged in developing the core underpinnings of Market Expansion Partners' approach and methodologies for innovation over the last 10 years. He and Letelier developed the theoretical approach to and the practical application of MEP's Listening-Based Innovation (LBME), Articulative Interviewing, Value-Conflict Identification, and Bridge Practice Application. These techniques grew out of his interest in developing practical commercial applications of his understanding of people as conflicted, historical beings who innovate in order to live good lives.

Charles's work in helping clients develop new offer concepts calls on his experience and training as a professor of philosophy and literature. He draws on his broad understanding of the historical development of values to identify the value conflicts in customer segments and to identify potential bridge practices for easing the conflict. He has developed a particular expertise in understanding human behavior in Latino markets and in developing innovative, offer concepts suited to these markets. He has published widely in academic journals on how we have made sense of change over the past 600 years. In particular, he has studied how identities and communication strategies have developed in difficult historical situations. Charles has applied his years of research and expertise in the philosophical understanding of human behavior to help clients expand and create markets by developing value-based instead of need-based products and services.

Charles has worked with diverse clients, including the Warner Music Group, Bancomer (one of Mexico's two largest banks), CEMEX (the world's third largest cement company), and ABB-ALSTOM Power (a world leader in power generation), the Bank of Ireland, Compañía Telefónica de Chile, KSTS-TV Telemundo Group, and the Inter-American Development Bank.

Charles received his doctorate in English literature from the University of California, Berkeley, and his bachelor's degree, magna cum laude, from Columbia.

Paul Wang is assistant professor in the graduate direct marketing program at Medill School of Journalism at Northwestern University. He is also the technical editor of the *Journal of Direct Marketing*. Wang specializes in database and direct marketing issues, and serves as a research consultant to a variety of companies developing database marketing programs. His PhD is in communications studies from Northwestern University.

Index